Must • Girls • Love
a memoir

Sabrina Must

Chapter One

Email From: Mom
To: Sabrina
Subject: Come Home Immediately
Date: Thu, Nov 15, 2007, 03:09 AM

Sabrina-
Miya hung herself. Dad and I are leaving for Gunnison this morning.
Love you,
Mom
I've been trying to call you.

******

     July 2, 1957, a perfect summer day. Not too humid, bright, or cloudy, just typical. Uncle Robert was eight, Aunt Debbie was five. It was a father and kid day, a canoe trip down a river in East Tawas, Michigan. My mom, Monni, the youngest Jacobs, was only three years old and therefore left behind.

     I had heard this story a thousand times. Or, at least had heard the result of the day's event. It wasn't until tenth grade, when I interviewed Grandma Maggie over the phone while she was in Boca Raton, that I finally got all the details and began to understand the repercussions of such a tragedy.

     I could see it. Grandpa driving the Chevy up to the river's edge, his eyes twinkling as usual, with Robert and Debbie in the backseat. Unloading the canoes with the other dozen or so fathers, they secured all the children into them as they knelt with over-sized paddles, their faces painted with contented, eager smiles.

     The fathers were the stern men, the children their crew. In no time they were off, mirroring the river's pace. I could see each kid attempting to imitate his or her dad's stroke, which inevitably turned into laborious lilly-dips, just like I used to do while canoeing South Tea Lake at Camp Tamakwa with my trip leader.

     I could see their band of canoes, proceeding down the tumultuous river, even see the beginning of the struggle to maintain control as the river's current flowed more feverishly. And, eventually I could see all the boats tipping, hitting tree stumps, surrendering to the river, everyone thrown in the water, helpless.

     I could see each father desperately reaching for and gripping his children. I could see Robert within Grandpa's reach, while Debbie was not. I could see Robert, whose hold was much stronger, more passionate than that of the river, refusing to let Grandpa go on shore. I could sense Robert's overwhelming fear. I could imagine Debbie lost in all the confusion, unable to swim, without a life-preserver, tossed like a rag doll from one current to another.

As soon as Grandpa escaped Robert's fearful grip, diving back in, the other men joining the search, bobbing every four seconds above water for a breath of life, I could see Grandpa rewarded with nothing other than a torn soul, as he crawled onto shore, wasted. Robert's hero, not Debbie's.

Mom had always said that after Debbie drowned, their house fell silent. No one spoke, no one interacted. The house itself became dead, having drowned in everyone's tearless sorrow. Grandma blamed Grandpa (even if she never outwardly said it), Grandpa blamed himself, and Uncle Robert did as well. They tortured themselves with guilt for the rest of their lives. Guilt which I couldn't decidewas or was not warranted. Both tried to suppress their pain for what could not have been. Grandpa saddened, just like my dad was, by knowing that he was unable to save his little girl from the undertow. Robert pleading with himself to know, *Why didn't I let go? How could I have been so selfish?*

Debbie's name was never spoken thereafter, nor was the memory of her ever cherished. She was pushed under the rug in a sense. It was probably what many would do in such a situation and what my dad wanted to do at times, if only he didn't have us consistently cherishing Miya's presence and forcing him to breathe her in every day. The denial might have seemed easier at the time, but it was what, in the end, would bring much greater pain.

Swimming had always been Mom's therapy. The monotony of the pool, lap after lap, the silence, the motion of the water enveloping her body. It was the precursor to her daily workout routine in order to loosen up her body as well as her mind. Her stroke was the most beautiful stroke I had ever seen. I used to, and even now as an adult, sit at the edge of the pool, just watching. Sort of how Miya would sit at the edge of my yoga mat, absorbed in my dance, I would absorb myself in Mom's. After Miya died, Mom felt like she could connect with Miya most while she was in the water. As though it was the only place in the world that she could feel the silence.

I had never really thought about it until recently, as I began to piece together family history and why things were the way they were growing up, but it was interesting that Mom's sport was swimming. I felt that if one of my children drowned, I would be terrified to allow my other children near the water. But Grandpa was not.

Mom's love for swimming seeped into our DNA. Growing up in the Jewish Community Center's pool, morning swim workouts with Mom, summers on the lake, relying on the water for rehabbing sport injuries. Mom supposedly even swam the morning she went into labor with me.

When I was a mere eight months old, I also had a near drowning experience. I was standing at Mom's feet and the next thing she knew, I was sitting, calmly, on the bottom of the pool. She dove in instinctively to save me. It was July 2, the anniversary of Debbie's drowning.

It was also interesting that Miya was named for Debbie: Debbie Jo, Miya Jo. As though the name carried with it some genetic predisposition for an early death.

Journal Entry, November 14, 2007, 7 p.m. during class at Hopkins:

I woke up at 4:30 this morning. I had peed and when I saw Miya's missed 2 a.m. phone calls I knew something was wrong. Matthew told her at counseling that night he wants a divorce. She cried and cried—sleeping over at her friend's house. She asked Mom, Dad and Nancy (Matthew's mom) to call Matthew and tell him that he took a vow and must keep it—but I disagree with that. It's not their place. Other people shouldn't have to convince Matthew to stay married.

I feel so depressed for her. Miya's whole life is crashing down.

How could she stay in Gunnison, where Matthew lives, where his business is expanding and she can't make a living for herself? Her happiness has been centered around being married and her plan to get pregnant. 28 seems young in general, but for Miya it seems old since she's been through so much.

Part of me wants to fly down there tomorrow; part of me wants her to come home for Thanksgiving. But, selfishly, I don't want to be around her. Hopefully being around Miya will be great—"I miss you so much, Beins!" she'll say. But then I fear it will be a judgmental/detrimental visit, as it was in August for Mom's birthday.

Some thought Grandma Maggie went crazy when Debbie drowned, but Mom insisted, "She's always been crazy." (I agreed, though in retrospect I hadn't realized this when I was younger.)

Grandma had hated Mom since she was born. To put it bluntly, they had always been enemies for reasons unknown.

I assumed an outsider could never fully understand the reality of such hatred. But, to skim the surface, imagine your mother ignoring you for months at a time for absolutely no reason at all, looking past you like you were invisible, and only, if absolutely necessary, speaking to your friend to tell you what she wanted you to know or do.

Debbie's death greatly altered the family's dynamic. While Robert became Grandma's child, Mom (Monni) was Grandpa's. In a way, they almost split up their love, maybe as a means for survival. Or maybe to balance the loss of Debbie. Or maybe to put complete responsibility on one parent for that child, so if he or she did screw up, everyone knew whose "fault" it was. Or maybe, since Grandpa knew the extent of Grandma's meanness and hatred for Mom, he "claimed" her for her own protection, as he was unable for Debbie from the river.

Grandpa did anything and everything for Mom. She needed him to drive her somewhere, he took the whole day off from work. If she needed money, he sent her five times for what she had asked. He didn't neglect Robert though; only overly protected Mom. Grandma's love for Robert was not as sincere. Sometimes she babied him, other times she publicly humiliated him. Robert didn't talk until he was five years old. Grandma was his dictator.

She always tried to imply that Grandpa's relationship with Mom was not healthy, as if she wanted their relationship to look creepy in the public's eye, as though being too close and loving was corruptive to a child's development.

Why Grandpa *ever* married Grandma was unanswerable. Opposites do attract apparently. Maggie was the insane, charismatic, ostentatious one, and Billy was the kind, reserved, generous, loving one.

I experienced Grandma's meanness firsthand when I was 14 years old. At that time, Grandpa was still living in Boca Raton with Grandma. On the phone one afternoon, I reminded him, like I did every day, "I love you, Gramps! Why are you soooo cute?" More than half the time, he didn't even know it was I. He always assumed I was "Monni", a consequence of his Alzheimer's. I didn't care though. In a way, since Mom was his life, his reason for being, it felt like a compliment.

Finishing our conversation, hesitantly holding the phone outward, I heard Grandpa ask, "Maggie, would you like to talk to your daughter?" With the phone still glued to my ear, I heard her shrill voice scream, "I don't have a fucking daughter! My daughter disowned me!" Her voice pierced me unexpectedly. Stunned, I listened to Grandpa stumble over his words. I tried to comfort him, "Grandpa, don't listen to her, it's fine. Don't worry, ignore her." Distant footsteps pounded the floor, getting closer and closer, and then she slammed the phone down. I stood unprotected from her harsh words.

Her final blow to Mom was having Grandpa, who was incapable of understanding what he was doing due to the Alzheimer's, sign papers, placing all legal assets and power in her name, as opposed to joint ownership. Grandma wanted to ensure that none of us, neither his daughter nor his four grandchildren, would get any money. This was something Grandpa would have considered his greatest failure—not being able to provide for his family and make sure they were well cared for when he was gone.

By that time, Grandpa was completely dependent on someone else's care. During one of our visits to Boca, I remember being left in the hotel room with my sister Kacee and Grandpa while Mom did some errands. (We weren't allowed in the condo, so visits were restricted to the hotel and surrounding shopping areas.) Thirty minutes after Mom left, we realized Grandpa had gone to the bathroom in his pants. Having your grandfather stand, leaning against the bathroom counter for support, with his pants and underwear around his ankles, poop smeared all over his butt and inner legs, waiting for you to wipe it up with wet towels alongside your sister when you're a teenager was a sobering experience. It was our initiation. Anything after that was no big deal. It was also the first time I understood what true love really meant.

He was an annoyance for Grandma. Everything was justification for scolding: if he spilled food while eating, if he wet the bed, if he couldn't remember someone's name, if he was unable to stand by himself. She passed over any and every care-giving duty to the 24-hour help Mom made sure he had. Somehow Grandpa was still crazy about her, unconditionally loving.

With a civil lawsuit against Grandma in full swing to reverse the effects of the legal paperwork, and when she finally agreed to relinquish guardianship of Grandpa, we flew him back to Detroit to live with us. Three caretakers worked around-the-clock, including Jimmy, who had also cared for my Papa Mike for four years when he was ill. It was a blessing, especially for Mom. He was out of Grandma's reach.

By summer 2002, Grandpa moved to Sylvan Lake where I spent summers since I was six years old. Not only was Sylvan a great escape, but it also was only a 15-minute drive from our permanent home in Bloomfield, the Big House. More than convenient. Mom didn't ever want to do the five-hour drive up North others made for their vacations. No, we kept it very realistic…homes only seven miles apart from each other. Genius!

Mom and our former next-door neighbor had made a joint promise that if either was going to sell she or he would inform the other before putting the house on the market. Our neighbor did just that in 2000. The two properties were directly next to each other on the Point, the peninsula in Sylvan populated by about a dozen or so families. One house was designated for the "adults," the other for the "kids." Which in turn became the "quiet house" and the "party house." Or, the Lake House and the Cottage. Mom had always fantasized about building her dream house on a lake. The purchase of the Lake House got her one step closer to this reality, so we could eventually tear both houses down and build one home on the joined properties.

That summer, while I slept in my bunk bed in the Cottage, Mom and Dad slept in the master bedroom upstairs and Grandpa took over the bedroom on the main floor of the Lake House. I loved it. I'd spring out of bed by 7 a.m. and sprint the ten meters from the Cottage's back screen door through the Lake House's garage door. On rare occasion, Grandpa would still be sleeping, his mouth slightly ajar, lips chapped. I'd hear Jimmy in the kitchen preparing breakfast: cereal with bananas and the fresh-off-the-press newspaper already at the kitchen table.

"Grannnnnnnnnnnnnnnnndpaaaaaaa!" I'd beckon into his ear, a low, soothing whisper, as I took my position, cuddling with him in bed. "Good morning. Are you going to wake up?" His eyes would gradually blink open, and he'd reply, "Ohhhhhh….Miss America!" Or he'd just chuckle. Or he'd mumble utter nonsense, as though finishing his dream's storyline.

I'd help him out of bed into the bathroom and while he was on the toilet, I'd brush my teeth and begin planning out our day's events. I knew Mom would be home after working out around 11 a.m. to take him to the JCC pool for rehab.

When we finally made it to the kitchen table, we'd sit, hand in hand, the morning sun beaming into our eyes. Grandpa would be chomping, and I would be chatting with Jimmy. If I thought he needed to eat more than he was, and he'd already told me he didn't want it, I simply would say, "Grandpa, eat this. I made it."

"Ohhh…you did, did you, sweetheart? Okay." He never wanted to disappoint me and insult my cooking or baking abilities.

Nights were probably the most entertaining. I'd find myself plopped onto the couch in the Lake House's office, channel surfing. Like clockwork, right around midnight, "HELP! HELP!" would startle me. I'd scurry into the bathroom, the light seeping into the hallway as the rest of the house was silent and dark, Mom and Dad having fallen asleep long before that. Grandpa would be on the toilet, arms flailing in a punching fit toward Jimmy.

"Grandpa, what's wrong?"

"I'm being shanghaied!" he'd proclaim, his voice altered, in a squeaky teenage tone. Jimmy would look at me, smirking, shaking his head.

"No, you're not, it's just Jimmy. Nothing's wrong. You have to let him help you up. No one is trying to imprison you, Grandpa."

"Yes, yes they are." He'd look from the wall to me, back to Jimmy. Fists ready, sometimes even forcibly gripping Jimmy's arm if he came too close. Jimmy and I would switch positions, and I'd take over.

"Okay! Are you ready to go sleep? I'll help." I'd encourage, "One-two-three, and up!" I'd lead him to his bed, help him lie down and in two minutes flat, he'd be out cold until the next morning, snoring, mouth agape.

I was never prepared for Grandpa Billy to die, but I knew it was coming. Knew I should have been okay with it when he finally did, as I watched his once athletic, meticulously groomed body wither away from the Alzeimer's, and heart-monitor and hernia ailments.

It was December 5, 2002. I was eating breakfast, about to leave for school when the phone rang at the Big House. Grandpa's caregiver directed me to call Mom immediately and send an ambulance. I jumped on it, calling the Sports Club since Mom was already in the pool. Then, I rushed Kacee and Dad into the car and over to Sylvan.

When I arrived, an ambulance and police cars were already lining the driveway at the Lake House. I sprinted through the garage door and clung to the doorjamb at his bedroom, staring at his body on the floor, Mom over him, not allowing the medics to resuscitate him any longer, saying to me, "It's okay, Sabrin—he's no longer in pain." I melted down, didn't realize the night before that I was *really* giving him his last kiss goodbye.

At his funeral three days later, Grandma wouldn't even look at me. That marked my 16th birthday.

Journal Entry, November 15, 2007, on the plane from Baltimore:

I woke up at 3 a.m. and saw Matthew's and the Big House's missed phone calls. I knew something was wrong—actually thought Miya had called me from Matthew's cell. Dad was silent and then bawling, "Miya killed herself." It's difficult to even write those words. It seems like a fictional statement that would start a story—not a journal entry.

I called Matthew—he seemed calm—asked, "What do you want to know, Sabrina?" I asked how, but then cut him short, saying I didn't want to know—hung up.

I kept saying [to myself], "I'm going to kill you." He did. Their marriage did this—his inability to be emotionally open—his broken promise. His trick that he changed.

I spoke with Miya on my way out of the apartment to 4:30 yoga yesterday. I was going to bike down, but I needed to stay on the phone with her. I knew that. I caught the shuttle instead. She kept repeating, "I love you so much, Sabrin; I love you so much. I want you to know that." I told her I did. And hung up. She wasn't answering her phone all night when I was calling. That was the last time we spoke— "I love you so much"— "I know, I love you, too."

She hung herself.

I thought it would've been much less harsh/painful/violent/desperate. I guess pills came to mind—I don't want to know how, where, who found her, how many tears were gushing down, what her body looked like after—but I do. I want someone to just say, just kidding. I want to wake-up and the past 2 days to be a dream. I feel guilty about what I

wrote last night during Kane's class—admitting I didn't really want her
around Thanksgiving break. I was writing that during her last hour of being
alive—how could I?

> *We're no longer 4 girls—or at least in the physical sense. Miya*
> *always thought she didn't fulfill her oldest role—she always did. She forced us*
> *to really unconditionally love.*

Mom never wanted children. The thought of creating anything resembling her mother terrified her. Plus, she was scared she would somehow turn into Grandma and be just as mean and ruthless as she was as a mother.

When she unexpectedly got pregnant a few months after her and Dad's wedding, she was, to say the least, disappointed. Little did she know how reliable and honest she would be as a mother. If it wasn't already in her nature to be nurturing, learned from Grandpa Billy, her fear of becoming Grandma generated an obsession with being the best she possibly could be for us, tagging Dad along for the ride. Nothing ever seemed too time consuming or too impossible for them where their children were concerned.

It was this devotion that influenced the way in which they dealt with caring for Miya. While Grandma had been and will always be in denial that she needed treatment and medication (for what exactly I was unable to determine), Miya was forced from the get-go to face her issues head-on. My parents made sure of it.

It was our perfect six—Joel, Monni, Miya, Emma, Kacee, Sabrina. But we had perfection in a very imperfect way, since Miya had not been easy. She had her issues, such as being diagnosed as bipolar, sent away to boarding schools in Oregon and northern Michigan, signed into hospitals in New York, lifelong psychiatrists, eating disorders, and prescribed meds. But she was in your face about her issues, up front, not afraid of them. Instead, she used her issues as a way to better understand, relate to, and help other people.

Any and every problem someone had, or anything someone was experiencing, Miya seemed to have been through it, too. She had done the hospitals and therapy sessions, done the eating disorders and mental illnesses, done the heartbreaks and deaths. No matter your shit, she was or had already been there. She could relate, made you feel alive, understood, heard, not alone.

Living on the edge, Miya had trod the fine line between acceptable and unacceptable, her expression of feelings coming out much more intensely in her than others. Miya's intensity helped to define her, which in some cases, with her diagnosis and chemical and neurological instability, would have been enough to cause her to be institutionalized. It merely defined the Miya that so many people loved.

I always wondered whether or not Grandma was manic depressive. Were we genetically predisposed to being "crazy" because of Grandma? Did Miya just get screwed? Could it have just as easily been one of the other sisters? Probably, but there was always a glaring difference between Grandma and Miya. Grandma was mean. Insane? Yes, but also mean. Miya was just suffocatingly kind.

Chapter Two

The four of us were a unit—Miya, Emma, Kacee, Sabrina. Each two years apart from the other, we were playmates and best friends. Dad and Mom made sure of it. We even slept together until Miya was ten. Every night, we'd scurry into our parents' room, Miya carrying me by my diaper so it wouldn't squish. Mom swore she did not have a full night's sleep for ten years, because despite our attempts to be completely silent, she always heard us, whispering and giggling in the darkness. In the morning, my parents would wake to see four little bodies sprawled across the floor, outlining their bed.

My parents weren't only sleep deprived though. They didn't even go out to eat alone for a decade. It was mostly by choice, since Mom never wanted to escape our little clan. We were her escape, her permanent vacation, partially because Dad was rarely around when we were young, leaving for work in those days by 5 a.m. and not returning home until 8 p.m. or later.

The first time they left the four of us alone, I locked myself in the car naked on the hottest day of the summer. We had just started a game of hide-n-go-seek. The teams were always the Ends vs. the Middles: Miya and me vs. Emma and Kacee. Fearful of being slowed down, Miya stuck me in the car and said, "Stay here, Beiners," and I did. But I also locked the doors. By the time my parents arrived, the police were already there, interviewing our neighbors, asking, "What exactly goes on at that house?"

We weren't prim and proper little girls. Scraped knees, tangled hair, stained and ripped T-shirts were common practice. Nothing was ever a big deal.

When we weren't playing at the house, we were most likely at the JCC. The four of us grew up there. Our clan, along with my Mom's friends—Al, Cindy and Debby—and their gangs. I didn't know how we spent so many hours there—tag, hide-n-go-seek, sharks and minnows, riding Mom's back for "dolphin" in the pool, squash, hours of shower-time fun...and the swimming-pajama-Thursday nights at Buddy's Pizza, Grandpa Billy's restaurant chain. All I knew was that those endless days were intoxicating, our paradise.

I remember piling mat upon mat at the JCC, one on top of the other, a monstrous mound of fun and mystery for my four-year-old eyes. Emma first, then Kacee, and then me, Miya hoisting me up by my *tuchis*, as she scrambled up last. *When* we were done playing queens of the world, I peered over the edge of the mound, Miya ten feet below, encouraging, "Jump, Beiners! Jump! I'll catch you!" and there I'd go, crashing down.

I was certain part of me knew the inevitability of my plunge, just another ding in my chin to add to my impressive record of stitches and scars. The other part of me believed she would catch me; or at least have known that the fall wouldn't be as bad, since I knew Miya was right there. Miya always had grand plans for us four girls; she was the innovator. She envisioned an enormous home built out of wood and stone in Gunnison, Colorado, where she lived. With a well-equipped kitchen, cozy living room, a communal bunk-bed room for our children, five wings, one for each of our families and one for my parents, and acres and acres of land and rivers where we could hike, swim and play, the Gunni Cabin would have been our safe haven. It was going to be a place where all of our little ones could frolic around in their naked splendor, as we did when we were kids.

Her ultimate goal was to force me, *when* I was done with school and traveling, to move out to Gunni and settle there for good. And, of course, to marry her best friend and Matthew's business partner, Brad. Every phone call *during her* last two years alive would end with, "Okay, so when you move out here and marry Brad, we're going to do this..." and she'd continue to plan out our lives together.

I would reply, laughing, "Miya, I'm not marrying Brad. You can't just plan that out." If I started to date or hook up with a new boy, Miya would adamantly object, "No! You're supposed to be together with Brad. What are you doing?" I'd counter Miya's demands, but secretly it was always an attractive idea to me. Sunny days in Gunnison for what seemed like 365 days a year, mountains and rivers to play in, and Miya. Brad was always the kicker that seemed to make the plan workable. I knew that when I needed a break from Miya's incessant hugs and kisses, I could just go to Brad and indulge in my marriage. What a life!

Every time I met someone, they routinely asked whether or not the four of us were similar. I would begin with Miya, but get so caught up with trying to describe her that I would forget to even mention Emma and Kacee. I'd begin by saying, "Well, Miya is overwhelming, all over the place; you'll want to punch her but then hug her and then punch her and then hug her, because she'll annoy you like a puppy dog." That's how it was with Miya—always extremes.

We were either on opposite ends of the country or she'd overwhelm me with kisses and hugs whenever we were together. It was either no returned phone calls or emails for two weeks, or a stream of pestering calls on one sporadic day. Call after call after call, until she reached me, and once she did after five missed calls, fifty more followed to provide me with minute-to-minute updates on how her day was going. Our morning conversations always sounded like this: "I'm lying in bed about to take the dogs out, then I'm going to go bike. No wait, I haven't practiced yoga in a while, I need to go practice instead and then I have to teach a yoga class and then I'll jump on the bike." By the end of the day though, this 6 a.m. plan had failed. No longer was it the walk-yoga-yoga-bike plan, but the swim-bike-walk plan. Everything in perfect disarray. She never learned the skill of filtering out what was and was not important. Tact was a foreign concept. If she had an audience, she went for the full monty.

My only response to these mind-numbing plans was: "You're driving me crazy! Just choose something!" Or, "What about doing *two things*, Miya, not twenty?"

But she'd object, "No. I want to plan all of these things, because then when I plan for twenty, there's a better chance I'll do some of them than nothing at all."

Miya was that kid you couldn't take your eyes off. If you did, for even a split second, she would be halfway across the mall, or had already ripped and torn open every drawer in your closet and thrown all the clothes onto the ground. Mom laughed about the time when she and Dad had taken *her* to a psychologist when she was two and a half, hoping to figure out why she wouldn't and couldn't sit still. In the office, just as Mom was explaining that Miya was "always constantly moving," the three of them turned to face her, only to find that she had shimmied to the top of the ceiling-high bookcase behind them.

Miya's Journal Entry, 1995:

> *How do I annoy people or push them away? Be simple and honest.*
> *I play a lot of games. I need to always have attention and a lot of the times I don't feel as though I'm good enough and I don't get recognized for what I do good. So I do stuff like be loud, interrupt, refuse things, and act like a victim, etc…I push things onto people and I don't take no for an answer. I blame my stuff onto other people and if I feel a certain way about someone bad then I make them pay even though I am the one at fault. I don't give people chances and space to let them understand me even though that is probably what I need…and then I complain and get mad about and at them for not being my friend. I also play games to see if people really want to talk and be my friend by letting them get away when they ask what is wrong and if they don't leave they can be with me. I can be really selfish and get in the mood of me, me, me. I complain when I have something that others don't and I want more. I am really judgmental and can be the biggest bitch and give the dirtiest looks.*

From the get-go, she struggled socially with other kids. She was never mean, just extreme, hugging them too hard, playing too rough, wanting the other kids to feel her love as intensely as she felt it and could give it. That was primarily the reason why Mom kept us four girls as a unit. Just so Miya would not be left out of any playgroup due to her struggle to suppress certain instincts and urges to be overbearing.

12

Initially, Mom was entirely opposed to medication. While she wasn't in denial that *something* was wrong with Miya, "fixing" her with drugs was never considered an option. In those days, doctors weren't diagnosing kids as having ADHD, nor prescribing Ritalin at the drop of a hat. Back then, being on meds was a big deal, almost a sign of failure, not seen as a means to regain normalcy. One afternoon at a local playground a woman, whose husband was a doctor, told Mom that Miya should be on Ritalin. Mom was horrified.

Slowly, that horrified thought became acceptable. A couple years later, at dinner alone with Miya when she was eight years old, my parents explained to her that she would begin taking pills in order to help her focus. As much as the Ritalin was an attempt to make Miya "normal," it also was one more thing that separated her from the other kids.

When Miya was off her meds, you knew it. Mom told me one day while in the car years ago, Miya had admitted, "When I'm on the medicine, Mom, I can see the leaves on the trees." She knew she needed the meds, but occasionally "forgetting" to take them was her way to rebel. In a sense, against herself, since it threw her into a downward spiral, a spiral which left it merely impossible to communicate with or be around her.

Miya never had a choice of not needing medication. It was obvious most of her issues were rooted in chemical imbalances and discrepancies. Accepting her reliance on them was another issue though. A child never wants to be different. You want to match your best friend, wearing the same color T-shirt, sweatpants and style of Converse shoes. You want to tie your hair the same way in a pony-tail. You want to order the same hamburger and fries. You'll stick out as weird if you *don't* like the "matching game." Taking medication in the early '90s definitely fit into that un-matching category.

No kids ever envied Miya. There was no oohing and aahing at the thought of tossing down pills daily. If anything, this was what alienated her. A symbol of sickness and unwanted difference.

Ritalin was not the only tactic my parents embraced. Montessori and her tutor, Lenard, also factored into the "healing equation." A website that outlines the philosophy of Montessori as an institutionadvertises the school as:

A revolutionary method of observing and supporting the natural development of children. Montessori educational practice helps children develop creativity, problem solving, critical thinking and time-management skills, to contribute to society and the environment, and to become fulfilled persons in their particular time and place on Earth. The basis of Montessori practice in the classroom is respected individual choice of research and work, and uninterrupted concentration rather than group lessons led by an adult.

However, Montessori was the worst decision for Miya. She needed structure, not complete freedom. She needed boundaries, not open fields where her individuality could pasture.

From kindergarten to fifth grade, she was considered the Terror of Montessori. She spent more time in the hallway than in the classroom. More time being told how to repress her urges than how to express them. They didn't teach her how to socialize with other children productively and successfully. Instead, Montessori isolated her more.

My parents finally gave up on the ideal of Montessori. If anything, Miya seemed to be regressing.

Sabrina's Letter to Miya, November 12, 1995:

Dear Miya,

    I miss you. Miya, I can't wait to see you. When you come home will you go right to the boarding school. I'm in your bed listening to enya and enigma. Say hi to Megan for me. What are you doing right now. I want to know if you got the letter that I wrote you. Well, I love you and I need to see you soon. Sisters forever. I love you, Monkey. Beiners Rae.

    p.s. Emma, Kacee and Sadie says hi. I love you a lot.

Parent's Visiting Day at Cranbrook, from where I graduated high school, is synonymous with three things: stocking up on free muffins, bagels, orange juice and coffee outside of the Dean's Office, reserved for parents and, therefore by default, students; having both the Cranbrook and Kingswood campus dining halls miraculously transformed from inedible, monotonous cafeteria food to gourmet, healthy and fresh food; and having all-day, get-out-of-jail-free-cards for being tardy.

Somehow my initiation into the world of substitute teaching at Cranbrook was also, just my luck, Parent's Visiting Day in February 2008. I knew the drill. Not only would 20 or so students test the teacher, but their overbearing parents, who wanted to ensure theexpensiveyearly tuition was well spent, also would scrutinize me. Despite not having teacher certification and therefore no real training for being a substitute teacher, I felt somewhat prepared for the five hours of Latin ahead of me (Levels 1 through Virgil AP). Mainly because I had studied Latin from seventh to twelfth grades at Cranbrook, had suffered through memorizing one declension after the next and all those damn verb tenses, not to mention those painful AP exams that promote anything but building confidence in your ability to intelligently decode tangled Latin poetry and prose.

However, I wasn't prepared to run into parents of my high school classmates, whose younger children were now in high school, offering their condolences for Miya. I definitely wasn't prepared for Miya's childhood psychiatrist to be one of the "students" in my first-hour Latin class. While I patiently waited for the remaining stragglers to arrive, Dr. Whitaker approached my desk and introduced herself. I would never have recognized her. I would never have realized this was the same woman whose old office was where I spent many afternoons waiting outside in Mom's car when I was seven years old while Miya finished up her weekly appointments. I would never have realized this was the woman who had guided my parents on their journey of seeking out the best possible treatment for Miya during her middle and high school years amidst major blunders in behavior.

Her eyes shone with compassion, with a longing to rekindle a connection to the youngest sister of her client she once considered her greatest success story. A client who now might be considered a complete failure. But at the same time, maybe not, since Whitaker had warned my parents Miya would either end up in a hospital or prison for the rest of her life by the time she was 18 years old. Miya fulfilled neither of those claims. I almost wished she had rather than the reality.

I followed Whitaker out of the classroom, and she embraced me in the hallway. Tears began to flow. "I couldn't have sat there the whole period without saying something to you. I almost didn't recognize you. But there was something so familiar about you. And then I overheard someone speaking to you about Miya." I thanked her and gave a quick two-minute rendition of what I had been up to the past few months, post-graduation and post Miya's death. She offered, "If you ever want to talk, or even send me something you've written to read, I'd love to. Here's my card." As I tried to compose myself, I reentered the classroom with reddened eyes. A great first day introduction.

Three months later on a Sunday evening, I finally took Whitaker up on her offer and met at her office. I sat on her exhausted, brown leather couch, barefoot, Indian-style, with pen and scrap paper in hand. She sat upright in a collapsible chair, in a dress suit, hands cupped over her crossed legs. Together, we began to recreate the past 28 years, which inevitably turned into the past 50 or so years, as we considered Mom's and Dad's family histories.

Dad's Letter to Miya, November 1995:
Dear Miya,

I want to first tell you how happy you make me. After all the pain we all felt, to see your life flowing so well is so great because of the way you were a few years ago, and I was so afraid that your Mom and I wouldn't be able to help you. I am going to tell you why I was so afraid for you. I don't think I've ever told you about my own unhappiness. I know that you know there are things I have kept from you about myself—but now I feel you are old enough and mature enough to understand. For years I saw a doctor to help me get in touch with myself and reality. I had hit an extremely low point in my early twenties and needed someone to help me get out of what seemed a bottomless pit and that is why I didn't stay married to L. But got married to your mother years later. I couldn't handle the relationship in the state I was in! To make a long story short—when you started to have problems, it scared me to death because of the Hell I went through in my own life. Working in family business was very, very tough. I was so pained to see you so unhappy.

Well, this weekend, let me tell you how proud and happy you have made me. I know in my heart that the best is yet to come. You never have to feel alone with your mother and I standing behind you.

I love you, honey.

Dad

Whitaker nailed it. "She had a complete lack of boundaries." When Miya was a child, she had no self-awareness when considering the consequence and outcome of her actions. It was as though any impulse translated to, "In the thought and out the action." Completely bypassing her brain.

Whitaker told me about one specific appointment when Miya simply ran out of her office on an impulse to rollerblade down the street. For whatever reason, Miya decided she needed to rollerblade at that exact moment, having brought her blades with her that day, the laces tied in a knot, allowing her to sling them over her shoulder for easy carrying. She didn't stop to think that it was probably more logical to merely wait 20 minutes until their session was over and then rollerblade. She just acted on the fleeting desire.

The highs for Miya were defined by impulsive physical or verbal activity; the lows were heart-wrenching bouts of sadness and depression, which were closely linked to her shame. A shame about her inability to suppress and sift through her thoughts or actions and recognize which were and were not appropriate.An ability, as Whitaker noted, a typical 12-year-old should master by that age.

The shame of what she "was" was only the surface of her issues. Only the pus of an infected wound. There was something, some sadness, that had always inherently been a part of Miya. A loneliness and need to feel accepted, which seemed to me to be almost completely unwarranted. Miya was never abused or sexually molested or abandoned. Instead, her upbringing was the complete opposite—one of unconditional, unfaltering love and devotion.

As Whitaker and I continued our conversation that evening, I became more and more aware that this theme of shame did in fact permeate every aspect of Miya's life and consequently her death. The shame she always had due to the feeling that she was the cause of any of our family's problems. The shame she felt for being too loving and needy. The shame she felt when she realized her marriage was crumbling and divorce, what would have been her life's greatest failure, was looming and inevitable.

Mostly when she was younger, the shift in her mood inspired rage. When she would get angry, there would be a swing of viciousness. Like morphing into a preschooler who couldn't step back from the situation, screaming and reacting. Her sentences were laced with the F-word. That's when Mom knew she was off, completely removed from herself. That she just wanted and needed whatever it was at that exact moment and would get angry with whomever or whatever got in her way or disagreed. Maybe such frustration was so great because Miya realized she couldn't control herself. Or maybe assuming Miya was aware that she lacked control is giving her too much credit. Maybe she wasn't even aware of how she was reacting at that moment. But the anger never lasted long, it was just as fleeting. Then she would feel intense guilt for hurting anyone affected by her actions or words.

One afternoon at the JCC, when I was six years old, the four of us were showering, playing our usual game of Spitting Water Wars. The rules: annoy your opponent by whatever means possible. Our naked bodies, shielded by the shower curtains, maneuvered from one shower stall to the next, spitting and splashing water at each other. Kacee and I were going at it, screeching and yelping. Then all a sudden the fun stopped.

I shot around to face Miya and Emma in the corner stall. Miya was gripping Emma's head, banging it against the tile wall, her fingers tangled in Emma's shampooed hair. I stood motionless, the hum of the showerheads drowned out my whimpering. Kacee was pleading, "Stop, Miya, stop!" It was like something took over, and as soon as it stopped, Miya returned, feeling defeated.

Just as I thought about the JCC fight, Whitaker next spoke about Miya's "enormity of kindness." She told me about conversations when Miya would exude her motherly love toward her three sisters, expressing her concerns of how, why, and when we were being cared. She loved us so endearingly.

BipolarDisorder, although there are different types and degrees, is essentially an imbalanced fluctuation of extreme mood changes—high highs, low lows. It was this fluctuation that made having any sort of consistent connection with Miya extremely difficult at times.

In the 80's and 90's, people were not diagnosed as bipolar until they were at least 17 years old. However, every psychologist unofficially considered Miya to be bipolar. They also claimed that Miya was such a severe case that she would probably end up in a hospital for the rest of her life. My parents would not allow that to happen. They knew they needed to do something and committed themselves to do anything and everything in their power to help her, driven by the fear of Miya growing up undiagnosed and untreated like Grandma Maggie. In the early 90's there was *only* a suspicion of genetic connection. But by the late 90's the American Psychiatric Association finally decided that personality disorders can be genetically connected through a family's lineage.

In 1991,by the middle of Miya's sixth grade year at Bloomfield Hills (BH) Middle School, my parents were beyond desperate. To put it lightly, Miya was struggling to get along with many of her classmates. These 12-year-old girls were so vicious that their day's pleasure became tormenting their one, vulnerable victim: Miya. As soon as the morning school bell rang, they seemed to morph into "We Hate Miya" swarms and cliques. Whitaker explained the girls were "so mean spirited and your parents couldn't get this through to the administrators." No one was there to protect Miya from the taunting and put-downs. No faculty made themselves accountable for how these children were treating one of their peers. Instead, my parents alone had to clean the wounds and stitch her up daily. They were trying to conquer that uphill battle as best they could, but eventually the steepness became too intense. This was when Whitaker came into the picture. My parents, facilitated by Whitaker, began the process of teaching Miya how to really "look" at herself and her actions.

I was well acquainted with the tale of BH. Had listened to Mom over the years talk about illegally removing Miya for the remaining month of that infamous school year, until she could start sixth grade again at Kingswood the following fall. Miya became Mom's new tag-along for a few months while Emma, Kacee and I were busy at school. Hearing it from Whitaker stung me differently. I got it. Understood where Miya's need to please and feel loved had marinated. The torture she endured while at BH was just one more bite scaring her ever-increasing, deep-rooted wound of shame.

Mom's Letter to Miya, November 1995:

My dear, sweet Miya,

When I think of you, I smile. When people ask me how you're doing, it's often difficult for me to express without choking back tears at how incredibly mature, sensitive, generous a kid you are. The person who has surfaced through all the anger and confusion is the true Miya. A Miya that we had hints of, but I didn't know how to help come out.

If I was asked to use this paper as a palette to create the kind of child I wished for—you have filled my dream. I have, in the past, shared with you how important it is for my child, my daughter, to have a friendship with me. That, we have. I wished for an athlete—you are. A person with real values. A non-JAP. A daughter who is kind, sensitive and generous…boy, do you ever possess those three virtues. Smart—well, I didn't really wish for that. I just wanted a child who wasn't "dumb." You may struggle in school—But it's certainly not because you're not smart enough. You are loaded with "street smarts"—common sense and, that my dear Miya, will get you much further along in life.

Miya, being the oldest has its advantages and disadvantages. One of the disadvantages is that as a parent you have helped Daddy and I become better parents. You have shown us the things we needed to improve, the changes that we needed to make to help our other girls. You have taken over your big sister role with grace, maturity and with pride! Your sisters absolutely adore you—I absolutely adore you. Thank you for appreciating and understanding who I am, for being my friend—sharing your feelings, your desires, your wishes with me—and knowing that I will understand—taking that chance and opening up.

You are a wonderful daughter. There is a reason that you were named after my sister—you have filled that void for me. I'm glad that you have sisters. They are your best friends.

I love you,
Mom

A few days after speaking with Whitaker, I joined Mrs. Yeager in the dining hall for lunch in hopes of filling in more gaps. In the back corner, at one of the round tables, the two of us sat a bit removed from the students and teachers.

Mrs. Yeager was the sixth grade geography teacher for me, as well as Kacee, Emma, and Miya at Kingswood—the girls' middle school at Cranbrook. But "teacher" did not do her justice. Mrs. Yeager was, and still is, much more. Especially for Miya. When I started kindergarten, Miya began sixth grade. I remember sitting in the back of the carpool van heading to school and being nervous for what Miya might say or do next, something inappropriate or aggressive. I felt embarrassed by my oldest sister. Even as a five-year-old, I felt more controlled than she.

Yeager was one of the main components in making her two years at Kingswood a success, despite being a hyper-active, semi-uncontrollable 12-year-old. "She and I developed sort of a mother-daughter relationship, instead of teacher-student," she said. "And I mean that the daughter fights with the mother, but the mother doesn't get mad because it's her daughter." Giving Miya her daily doses of meds, Yeager, in a sense, also took on the role of Miya's therapist since there was no school psychologist. "Miya was the first relationship I had with a student that I didn't worry about the right way to say it; I just did it from emotion. I was just safe [for her]. In her own way, it was the biggest compliment she could give me. Maybe it did or did not make my role effective, but it did work."

When the issue was discussed as to whether or not to allow Miya to return for her second year at Kingswood, Yeager declared to the other faculty, "She needs another chance." So round two began.

Repetition of sixth grade. My parents and her teachers hoped the previous year would make Miya one year wiser and a step above the other girls in performance and maturity, or at least perform better than her previous year and set her on an even keel with her peers. Being the "experienced" sixth grader, Miya was always "looking for that edge." She'd show off, "Oh, I did that before," whenever one of her teachers would introduce a new chapter or topic. It bothered the teachers, who would complain to Yeager, annoyed and confused, "Why does Miya repeatedly respond in this way?" Yeager would back her, though, explaining to those teachers that Miya simply needed to reassert her older, wiser, cooler status with her peers. She needed to feel intelligent since, in most cases, the catalyst for being held back in school is due to being intellectually inferior to the status quo. This wasn't the case for Miya. She was very bright, although extremely Bipolar. So she needed to be "redirected." At school, "some days she'd talk out loudly, was disruptive. But she was never unkind. I just remember her being impulsive."

My parents were the reason why Kingswood was able to "work" with and around Miya. Instead of being defensive, they were "so easy to handle," explained Yeager. When she called the house to discuss Miya, both Mom and Dad would pick up and take part in the conference call.

"They just wanted help; they just wanted advice; they just wanted to know what to do…If I told them to stand in the middle of the room and bark like a dog, they would've done it."

The blame was never solely put on Miya, nor the other students, nor the teachers. Dealing with Miya was a bit of an art. There was no pre-calculated curriculum.

During those two years, Mom and Yeager formed an automatic bond.Yeager told me, "That's the best relationship to have between parent and teacher when trying to deal with a needystudent—the one your mother and I had." The two of them understood and respected a mother's passion for their children. Yeager and Mom had the same protectiveness over their kids; Yeager joked,"It is not necessarily the healthiest thing." They were and are those parents who love their children so deeply they will literally do anything and everything in their power to protect, love and provide for them.

Yeager was right. This was what Mom and Dad did for us girls.

"The four of you were so different, yet all looked the same. You were all built so beautifully, but sexuality was not an issue." Mom respected our differences. As Yeager put it, Miya was impulsive; Emma was extremely school-oriented and smart; Kacee was Ms. Sensitive, more concerned with popularity, not realizing how bright she really was; and I was driven…to the extent that my parents and teachers sometimes worried about me, since I was very hard on myself.

Yeager told me that she had always associated my driven personality with Mom. She admitted, "I picture your mom having a little of that. I think of your mother as just such strength. That's my thought as to how Miya probably lasted so long."

By the end of Miya's second sixth grade year, my parents and Whitaker were considering different options, though. Miya's time at Kingswood seemed to have been exhausted. Mount Bachelor Academy, a boarding school for struggling teenagers in Bend, Oregon, was their next step.

Miya's Journal Entry, Mt. Bachelor Conquest Solo, 1999:

What do you need to forgive yourself for?

I need to forgive myself for hurting my sisters. For beating up on them with anger that was bottled up from other times in my life. For making a bad example for what a sister should be. For blaming things on my sisters. For ganging up on the people who are supposed to be the ones in my life that will never ever leave me. Not being Monkey [Miya] to them, physically hurting a six year old. Not being someone they could count on or turning my back on them. For turning my back on my friends. For lying to them + my parents. For hurting them. For hurting my parents. For hurting my grandpa Billy + Grandma Maggie. For being irresponsible. For blaming things on people instead of myself when I'm the one in the wrong. For hurting all the people that care about me when I do foolish things. For hurting Miya when I messed up so I had to come here + for running away + affecting her how I did…For hurting myself (Monkey).

I remember staying at my grandparent's apartment, right up the street from the JCC, while my parents and Miya visited Mt. Bachelor. The original plan was to fly out to Oregon and check out the school. But as soon as my parents realized it was a perfect fit, they decided at the last minute Miya would not come home for the summer. Instead, she would begin the program right away. I remember Kacee, Emma, and Grandma crying. I didn't understand it, though. I figured, *She's coming back in a week, tops.* She wasn't. She was there alone, without us, for two and a half years, a long time for a lonely 13-year-old.

When Mom and Dad told her she would be staying for good, she ran away, sending everyone on a wild goose chase around the town. Miya was infuriated with them; the thought of living away from home and not being by her friends and family was unbearable. Yet when she called to say goodbye to Lizzie, one of her best girlfriends whom she met at Kingswood, she finally admitted, "I don't listen. And I can't make myself listen."

I never blamed my parents. They needed to do something to help Miya deal with her issues. She was out of control in those days. Not only hyperactive, but kind of violent (primarily because she was so intensely frustrated by her inability to control her impulses and ups and downs).

Mt. Bachelor taught her how to talk about her feelings, that there were other kids just as lost as she was, how to open herself up and heal herself through her words, art, listening, and mostly through writing. Miya journaled like I journaled—religiously, deeply, uninhibited, baring her soul.

The few times I visited her I became everyone's youngest sister. We'd walk around, go to her room, eat lunch, pick her up and take her out for the day in Bend. It was like parent's visiting day at Camp Tamakwa. The goodbyes were always the most difficult for me. I would torpedo my seven-year-old body into Miya's, clinging and gripping onto her. I didn't want to leave. Didn't want to let go.

Two and a half years later, she graduated from Mt. Bachelor with life-long friends and lessons. On her graduation plaque, these words were engraved:

I have changed. I will never change back. I have come this far forever.

But her transition back into Bloomfield Hills was far from easy. All her friends had moved on. They were at different places than she was. My parents thought the next step should be a boarding school in Leelanau in northern Michigan. That was a disaster, because she was too homesick and miserable. After spending only six weeks there, Miya returned home.

My parents instead enrolled her at Andover, the public high school. Miya took the majority of her classes at Model, an alternative program associated with Andover, allowing its students to learn in a more non-traditional way where they could illustrate their knowledge through a more hands-on approach as opposed to standardized testing. Classes were easier, and the teachers were more aware of their students' needs. In all honesty though, both Andover and Model were a complete joke. How the school actually felt justified to graduate her in June 1997 was beyond me, since she only attended class and did homework the last two weeks of her senior year. The administration and teachers just wanted her out.

Mt. Bachelor never "cured" her. She was definitely still difficult in those days. But it was all part of the plan, a step-by-step gradual treatment, to lessen the number of major roadblocks in the way. This was also during her days as Miya Jo "Marley," with one disgusting dreadlockclump on the back of her head, wearing Mom's 70's vintage tan leather jacket, found in our "costume closet", with fake fur around the edges that looked more like a mane.

Whenever I ran into Miya at the top of the staircase by our rooms, I'd stand on my tippy-toes, sniffing her, commenting and interrogating, "You smell like cigarettes. Were you smoking?" I needed her to know that I disapproved, and I hated that she wasn't living "like Mom." That even a 12-year-old was disappointed in her behavior. She started to get heavy into drugs and alcohol. And characteristically, Miya took it to the ultimate extreme.

I was 11 when Miya was sent to the Cornell University Hospital in White Plains, New York, housed on the 5th floor of the psychiatric ward for bipolar patients. She had been at a concert at Pine Knob, an outdoor venue near Detroit, where she had eaten a brownie mixed with a cocktail of dangerous drugs. As she was foaming at the mouth on the ground, some friends luckily had enough sense to grab the police.

I was at sleepover soccer camp at Eastern Michigan University that week, miserable and homesick myself, calling and calling, crying for Mom to come and save me. Little did I realize that while I tried to get hold of Mom, she was dealing with Miya in the hospital, the release stipulation being a treatment center. White Plains was the best option, at Whitaker's suggestion. (Whitaker had come in and out of the picture whenever Miya had a crisis.) The facility was associated with Cornell University, providing internationally known in-patient treatment with onsite foster home/out-patient opportunities.

I didn't know how Mom did it—juggling Miya and a crying 11-year-old at the same time, driving the hour to Eastern's campus a few times that week just to watch my evening soccer scrimmages, and transporting Miya to White Plains, in addition to caring for her two other children. Never once did she mention what was happening with Miya, nor did she make excuses for why she couldn't come "save me." It wasn't until I was back at home after camp that Mom told me a PG-version of what happened. We flew to visit Miya a week later.

Her floor was on lock-down, the entrance doors opening only from the outside, a peephole separating insiders from outsiders. No patient was allowed to have any pens, strings, jewelry, belts, shoelaces. Nothing that would conceivably be used for suicide. She was stripped down as though she was a prisoner in jail.

I sat on the floor of her room, only a small cot pushed into the corner. I wouldn't look at her. I couldn't. Felt horrified that she would've done this to herself. Done this to me. It had taken me years to get over the regret I had built up when Miya left me for Mt. Bachelor, years to get over the pain I felt when I visited her at the hospital after she OD'd. I felt betrayed, as though she had abandoned me, but I didn't realize until years later that she had blamed herself far more than I ever blamed her.

Whitaker told me that "Miya desperately wanted to fix herself." Mom had told me about the time Miya spoke with one of her photography clients whose daughter was "sick." Miya knew the drill, knew how people react to "problem children." They always wanted to fix them, heal them, find the cure, be their savior, make them normal. What people forgot, but what Miya lived and understood, was that there should be no "fixing," only accepting and working within that individual's limitations.

Miya patiently spoke with this mother for four hours about "not trying to fix her daughter, but instead work with who she is." Miya wanted people to see the greatness in individuality and difference, not the disappointments and struggles. Since who's to define "normal?"

Miya encouraged the mother not to fix her daughter, yetMiya wanted to fix herself? I wondered.If this was true, was it because Miya felt she was "broken?" And, more importantly, why did Whitaker's statement catch me so off guard? Hadn't I known this? Why else would someone work and work and work to become more in-tune with herself and learn how to tweak her "imperfections"? Or, was Miya simply encouraging this mother to not fix her daughter in the way that society wanted to fix them, the sick ones? Did Miya instead want the mother to work with what she's got, like my parents did for Miya?

Either way, as I compiled all of Miya's treatment history, I questioned the motives. What was the purpose of all of this treatment? Was it to fix Miya? If anything, I felt it made Miya feel even more sick at times. She always blamed herself for our family's issues; but in truth, she was our central axis.

She had come so far that her suicide was the last thing I expected. She kept telling me the last time I spoke with her on the phone the afternoon of November 14: *I love you so much, Beiners. So much. Do you know that? I love you so much. I want you to know that.* And she did. And I knew.

Chapter Three

Gunnison, Colorado is a town of about 8,000 people. The airport is a five-minute drive for every one of them. The two main streets—Tomichi and Main—split the town. Downtown consists of a row of second-hand clothing stores, coffee shops, eateries and the police station, dominated by the campus of Western State College of Colorado, which many attended primarily so they could ski or snowboard every day in the winter. That's where Miya graduated in 2002.

After a snowfall, playing hooky from class is expected from both students and professors alike. There are the townies, who grew up there, and the college kids who end up staying after an extended, seven-year college experience and try to fit in. It is a town of a bunch of world-class athletes, who are into extreme sports like rock-climbing, snowboarding, 24-hour bike races, and triathlons, trying to make a living where the average income is most likely around $20,000. Everyone in Gunnison works two or three jobs. The cook at The Bean may also be the custodian at the university as well as one of the airline attendants at United. This may be the only place in the world where you may see someone driving around in a minivan with a llama in the backseat, which will be tied up later to his or her double-wide.

Miya's heart was in Gunnison. That Rocky Mountain high, which Mt. Bachelor had instilled in her, had become her oxygen and permeated every aspect of life in that small town. Spending five years in Gunni wasn't enough. She moved back after her two-year hiatus in Detroit, homesick for the comfort of endless sunny days. The Gunnison community accepted Miya, didn't judge her simply on the title of her mental illness, but by her actions and words. Actions and words that were consistently endearing and sincere. Her onetime therapist Caren described the attachment. "Yes, she's a little neurotic in some of her behaviors, but who isn't to some degree? So instead of reading the label to decide who the person is, people in Gunnison step back and really get to know the person.Except for the old timers, who are few and far between, people come here and every one has their own story. And Miya had her own story. So many people had identified with who Miya was because they all had a story. Miya was not different, just unique."

And that was it. The idea of being different and sick had tormented Miya her whole life. The reassurance that she wasn't drew her to Gunni. As Mom joked, "She could take a U-Turn in the middle of the street while her dogs chased her down the street and no one would care. That's why she loved it."

Miya's Journal Entry, January 15, 2002:

The first semester in four years that I've been a student at Western, yoga class has openings.

The last time I took yoga I remember, I went all the time, but I think in some ways I wasn't ready.

Jonny pushed me and my hips released, along with so many tears. That memory was maybe meant to be information. It was the scary kind. I want to go to yoga, get a credit, and be done. Maybe it's my path. The thing is that it is inward and for me that tells me it's going to be hard.

So I want from yoga so much, that maybe before I just wasn't able to step away from my patterns and let go.

Only once before have I let go, but when Brenda talks about that yoga is the non-violent path, I see that all the other paths, including that one, wasn't positive, only hurtful.

I'm promising myself now to work hard, practice, and always be honest in this journal. I can't do this when half the truth is untold. I'm hungry, and the thing is I don't know how to feed myself. I don't want to hate myself. It's coming out onto others.

This is the start of my first, hopefully not last, yoga journal...

Since I could remember, yoga had been a part of my family. As the baby of four girls, I was naturally dragged around as Mom's tag-along. I was attached to her hip, her little sidekick. Seven in the morning swim workouts or two-hour dog walks at 9 a.m. were standard practice. When Mom began to practice yoga in the mid-90s, I joined her too for weekly Wednesday night classes.

Jonny, our original teacher, taught class in a rented office building in Southfield. As a ten-year-old, yoga meant being packed in an over-heated room with a snarling, overweight man next to me, *ujjiahi* breathing, sweating profusely, as I fell asleep every class without fail during *shavassana*—some things never change—and picking up Boston Market on the way home. I loved it; I looked forward to it. It was just one more thing Mom and I did together. Soon though, it turned into a family event, and each one of us discovered the value of our own practices, especially Miya.

Miya's Journal Entry, January 29, 2002:

Yoga tonight was difficult...I hold all my emotions inside. I know I am, or my pattern to act violently toward myself is beginning to change. I feel it and my thoughts are being corrected.

Going inside is kinda like opening the path for a free flow. The negative moving out and giving room for my true self that always feel cramped up inside. I've been looking for something. All the self-discovery leaves me knowledgeable and stuck in my head.

I've been in the moment more in the past two weeks than I have in years.

After finishing up her Psychology major at Western in 2002, Miya moved back to Michigan to pursue her Masters. Of course, she changed her mind six months later and embarked on what I soon realized was her life's journey and purpose: yoga. She didn't falter from that path. In fact, she pursued it relentlessly.

In 2003, she began Jonny's yoga teacher training program. Having broken off her previous marriage engagement to her fiancé Ben, Miya's escape was her mat. Her heart was torn apart, but yoga allowed her to deal with her open wounds in a safe environment. Living in the Cottage, our little cabin became her library, a place to study the ins and outs of the practice.

I'd drop by occasionally and sit in the living room, staring at the hundred or so multi-colored note cards taped to the glass doors which separated the living room from the sunporch—poses written in Sanskrit, statements of her successes, failures, fears and dreams. It was Miya plastered on the wall. She became the practice; as she studied the postures and shakras, she dwelled into studying who she had been, what she was becoming. That transformation inspired her to pursue yoga as her life mission. It was always more than a physical practice for her. It was her most effective therapy.

Miya's Journal Entry, March 13, 2006:

When I look back at how much awareness I have gained since the yoga course in college w/ Brenda—truth is that (this I just realized) I am running from the truth. Accessing all the openness up until now—it's easy—the path is cleared, but I don't find myself taking it. Just writing this turns my belly, the taste of truth, the feeling of standing on the other side of the river and not choosing to walk on the bridge I worked so hard to build baffles me. All I can decide is that there is a lack of motivation. I am still up against this same wall. I can only connect so far, give so much, feel so deep w/o giving to myself. Completely self-motivated, lovingly giving. Not b/c of needing to exercise to not gain weight—that's gone. Not going to Jason's class and have that push in me, but I realize every time I begin doing something—swimming, yoga, running—I feel or think that I have other things, more important things to do and I struggle to stay present w/ me. Something w/ meditation, maybe meditation can teach me this thing I am struggling so hard to do. Just be w/ me b/c I choose to, not b/c I am made or expected to. Not b/c I must prove or prevent something but can I give to me for no reason at all?

Loyalty to myself? What defines me, I am lost inside still or unable to grasp or define myself. Why does this leave me w/ emptiness?

Miya didn't have to study Psychology to "get" the psychology of the mind. She intuitively knew how to relate to and be empathetic toward others. However she might have struggled mentally, emotionally and physically within her own practice, Miya used her own lessons and realizations to dictate how to lead others through their practices. No matter what was going on with her, the moment she walked into the studio everything evaporated. Her persona would instantly transform. She became grounded, rid of all the day's muck and chaos. Her words went much deeper than merely teaching poses. They rang with understanding and experience. Her flows inspired soulful dance.

I remember a Saturday morning Vinyasa class when Miya helped instruct. She and a fellow classmate walked around the room, observing people's practice, as Jonny taught. He passed over the class first to Miya who led us through Sun Salutation A. At first her voice was a bit shaky, her energy scattered. Then it became soothing, sturdy, unaffected and real. Halfway through the class, she situated herself in *Padmasanam,* sitting cross-legged at the edge of my mat. As I flowed, she watched, both of us absorbed in my dance. She told me after class that she had never seen something more beautiful, that she was intoxicated by my practice.

When teaching training had finished, Miya moved back to Gunnison to open up and build her own studio, The Yoga Room.

The Yoga Room's Mission Statement:

My practice began in 1995 when my mother introduced yoga to me and my three sisters as a way for us to grow as a family. The benefits began to appear in my daily life. It was clear to me how yoga was the centering force, helping me become more comfortable with myself.

Naturally, my practice progressed the more I felt in balance on all levels.

My dedication is expressed both on the mat and in my life. Certified at a yoga school in Michigan, I decided to take the one thing I'm most passionate about—yoga—to the Gunnison valley, the one place I love the most. My commitment lies in teaching this ancient system to any and all with a motivated spirit and a compassionate heart.

After her death my sweat and tears became one and the same. Both would trickle down my protruding, hyper-extended shoulder blades, both would rest on my forearms, both would drip onto my mat, both would run down my cheeks. It was hard to pinpoint the exact moment when I could no longer differentiate between the sweat and tears. It was merely impossible to differentiate between moments of pure bliss and utter sadness. All I knew was that my mat was soaked in my very own natural detox, trying to cleanse myself of this toxic energy, but also to figure out a way to live with it.

Whenever I practiced, I felt her. Wherever I was, I encouraged myself to be most vulnerable. I felt like I could allow my un-healable wound, my punctured soul, to be completely exposed. Every time I went to my mat, I would gaze up while raising my arms up in *urdvah hastasana*, hoping that she'd be looking down at me, smiling. Hovering above my sweat-and-tear-soaked body. Or, I would imagine her kneeling next to my mat, watching. Or, I would hope to feel her hands, not my teacher's, adjusting my body. Or I swore she was practicing a few mats away, that unknown girl's shoulders so similar to Miya's, her hair tied back in the same way. I longed for her touch when I would melt into child's pose, my body convulsing with steady rhythmic beats as I cried. I wished she were there just one more time to soothe me while I was resting in *shavassana*, the corpse pose. And when I would extend my hand to my side toward the person next to me, I prayed she'd be there to grasp it.

Miya's Journal Entry, March 20, 2007:

I have deep-seated fears about being thrown out in the trash and forgotten. That there are things I can do to make someone not love me & want me. I wanted to disappear—be small, contained w/o any cellulite, fat, anything imperfect so that nothing can be hanging out to make me rejected.

I think in my mind I think it's ridiculous. Maybe I need to go through this w/ Matthew. Honestly that is where my deep trust w/ Mooks, Sarah, Margo comes from. Lizzie, Kari, Caren—I don't feel they will stop talking to me if I do something. I have this very sad, scared, & needy girl inside I ignore. Desperate for safety, the trauma was huge every time I felt left and abandoned. But then in my mind I diminish it.

- left at MBA [Mount Bachelor Academy]
- left out of Nicki's house
- Emma ditching me at camp
- my dad forgetting me at therapy
- every time I was dismissed as problematic or stupid
- left out during BHMA, hiding from kids at lunch
- being told by my mother I am disgusting, embarrassed my mother
- talked about me as though I was a disease in third person
- taken to NY hospital for assessment
- left at NY hospital
- my dad/mom visiting me in NY and dad saying he didn't have time to come & angry he did
- left at other hospital and told I have problems
- all the problems I was pushed to believe

*- being talked about like I'm this idiot & making big deal when I
do something normal
- forgotten about at Christmas '94—family went on vacation w/o
me
I am writing this down. I feel sad, emotional—but in my head,
ridiculous. The sadness is deep. The hurt is real & endless and I talk myself
out of it during the day. But my dreams are free range for expressions.*

I loved Caren, Miya's therapist in Gunnison. I loved her because
Miya loved her, even though I barely knew her. I had only met her a few
times: first when I was a timid 16-year-old at her office at Western, then as
a 21-year-old at Miya's wedding, and then twice more that same year, while
picking up Miya's body and attending her memorial service. I was well
aware, however, she knew me much better through Miya's eyes and words.

It wasn't until six months after Miya's death that I finally
understood the reason for the extent of Miya's love for her. Caren *got*
Miya...as much as I got her.

Email from Caren to Sabrina:

*Initially, when Miya first came to Gunnison, she became my client. I
saw her regularly for several years and our relationship was purely
client/therapist. I have not revealed to you anything from those sessions because
they were, and they remain still, confidential.*

*When Miya left Gunnison to go home to Florida with Ben [her ex-
fiancé], and back to Michigan after that, we talked at length about the fact
that I could not do an adequate job from such a distance and that she needed to
find a therapist, wherever she was living, to see her on a regular basis. She
agreed to that and because it didn't seem likely at that time that she would ever
return to Gunnison full time, we decided that our relationship could evolve into
a friendship. We agreed to keep in touch with each other by phone, which we
did regularly, and although many of our conversations were therapeutic in their
content, the tenor of our relationship was definitely different. We joked and
laughed and talked about silly things and probably the most significant change
for me was that I shared my life with her. She came to know me in a very
different way and I shared things with her that I had not done when we had a
therapeutic relationship.*

While Miya was living at the Cottage in 2005, in the wake of her
engagement break-off, Caren sat on the phone with her. Four hours of
talking and crying about how sad she was, how she never thought she
would find someone like Ben again, why she let him go. As well as asking
why she did let him go.

Ben was too good to be true. Miya had always said, "He doesn't deserve me. He deserves someone easier." And this was what I believed tore them apart. Miya didn't believe she deserved the best.

If I could have married Ben, I honestly would have felt like the luckiest girl in the world. I knew falling in love with my sister's boyfriend wasn't normal. Especially when he became her fiancé, soon to be my brother-in-law. But I couldn't help it. I loved how kind Ben was, how nothing was ever a big deal, how utterly handsome and athletic he was, and mostly how unconditionally wonderful he was to Miya.

Caren made her promise she would not do anything. She believed Miya wasn't serious about suicide primarily because Miya never really had a plan. Just spoke of her sadness and wanting to end her life. How? She never once mentioned.

Email from Caren to Sabrina:

> *She just knew that she was in terrible pain and thought that the only way out of that pain was death. It took a lot of talking, but eventually she came to agree that that was not the solution to the problem.*

> *But I do know that if I had thought for ONE MINUTE that she might actually do it, I would have called everyone: your mom, your dad, 911, whomever. She had no plan, no specifics, she just was, as I said before, unable to see past the pain.*

Miya and Ben weren't ready for marriage. They both wanted to give themselves completely to and be the best they could be for each other. Miya was struggling with her eating disorder and inability to grasp control over her mental illness. Ben was still figuring out his plan—should he or should he not pursue becoming a commercial pilot, and if not, what then? They both considered the other to be the greatest and kindest, but Miya knew she needed to sort through her own shit before she could commit to someone else. She wanted to give Ben nothing less than perfection. Plus, the thought of being married to a pilot, alone week after week, tortured her.

Six months after Miya's death, Mom discovered a poem she had written about Ben and herself. Sitting on the kitchen floor, surrounded by random letters, paperwork and photos, Mom read me the poem out loud.

"A Broken Heart":

> *Have you ever had a broken heart, felt that pain inside, dull and never ending? I find myself holding my breath hoping the pain will go away and leave me alone. Stop me from recreating memories in my head and thinking about those eyes, those sweet beautiful eyes that look at me so lovingly. And then I take a breath and the pain soaks back*

*in. Has anyone else ever hurt like this; it's hard to know because lately
looking into others' eyes has been too hard to do.*

*And so I keep hoping that one day he will come back to me.
That we will pick back up and live out those dreams we have spent
hours upon hours dreaming. In this moment I am on a journey of
change, and I am scared. Yet the fearing that I wouldn't ever have him
again is much worse. So I take a breath, let it out, and then do it all
over again, maybe it will help me through this painful time. I really hope
it does.*

Miya believed this: *If you love someone, set them free; he'll come back to you.*
The day Ben drove away from the Cottage when they broke up. The day he
flew back for his grandmother's wedding ring he had given to Miya for their
engagement. The day Miya drove to Florida for her belongings she had left
behind when living with Ben while he studied at pilot school. Even the day
Miya found out Ben was engaged to a girl from his hometown.

She always *knew* he'd come back to her.

After the breakup, Miya was devastated. This was when she began
her yoga teaching training program. And this was also when she had that
suicidal conversation with Caren.

Caren was so shocked by the news of Miya's suicide because their
conversation earlier that morning of November 14 had ended so similarly
to the one while Miya was at the Cottage.

Email from Caren to Sabrina:

*When she called me from Michigan in such a severe state of
depression that I was concerned for her safety, I acted as a friend, not a
therapist. I stayed on the phone with her for several hours until I was as sure as
I could be that she was ok and then insisted that she call her therapist the next
day and make an appointment. I also called her the next day and she was fine.
I might have handled the situation differently had I been her acting therapist,
and certainly, I would not have shared that experience with you.*

In 2005, Miya moved back to Gunnison to start her yoga business
and transformed a house a few blocks off of Main Street into an escape.
Gorgeous wooden floors, custom-made doors, a standard-Miya, chaotic
office tucked around the back, and the walls adorned with photography
courtesy of Mom from her visits to see Emma while she was living in Laos
and Thailand. The Yoga Room was her creation. Just as she described on
her website, it was a place to recognize and invite that:

*When we spend our lives trying to fit into the box, we begin to
slowly lose our own unique shapes and ways of being. When you
lay down your yoga mat, do so with the intention of stepping into a*

*space where your breath creates your boundaries and where who you
are is defined from one moment to the next as you unlock doors
and allow yourself to just be.*

Email from Caren to Sabrina:

*So, when she did in fact return to Gunnison to live, we spent quite
some time trying to figure out what our relationship was going to be like. We
had definitely gotten to a point where we could NOT return to the
client/therapist roles we had had previously. The "dual relationship"
implications were too powerful and ethically it was wrong for me to do so. So we
continued as friends- and even that relationship evolved. She and David got to
know each other and she often came over for dinner or just for an evening to
talk. She became part of the family- very much like a daughter to me, and I
know that she often referred to us as her Gunni parents.*

In 2006, during winter break at Johns Hopkins (where I attended
undergrad), I flew to Colorado for a long weekend to visit. Miya had been
dating Matthew for only one month, but they were already in 5th gear. I
barely spent time with Matthew, only a couple of dinners or visits to his
office. We never had a one-on-one conversation about life or family or
hobbies. I "knew" Matthew only through Miya's words and claims. And
honestly felt a bit uncomfortable around him, the same feeling I had a year
later at their wedding.

The morning before I flew back to Baltimore, we practiced yoga at
her studio. Just the two of us. Flowing together as the room gradually
heated up. And, eventually after massaging each other and floating in and
out of *shavassana* for a couple of hours, we laid there chatting about
Matthew.

"This is the man I want to marry," she told me. I sort of rolled my
eyes and replied, "Well, Miy, just maybe slow down a bit. I mean, it's only
been one month. You're still in your honeymoon stage." I was used to Miya
always bouncing from one relationship to the next. Emma used to define
her as a "serial dater": Andy while at Mt. Bachelor, then Brian for two years
during high school and the start of Western State, then Dave for four years,
then Justin for a few months, then Todd for another few months, then
Jason for a few weeks, then Matthew—those were the big ones with
countless rebounds trickled in between. While I never had a boyfriend, she
never seemed to not have one. She played the field for both of us. I wanted
her to slow down, not rush into anything, learn to be alone for
once…which she herself deep down even knew she should have done.

Miya's Journal Entry, July 30, 2005:

Loneliness: It always is that same empty feeling right in the middle. I think that learning to soothe it myself is key. Maybe that emptiness is always there and by getting into relationships I find a quick fix. I think so much gets stuck there in my third chakra area. To be truly happy with myself and not say, "If only this happened or they were in my life or I had this". Happiness w/o attachment—that is the journey. So that is the cause of the pain. All that I hold onto so tight, so when it is gone I hurt.

Letting go—I can't figure it out.

There's so much I need to learn. I thought what it was is a test to see if I learned my lessons from Justin. But instead I am a lot like Jason w/ guys as he has been with women. I hate that about myself. I hate getting wasted and making stupid decisions. This is just what I needed to open my eyes up. I feel so much guilt and the guys could be another addiction. Trying desperately to escape the feeling of loneliness.

In my mind it all makes so much sense. When I think back to the beginning of relationships—I move in so fast—to connect, attach myself to security, and then have these huge reactions when they begin to pull away. Dave, Brian, Ben, Justin even, and now Jason. I am so strong. I can endure so much, but this release is what gets me hurting the most. I know that not until I heal this, I figure out how to let go w/o this huge struggle inside will I have a healthy relationship. All the things I am. It's still this little girl inside who desperately needs to hold on tight that has to finally choose to let go and trust. Even writing this I feel the emptiness inside. The pain, anger, and desperation to do anything to alleviate how this feels. It's like I need to work so hard at not doing anything. Then what is the fear…of feeling lonely, empty?

Despite knowing her pattern and what she needed to heal, Miya was still persistent and attacked her relationship with Matthew with fervor. She was on a mission: she wanted to fall in love, get married and have babies…ASAP.

Five months into their relationship, theyofficially moved in with one another. Miya had just purchased a house two minutes outside of town. It was her beautiful vision—a home that backed up to the nature trails where she could run the dogs or mountain bike, adjacent to Western's campus. She left her adorable, homey two-bedroom shack and Matthew left his two-story, run-down looking townhouse.

The honeymoon didn't last long. Vicious "shut ups" and thrown knives in the kitchen and chairs off the balcony were just the tip of the iceberg. Even arguments about how much toilet paper she used or how she chewed her cereal caused issues. He was so rigid and defined, while she knew no boundaries. She was trying to teach him to grow and see himself, but she felt more like a therapist than his girlfriend. And he felt more like a disciplinarian than her boyfriend—a job he abhorred.

One of their biggest issues was Miya's eating disorder from which she had suffered since she was 17 years old. It was a way to manifest her self-hatred, her mental tape that *I am sick, I am ugly.* When she would binge, it was like she needed to fill and satisfy her unrelenting loneliness, sadness and fear for not being good enough and getting thrown out. When that fullness caused her shame and fear to surface, because such behavior would cause her to be "fat," she'd purge the food, creating that blissful environment she longed for once she was empty in a different way.

In September, Miya slipped up, binging and purging. The episode caused Matthew to become hostile. Miya had wanted to hide it, because of her fear of being thrown out again.

Miya's Journal Entry, September 11, 2006:

What a disaster I have created. Last week standing in the kitchen with the bag of chips I had the same choice. What was different yesterday? Why could I stop the thought & not react last week but not yesterday? Maybe getting my period and the cravings are more. When I give in to the food— throwing up—the cycle has already begun. I know while I'm eating that I'm going to purge it. How do I walk away? I have to, this is IT! I am going to create such a detailed plan of action that walking away in that moment, putting down whatever it is that I feel guilty about.

These slips don't happen often—which really makes me believe that there is a reason that causes them. Lately the compulsive thinking about calories & about my body, the dreams I was having about Ben, him getting married, restricting my food intake, not having the carbs I needed yesterday & the reading on Saturday. Not to mention eating too many chips all lead to this. Matt's right. I need to talk to someone…

I didn't want to admit it is still there, just waiting for that weak moment to attack. And as I ignored it, some part of me allowed it to smack me in the face. This is really the truth. I hate it. I feel weak. I feel ashamed and most of all I know that this could destroy this love the way it did my last. I don't want to fail. Matt's right. This can never happen again. My body wouldn't recover. I want to live, have a family. Now I am not even fighting against my parents or anyone. Now my enemy is myself.

Miya told me the morning after it happened. "I just needed to put it all in me, fill myself up. Then, once I ate it, I didn't need that fullness anymore so I threw it up. I feel okay now. Don't worry." What she never mentioned though was that when Matthew found out he ripped apart the bathroom in a raging fit, tearing the mirror cabinet off the wall, punching holes in the plaster. During an informal conversation with Caren after the episode, which Matt joined, Miya admitted, "I didn't tell him the truth right away, because I knew he'd freak out, and he did."

Matt, in response, simply lamented, "This was the hardest day ever. I feel I was getting let down and lost my trust." As though he was the one who threw up and felt ashamed, not Miya. As though the eating disorder was controlling him, not Miya. As though he was the one who needed support and understanding, not Miya.

When Miya envisioned her future, she saw marriage and children. That was all she aspired to be, a wife and a mother. Happiness was the consequence of such accomplishments. Everything else would fall into place and allow for such a dream to prosper. Matt's words understandably destroyed her. He'd say, "I want a family. I don't want to bring a family up in this though." He feared Miya's inability to conquer her eating disorder would creep up and affect their children. Which, I believe, it would have. But there would have been a more supportive way to help her cope than by put-downs.

He talked down to her. She felt degraded, and he felt angry with himself because he didn't want to have to talk down to her and be her parent. There were so many discrepancies between Miya and Matthew. One of which was how Matthew dealt with issues. "He was very concrete always," said Caren. "*I want her to continue therapy; I want her to…* With Miya, though, it would be on an emotional level. *I feel sad, etc.*" What most frustrated the two of them, as Caren put it, was "they were not sure how to *be*. He did not know what to do with emotions."

Miya's Journal Entry, September 14, 2006:
> *Laying in bed. I had a good day, except being around Matthew hurts. He is so disgusted with me, intolerant, and is saying we have gone back 7 months. The consequences of my actions, they suck. It wasn't my intention— all I wanted was relief. I think I'd been building for a while. I feel sad. We are laying in bed, talking at each other, not even facing each other.*

By October 2006, things were beyond tumultuous. Miya had hacked into Matthew's e-mail account and cell phone log, discovering secret communication on a regular basis between him and Julie, some girl from Chicago where he grew up. An online relationship that began on *Yahoo! Personals*. Miya was enraged and hurt; Matthew was pissed that she read the e-mails and checked the call listings.

When Miya found out about Julie, she confronted the issue head-on. She began calling, emailing, or texting Julie on a bi-weekly basis. The two women formed an alliance by November. (Miya could befriend anyone, even if that somebody should have been her worst enemy). Only Miya.

Miya's Journal, November 16, 2006:

*Well, I fucked up again. My fear runs me too much of the time—
like now. I need a positive thought. I love myself and by doing that I can
embrace my issues w/ compassion & make changes. I don't do many things I
used to regret doing. Be gentle & kind to yourself, Miya. Whatever happens
w/ Matt is for the best, trust in the universe, ride the wave. Just b/c we don't
work out doesn't mean he wouldn't be part of my life. Choose to think positive
thoughts.*

*Why do I obsess over negative thoughts? Matt cheating, my body,
shoulds & nevers. Impulsive actions or acting in ways that I wouldn't want
everyone to see—that is what I need to do—live mindfully. Deal w/ the shit
my head convinces me is ok to do.*

They broke up in November. It happened to be an especially
opportune time for Miya to escape from Gunnison.

Chapter Four

For my 21st birthday, Mom and Miya flew to Thailand to visit me. I had just finished my fall semester studying at Mahidol International, a Thai university in a town right outside of Bangkok. This study abroad program topped off my seven-month excursion through Europe and Southeast Asia. I promised Miya that I would travel with her to Mysore, India to study yoga under Pattabi Jois, the founder of Ashtanga.

When Miya and Matthew decided to separate, we emailed back and forth for those couple weeks before she arrived. I reminded her to be strong, take care of herself, and not to worry. I also promised that we would talk exhaustively about the situation and rebalance her while traveling together.

In a way, emailing me was a way for Miya to work on and practice how to speak to Matthew and clarify what she wanted out of their relationship, as well as what went wrong. Not only would the trip be beneficial for sisterly bonding time and yoga, but also as a means to free herself from the heartbreak and her own insecurities.

Miya's Journal Entry, October 7, 2006:

I am terrified that I'm fat, that my back is flabby, that I don't know the truth about how I really look. My thoughts the past few days are obsessive. I hate it. Is it my period?

We are talking about biking. I don't do anything anymore. I feel like such a loser. I can't get going. Yoga at 6Am, primary series 2x a week. Vinyasa, 2nd series once a week. Why do I make these stupid goals? Why can't I choose what I want to look like and just look like that? It does make me feel more comfortable in my own skin. I hate my scars, hair, fat, teeth, hands, nails, length of my torso. Why can't I just be content? Why does this society push beauty so much as being so external? I am obsessive about it now. India/Thailand—hopefully I can find something more inside myself.

When Mom and Miya arrived, I was ready for change in scenery, too, having lived in a house with 25 other international students for the past four months. From Bangkok, the three of us headed south to vacation in Hua Hin, where the King had his traditional vacation home. It was a quick, but relaxing three-day hangout on the ocean, the three of us quite a team. Staying in one of the most extravagant hotels I had ever seen—the Dusit Resort—we swam laps, tanned, ate and held photo shoots on the beach. After Mom flew home, Miya and I had a week more in Thailand before we flew to India. First, I gave Miya the grand tour of Bangkok. The pace of the city excited her; I often described Bangkok to be the most "un-Asian Asian" city imaginable. Miya loved it.

Sabrina's Journal Entry, November 15, 2007:

I stood outside of the jet to Gunnison, the sun hugging me, wrapping around my thighs. I felt her, like we were back in Koh Tao last December.

We then spent four days in Koh Tao to get PADI certified in scuba diving. Koh Tao is one of the premier places to scuba in the world. The clearness of the water, weather, and diversity of the sea life made it an ideal location. On December 8, the night of my 21st birthday, we took the overnight train south.

Of course, our scheduled 9 p.m. departure soon turned into 10:30 p.m. Nothing in Asia is ever on time. If you realized this, life ran much more freely and easily. Somehow, even after four months in Asia, I still hadn't "realized" it, and failed to break my habit of always being on time and expecting everything and everyone else to be as well.

Thai time was either very delayed or very early. Two o'clock trains came at 4:20 p.m., taxis that should have taken 30 minutes take a mere ten, because of the stereotypical crazy Asian driving maneuvers. I once read a sign at a bus stop on my way to Mae Hong Son: "Sometimes the bus is late, sometimes it never shows, sometimes it broke down. Thank you." I decided to hitchhike the rest of the way through the mountains on the back of a motorcycle.

So, with time to spare, instead of 21 shots of liquor (which wasn't on the menu anyway since I wasn't a drinker), I took 21 plus photos of the half dozen kids Miya and I befriended. We played soccer and tag in the dark, and sang "Chuga, Chuga, Chu-chu!"

When we finally boarded the train, we set ourselves up for the night on our top bunks. The royal blue curtain that separated her bunk from the rest of the cabin tickled Miya. She continued to open and close it in a game of peek-a-boo. Apparently, I was turning 6, not 21.

At 5 a.m., we were dropped off at the train station in Chumphon and took the hour-long ferry boat ride to the island. We stumbled off the ship and swarming bungalow and scuba diving school salespersons swarmed us. We choose Buddha View Scuba and Dive School, located in Cholak Baan Kao, the south side of the island. The four days spent getting certified were possibly the best four days of our lives together. There was acertain magic that southern Thailand and the ocean and the sun brought us. It gave us an outlet to rediscover our childish ways. To rediscover each other—who we always had been and who we had become as women.

I remembered a moment while our dive group swam in pairs behind our instructor. Miya was next to me, the water so crisp that tiny blue and yellow fishes danced all around us, nibbling at our exposed calves. Dust occasionally clouded our group's wake as a fin or two brushed the ground, which sent the fish into a frenzy.

This test dive was particularly amazing because two whale sharks were at the dive site. As each group of divers took turns exploring these enormous, friendly beings, I watched as another school of gray-colored fish danced around the sharks. It was as though they were "dolphin-swimming," just as the four of us girls had in the JCC's pool with Mom growing up.

I looked at Miya, happily twirling in circles, taking in every sight and sound, her hair tangled in her goggle strap, pulling on the odd ends. I reached out, brushed her shoulder and smiled. Her face shone back at me. I pointed to myself, drew a heart between us and then pointed to her. Now, under the water, where words were impossible and only silence prevailed, I had never felt so much overwhelming love toward her. I wanted to swim to her and pour my heart into her salted palms. I wanted to incessantly kiss and hug her. I wanted her to know I was proud of her and at 27 years old she was in fact the role model she always wanted to be for me, Kacee and Emma. Where words were unnecessary, but eyes were everything, we explored the deep sea together.

I intended to talk out the Matthew-stuff with Miya. But looking back, we didn't spend much time doing that. I later realized we should have. I only recalled a few conversations. Mostly when Miya found out Matthew had invited Julie to celebrate New Year's Eve with him and friends in Chicago (expecting Miya to still be traveling instead of returning to the States two weeks early). I assumed if we kept busy exploring and having fun, she would not have time to obsess about the situation. I was naïve. I didn't really understand at the time what it felt like to have a broken heart, or to be inside Miya's head. I had only had a handful of three-week or shorter flings over the past three years. I kissed a boy for the first time when I was 18 (I was extremely picky). I thought I had gotten my heart broken before. However, they were just disappointments. Lost opportunities for something I wanted so badly to experience: Love.

Journal Entry, June 6, 2008:

Miya's broken heart. Something which rings so true for me right now. The fling with Carter lasted only weeks. I can't imagine the pain after years of love. I almost justify this heartbreak, which I have been feeling the past couple of months, as purposeful. The universe's way of educating me. Of allowing me to connect with Miya on a level I wouldn't have been able to. To understand that pain…even if it is only a minute fraction of what Miya had been feeling.

Therefore, I didn't realize in Thailand how much pain Miya was in. Unrelenting internal obsession about what she did wrong, how to fix it, how to not feel hurt, how to strengthen herself so she could be fuller.

It wasn't until September 2008, when I received copies of two of her journals that were still being held as evidence in Gunnison that I finally understood. Sitting, reading them that Friday evening, I realized I completely missed it. I was having a blast, and she was in pain. I thought I was doing my job by helping distract her. But what I should have been doing the entire time was allowing her to purge every thought, emotion, insecurity and fear she was feeling at that time about Matthew. As Miya herself admitted, she couldn't quiet her mind.

Miya's Journal, December 14, 2006:

I am so upset. Matt lied to me today when I asked about who he was going to be at the New Year's show with. Why does she have to be his friend? They don't have this long standing friendship. I am not going to tell him not to, but I would really like that to happen on his own. Maybe he planned New Year's w/ her at Thanksgiving & that is why he was so defensive before I left. Either way, I need to make myself take space, be here—go to India, get into this experience already. I feel myself struggling—thoughts about wanting to go home—& be safe—be w/ him. I am having nightmares—why?

Truth is something inside me I don't want to listen to, knows this isn't going to turn out good for me. I want to settle this inside me. What is this fear that bubbles? Why am I so terrified? So scared that these nightmares will come true—that I am a joke, nothing—that I have put my heart on the line and someone or Matthew will stomp on it. That I'm not safe—I am so vulnerable, I don't want to be this fragile.

This is the real beginning of my trip. I am taking space—right now. This is my spiritual time to grow. Every piece of fear, everything I do like yoga. I want to be here, be present. I want to feel secure b/c of me & not b/c Matthew e-mails me I love you. I need some growth from this experience. I need to make it happen for myself.

It's good for me to write. My thoughts need an outlet or else they just keep circling around in my head. I think I'm angry, or better yet, I know I am angry. How dare he lie to me after all the times he yelled at me for doing the same thing? How dare he make New Year's plans w/ her. What the fuck— why does he do this shit? I am really hurt, as though he has no regards for how I feel. This tells me he isn't committed. I don't feel this is right. He doesn't deserve me to be so loving when I did this stuff & he gave it to me. What should I do, how am I suppose to know he is being honest w/ me? How am I suppose to trust that he isn't fucking w/ me so that he can change his mind on this trip out of anger? We should do things to make each other feel loved. This shit is not ok w/ me.

We flew out of Bangkok on December 14 for India. Miya and I had planned to be in Mysore for one month to study yoga with Pattabi Jois, better known as Guru Gi, the Ashtanga yoga guru. For the past 30 or so years, he had shuttled Westerners into Mysore and had taught yogis the fundamentals of the practice. When Miya invited me to join her in Mysore to study with Guru Gi, I couldn't pass it up. I mean, how much longer was a 91-year-old Indian man, who's considered a yoga god, going to live?

I didn't know what hit me first when we walked out of the airport in Bangalore: the smell, the stares, or the constant badgering for our business. Each was equally annoying, each was wonderfully Indian.

"You need accommodation? I have room, very nice, very close to airport, only 10 minutes away! How much you pay?"

I remembered stepping back to try to regain my personal space, which constantly seemed absent in India, and breathe (something which I couldn't decide was a good or bad idea, as the dust and urine smell permeated my nose). "No, thank you, we're all set," I answered smoothly. I glanced at Miya and nudged her to follow me a couple steps to our right, asking, "What do you want to do?"

Miya's Journal, December 15, 2006:

    Arrived in Bangalore, India last night. The airport is 100x worse than Detroit airport. More shocking here than Thailand. We took a while to figure out what to do about hotel & train/bus to Mysore. This man let us use his cell phone to call a few places to stay in the Lonely Planet before we just tried to go. They either didn't answer or were full. The government official tried to get us to pre-book hotel w/ him. We decided to not give him money, but instead take a pre-paid cab to find it. I don't think it existed.

    Sabrina is determined to travel cheap, but here the standards are rock bottom. Our hotel last night cost 650 rupees. It was disgusting. The walls were all torn up, the sheets dirty, but there was TV/cable. Very weird. There is trash everywhere, we have gotten lots of stares. The people here have been very helpful. It's not a beautiful city (Bangalore) by any means, at least not this section. It's interesting to experience the world's bottom end from the world's top end. We just had our first meal. Everything is vegetarian, so it's easier than in Thailand to eat. I feel so nervous right now. I think it will take me some time to relax and feel confident at not getting really sick.

The Bangalore train station was a chaotic array of tracks, concrete landing points, and small groups of people standing everywhere, all waiting for something, something which was always late. As the train creaked to the platform, a mob of people rushed to its side doors—women in one place, men in the other.

Miya and I were amateurs at this "seat claiming business," so we were the last to board. Only two single seats remained, which happened to face each other next to the window. I set down my mini-North Face backpack (bought in Siem Reap for only six dollars) and shoulder bag on the floor, sandwiched between my calves, securing them. I had been warned, and warned again, and warned again to "watch your stuff, especially in India." My usual policy of tossing my belongings wherever and trusting that no one would touch them wouldn't slide here.

Settling in for the expected three-hour ride, which turned into four and a half hours, I began people watching, examining the other passengers. Women, clothed in sarongs, which wrapped around their waists and draped their shoulders, crowded the bare, metal encased train cart.

Miya and I sat with at least fifteen pairs of eyes scrutinizing our every move. If you thought you weren't being stared at, you were wrong. "Hi!" I smiled, inviting the women sitting adjacent from me to open up, too. They showed their not-so-pearly white teeth and lowered their shoulders as they began to feel more comfortable in the presence of Western girls.

"You from Mysore?" "Where are you going?" "What do you do?" "Is that your daughter?" "Why do the men sit separately?" The two of us asked and asked and asked, questions sliding off our tongues; they answered and answered and answered.

For the entire ride, Miya and I took in their life stories and travel suggestions, as the women also adorned us in Hindi dots. Two hours in, I wedged myself onto the top bunk metal bed to nap. Meanwhile, Miya, surrounded by at least five women, was outfitted in a sarong. I watched her, glowing with excitement and from a sense of belonging to these women. Even though their culture seemed so different and distant, to Miya their nature was so similar. She had that innate and freeing ability of being able to connect with anyone.

When the train arrived at Mysore, I hopped down with great anticipation. The women led me and Miya up and around the overarching stairwell to the parking lot. An overpopulated, dust-ridden area with rickshaws buzzing and ready for business, and at most four early 1990s Toyotas due for a major tune-up.

With our *Lonely Planet* open, I suggested and pointed: "Take one of these into town and then search for this guesthouse?" She agreed.

We headed toward the only woman rickshaw taxi driver we saw, climbed into her get-up, and held onto the guard railing. We were thrown to and fro in the backseat as she drove us through the city's main roads. Lanes were non-existent; cows roamed the streets at their leisure; honking was a must (a little toot here and there announced: "Hey, just so you know,

I'm right behind you."); cutting people off was synonymous with driving; whizzing by a pedestrian, brushing the lint on their right shoulder, was A-OK.

After checking out some of the hotels in the city center (none of which seemed inhabitable), we again hailed down a rickshaw and drove directly to the Ashtanga Yoga Center ten minutes out of town. Guru Gi's house and yoga center was in the most upscale area of Mysore. The homes were massive, multi-floor, flower-adorned buildings with gates. The class separation was astonishing.

For four nights we were guests at Mina's home, blocks from the yoga center. She was a financially well-off wife and mother of two. Her two little boys would timidly skip around the house, avoiding eye contact with us. Mina just smiled. This five-foot tall, voluptuously round, angel-faced woman fell in love with us. By the third day, not only had Miya and I become houseguests, but also Mina and Ramesh's marriage counselors. We mediated a conversation between them about what was and was not frustrating the other, and what could be done to make their marriage happier. Miya was in her element. Not only did she want to help, but she believed in marriage and just *knew* that all differences could be worked out.

Miya's Journal, December 17, 2006:

This morning was the first class w/ Guru Gi. It's just what I hoped for—amazing people gathered together in India to practice w/ their teachers, teachers, teachers…that's what it's about—sharing & connecting in a healthy & positive, energetic community. Guru Gi has Grandpa's energy. Eddie's right—he is so kind & humble. Being around him is worth the trip, then again they didn't have my grandpa. It took me so long to get out of my head— and even at the end—I was still judging myself. I wish I wasn't so overly focused on how I look and always comparing myself. I think separating from Bein will be good for me. I'll take time just to be alone—although I can do it—I always run from it. I need to find my strength. If not, this time is wasted. I feel myself uncentered—not grounded. I really need to slow down. Sit, write, meditate, relax, watch, walk. Shopping or what I dress like needs to be the least of my concerns. I need to really have yoga meals, really have my trip. I am happy to spend time apart from Sabrina so I can grow. I am so overly self-focused in my mind, analyzing everything. Relaxing my mind. That is what I need yoga for. Not trying to do anything in my head, but instead doing nothing—just relaxing. I need to simplify my life—really what is most important to me—it's the people and dogs I love. In order for me to love them I must love myself. So I will commit to Caren's assignment:

- *follow any thought of negativity toward myself w/ two double positives*
- *not get a phone*

- *write everyday (especially food journal)*
- *meditate for 30 min daily*
- *listen to a new person everyday*

We spent the four days in Mysore hanging out, taking pictures, exploring openmarkets, and changing plans. We had arrived with the assumption that we would feel an overwhelming energy at the place where Ashtanga Yoga was born. But such enthusiasm was absent. The Ashtanga Yoga School was actually a business run by Guru Gi's family, much more business-like and political than I would ever have imagined a yoga school could be. After taking class the first morning we were there, I realized the center was not for me, and I chose not to enroll and pay the $600 monthly. Instead, I decided I would spend the rest of the month traveling wherever I choose in India. Goa, Kerala, possibly a bit in the North. Miya was not so easily deterred, since she was so invested in what the school could offer her as a teacher. However, two days later, she changed her mind as well.

Miya's Journal, December 19, 2007:

> *I am on the train to Goa. So much has happened. I am glad I didn't stay in that cloud of ignorance, chasing an illusion. This idea of studying w/ Guru Gi is kinda like a myth or chasing an ideal—but really the guru is inside.*

Things changed again quite rapidly though. The morning we left for Goa, I woke up feeling like shit. My body was quivering with intense chills, my temperature skyrocketed, and I couldn't see straight. Preparing to leave Mina's for our 10 a.m. train, I tried my best to eat whatever Mina cooked despite my nausea—naan and plain mashed potatoes. From the moment Miya and I were dropped off at the Mysore train station, I quickly got worse. My world spun into a whirlwind of Indian sights, sounds and smells. My head ached, as though it weighed 150 pounds with a temperature of at least 104 degrees.

As we switched trains in Bangalore, I trudged through the hoard of people like a sardine, my mind set on one thing—not falling over. Taking breaks every 20 meters, my fingertips would brush the concrete floor as a reminder to stay upright. When I felt as though I was about to fall over, I'd kneel down, rest, hear Miya's voice, peering over the mass of people, searching for me, screaming, "Beins?!"

"Yeah, I'm coming. I'm trying," I'd mumble.

As soon as Miya situated me next to our bags on the station's platform, she hurried to switch our seating assignments, so that I was as comfortable as I could be for the ride. When random travelers would approach and check on me, I'd glance upward from my fetal position while hugging our bags, stare at them, my eyes glossy and dark, my skin pale and force, "Yeah, I'm just a bit sick. I'll survive."

The 15-hour overnight ride from Bangalore to Goa was torturous. I used to look forward to nights such as these while traveling since they had been some of my best night sleeps. With night trains there was usually no surprise—definitely sketchy and creaky, yet consistent. But the train from Bangalore to Goa was in a league of its own. Miserable did not begin to cut it. The smell of urine was unrelenting, the metal beds/seats were rusted, the train was unsteady.

I cruised between sleep and sub-consciousness for the whole ride, my temperature fluctuating with the train's speed. Whenever I had to go pee, I'd climb down from my bunk, sway back and forth, using strangers' laps and bags for support. Eventually, I would make it almost to the bathroom just to turn right around to go lie down again, since I feared I would otherwise fall into the toilet holethat dropped straight to the tracks and never get up.

As 6:30 a.m. rolled around, our plans for the beach were long forgotten. Miya focused on one thing: getting me to the nearest hospital. Walking from the train to the taxi was impossible; I stumbled onto my knees every four steps, clawing the ground for support, so close to the brink of cashing in and curling up into a little ball in the middle of the Goa station amid all the arriving and departing trains. The only reason I did not was because Miya was literally screaming at me to keep walking and get into the taxi.

Ten minutes later, we reached the hospital, my head pounding, the intensity beyond explanation. I trekked up the winding walkway to the help desk, sprawled across a waiting bench, and waited for Miya to return with a wheelchair. She escorted me directly into the emergency room and I crawled up onto the bed, relief draping over my body.

White curtains tic-tac-toed the room, separating the white beds from one another. Three Indian nurses cornered my bed, taking my temperature and blood pressure, while they asked questions about how I felt, when I first got sick, and what my symptoms were. I answered incoherently, all energy sucked away. So, Miya filled in the gaps as she stood, defensive and skeptical, at the head of my bed.

The Apollo Victor Hospital was considered the best-known Westernized hospital chain in India. In a third-world country, since you never knew what you're getting, and how safe and knowledgeable the staff and medications were—especially considering the language barrier—it was pure luck that we stumbled into this one. Not that it was comparable to the Mayo Clinic by any means.

My blood pressure was dangerously low. So, while Miya spoke with Mom and Dad on the phone, the doctor convinced us that I must not leave for fear of my blood pressure dropping any lower. Miya, intensely frustrated and on edge, snarled at him and asked me, "What do you want to do, Bein?" Her eyes were those of a worried mother, as I seemed to be on the brink of death. And, honestly, I felt as though I was on my death bed, my right arm slung over the edge of the bed, an IV sticking out, fluid being fueled into my blood stream, my stomach churning. "I want to stay here. Then see how I feel tomorrow. I can't move."

For the next day and a half, I was at the mercy of the Indian nurses and doctors. Every hour, they'd shuffle in and out of my private room—which they were charging up the wazoo since we were foreigners—checking my vital signs and progress. Not only was I feeling extremely nauseous, I started to have diarrhea. I felt so weak, my eyes sunken and glossy, my face Casper-white, partly from a lack of food because I was put on a liquid diet. If Miya wasn't paranoid enough about cleanliness, having her baby sister cooped up in an Indian hospital sure didn't help.

Journal Entry, December 15, 2006:

Things Miya and I have learned:
Miya is officially obsessed w/ cleanliness + it's driving me crazy!
She'd joke, "You're not nervous at all, so we equal each other out!"
Yeah, exactly, I was the one who barely washed my hands, while Miya did 50 times a day. I just figured, and always have, that you must "teach" your body to fight off illness and strengthen your immune system. Maybe such a theory was the reason I decided it would be okay to drink the "purified" water at Mina's house and the washed apple at the street-corner grocery store in Mysore. Probably not my most proud moment, and probably the reason for getting sick.

While in the hospital, Miya checked and double-checked every little thing the nurses or doctors did or didn't do to and for me: making SURE the needles were new and clean, or interrogating the nurses about how they were exactly inserting my IV, frustrated and confused why it was taking 45 minutes each time, painfully poking me over and over until both arms were bruised up and down, or complaining that my juice still hadn't been delivered after two hours, or pushing the hospital to know why no one would tell us exactly how much the treatment and hospital stay would cost, and on and on. She sat vigil at my bedside, only leaving me to sprint a mile and a half down the road every few hours where she had access to a travel agent and to a phone to report my status to Mom and Dad.

By the next morning, I felt a bit better—30% alive as opposed to 5%. Miya decided the best and only option was to fly that night directly to Mumbai, sleep over at a hotel, and fly out on a 6 a.m. the next morning for Bangkok—anything to get out of India.

After signing hospital release papers, paying, and filling prescriptions for follow-up medications, we left for the airport.

Miya's Journal, December 21, 2006:

Well...we are on our way home. Sabrina is better & I think I am going to change my ticket & stay. I want to go south again & dive.

I think it will be good for me to travel alone, have some time to myself, go to a beach, do yoga, meditate, swim, tan, write & read...That sounds great. I notice that maybe Beiner is an excuse to go home. I do miss Matt—but maybe traveling alone is really what I need to do. It feels good that Matt is so excited to see me, but it will probably be good for us to stay apart a little longer.

It's really weird being in this airport—all of these upper-class Indians compared to the poverty—talk about extremes. I feel sad a little my time here has been cut short. It's a hard place to travel—at least the way we are—seeing everything. This morning 6 am walking through Margao I thought to myself that I could've been born here—why am I so lucky? I walk around looking at the faces & people are surprisingly happy when they're not putting on a begging face. Simple lives really mean simple problems. Not to say they don't have them. They are just not all jumbles of crap in their head & more to do w/ survival. I don't want to leave so fast—not have time to slow down & reflect all I learned.

The most I saw of Goa was the hospital and the back seat of the taxi. Frustrated that our plans for the beach were shot to shit, I still was glad I survived India. Mom's certain that if Miya hadn't been there, I would've died. I have to agree.

Miya had always taken her job as oldest sister very seriously, never wanting to disappoint us. She always repeated over and over, somewhat jokingly, yet somewhat seriously, "I'm the oldest sister. I'm the oldest sister. You have to listen to me!" She'd remind me of her phrases: "Must Girls Love" and "Forever Sisters." She believed in them, wanted to teach us how to be the best we could to each other. She wanted that role. Anything short was unacceptable to her.

Miya's Journal, December 22, 2006:

Well, I'm sitting at a café in Khaocan and I notice it is taking me a little while to allow myself to be alone. This is really good for me—I am really happy w/ my plans. Don't understand this incessant need to run home to Matthew or my circulating thoughts about him & Julie. It's going to take me time to trust the love—in reality it's hard to know he gave someone else his passion—I hate it. I want to take this week to re-focus back on me—be strong, powerful & happy w/ myself. I look around her and truth is I have really spent a lot of time working through my stuff—Now I am really ready to give away everything & share everything. This is all very fun, but what no one else understands is where I want to be is in Matthew's arms. I just feel this trip was ending so abruptly & need time to slow down & process & reaffirm all that I have discovered about me. I feel an incredible happiness when I think about what I am about to come home to. I don't care what anyone thinks more than I have ever not cared.

When Miya arrived back in the States six days later, she flew directly to Chicago to meet up with Matthew and Brad for a New Year's Eve techno concert. Matthew had realized on his bike trip he "couldn't live without her," and Miya had "found" herself in Asia. Both were ready to give themselves unconditionally to one another. Julie's New Year's Eve attendance was axed from Matthew's plan.

Miya's Journal, December 28, 2006:

This is my second December 28—and we are about to land in Chicago. I don't like how obsessive I've been about my face & body and want to let it go. So worried—so stupid—doesn't matter just like it didn't matter in India. I am who I am. I feel good and weird too. Part of me questions if I should have stayed & then if I had I would have wanted to be back for this next year. I want to stop doing this in my mind. I want to be decisive & sure. Confidence starts with the simplest things. Live my changes—don't forget & don't get caught up in all the unimportant bullshit. Remember what matters, put life into perspective the same way I was able to walk through Margao that morning. I am so lucky—I have fussed a lot lately, & I see how fast I can be sucked back into my head & all that really isn't that important. I am ready to start anew. Even right now I am trying to feel something—fuck, maybe I'll not try & just relax and be. Traveling just reinforces me that no matter where you are, who you are, how you look, how much money you make, the most important thing is love—Period.

That's what I want my life to be about. Giving that to myself & to everyone I come into contact w/ & all the ways I don't just gives me a lifetime of things to work on & get better at.

There was (and will always be) certain things that remind me of Miya. Things that made me smile, things that made me cry, and things that put a sour taste in my mouth. Justin Timberlake's "My Love" was one of those things. When Matthew proposed to Miya on New Year's Eve, that song was playing at the concert in the midst of techno dance mixes. Miya had admitted, "If I had a ring, I'd ask you to marry me," and Matthew replied, "Well, I have a ring, so will you marry me?" Then, I could imagine

Matthew singing, "This ring here represents my heart. But there's just one thing I need from you; say 'I do.'"

Corny? Yes. Miya's ideal engagement scenario? Completely. Every time I heard it on the radio for months afterward, I'd get excited. Mostly for Miya, thinking about how happy she was. Some for myself, when I thought about her wedding. But I soon despised it.

It usually took me a moment to remember that I should despise "My Love." It wasn't an automatic response. I usually first started to tap my toes, then shook my hips a bit, then finally got pissed—the range of emotion jumping from joy to rage. I usually felt ashamed that I forgot what that song represented and that I enjoyed it for even three seconds. It didn't represent my sister's life, but her death. The beginning of her end.

Chapter Five

The happiest day of my sister's life and of our family's was Miya's wedding day—March 31, 2007. But it was also the seal of disaster. Getting married was the last straw. We didn't realize it at the time. We missed all the signs, everything that should've sent red blaring smoke signals, especially having Matthew demand the wedding take place ASAP.

On Tuesday, March 27, the six of us, plus Uncle Robert, arrived in St. George, Utah at the Red Mountain Resort and Spa. It would be our last hurrah together as a family. Miya stressed the importance of us, our family, devoid of Matthew, since it would never be the same after the wedding. Afterwards, Matthew would forever be part of our family and the original six would expand to seven.

Red Mountain had become our family's premier vacation spot. Mom loved it simply because it forced all of us to be together all the time, without a city and nightlife as an escape. No 5 a.m. arrivals after a night clubbing in Puerto Vallarta; Dad up all night, nervous, wondering to where Miya and Emma, 17 and 15 yearsold at the time, had disappeared. Red Mountain instead meant all-family breakfasts, three-hour hikes through the desert, lunches, aerobics classes where one of us would fart or uncontrollably laugh, massages, facials, pedicures and manicures, dinners, and early bedtimes. Mom's ultimate paradise. It seemed only her 10-egg-white omelets with double spinach, double mushroom, Rio wraps, toasted bagels with peanut butter, Costco animal crackers, and large frozen yogurt chocolate cones were missing.

I arrived at Red Mountain separately on a flight from Baltimore and a shuttle from Las Vegas. Kacee had flown in from Israel, where she had been living in Tel Aviv for the past few months, and Emma from L.A., where she was working for an online marketing website.

I couldn't wait to give Miya her gift. She and I naturally roomed together, while Emma and Kacee were paired up in the other room. I jumped on the bed, rubbing her arm, waking her up, "Hello! I can't wait. Open up your wedding gift!" I had made a photo album of our excursion abroad, using markers to color the inside covers—"Miya and Beiners, December 2007, Thailand and India, I love you so much! Forever Sisters, Congratulations!" I tucked the DVD of us scuba diving in a sleeve in the back of the album.

A couple days later, on Thursday morning, we all drove the four hours to Moab, Utah where the wedding ceremony and reception was being held. The seven of us piled into two rental cars. Emma drove the first one with Dad sitting shotgun and Uncle Robert in the back. We forced Miya to rent a second car, since no one wanted to be in her dog-hair infested Jeep

Cherokee, which Dad bought her in 2002 when she graduated from Western. Mom and I sat in the back, while Miya drove with Kacee as co-pilot.

We were obviously the more fun car. Who really wanted to listen to Dad's random comments about which tree this is, which tree that is, and what the benefits are of its growing cycle, or about the different crops on the side of the highway, or specifics about new corn growth and production technology, all the while having to listen to Emma pick arguments over politics and comment on foolish foreign policies?

Instead, our car indulged in a sing-a-long, dipping into our secret stash—Camp Tamakwian songs. Tamakwa was our summer camp in Algonquin Park, Ontario, Canada. Since Mom had spent twelve consecutive summers there as a kid, Tamakwa had become a Jacobs/Must family tradition. All four of us went. We'd board the buses for the eight-hour ride and wave goodbye to our parents, eager to smell the delicious freshness of South Tea Lake. Kacee and I always cried while we said goodbye. As we pulled into the parking lot to load the bus, we'd both say, "You know what, I changed my mind. I don't want to go this summer."

I always had a pattern: intensely homesick the first week, more than fine the second and third weeks, eager to see Mom and Dad with five days to go, and then mad I actually had to leave come departure day. If I was homesick, Kacee was too, just because she felt bad for me. When I finally wasn't any longer, she'd be mad because she still was. It was all my fault!

I was just a little pipsqueak. Being the youngest camper for my first three summers when I was five, six, and seven years old gave me an edge; the counselors adored me. With Mom and Dad absent, Miya amped up her sisterly/motherly role. When she couldn't sleep at night, she used to force her counselor to walk from cabin to cabin, checking on the three of us. She'd make sure that I was tucked into bed properly, I was getting along with all the girls in my cabin, and I had gotten Mom's package with candy secretly stashed into the stuffed animal. (Mom knew all the workable tricks, since she was herself a camper.)

Reminiscing about those golden Tamakwan days even a decade later, I felt intense joy and love.

We soon arrived at the Red Cliffs Lodge. Moab is known for its world-class mountain biking and rock climbing terrain. Only a four-hour drive from Gunni, it was a place Miya and Matthew had claimed as their spot. They would routinely vacation in Moab, often accompanied by Brad as their third wheel. Wanting the wedding to be intimate and "them," they chose Moab for the festivities.

There were only 80 or so guests, 50 of whom were Miya and Matthew's friends. The others were split between our favorite relatives and family best friends (who are also our pseudo aunts and uncles), and

Matthew's family. It was perfect. Everyone there became one big family. We spent Friday and Saturday hiking, biking, and doing yoga together, allowing everyone to feel close and comfortable, even though they may have only just met six hours earlier.

The morning of the wedding I joined Matthew and the "Colorado Crew" for quality bonding time—my first mountain biking experience. What was supposed to be a two-hour ride quickly turned into six. My crash course was much more than I anticipated. When I arrived back at the winery, I was completely spent, bruised all over from my one, glorious fall when I tried to "kick" a rock with my tire like all the boys had. I had a blast.

Another perk of the ride was a chance to scope out Brad's date, some girl he knew from North Carolina. Since she and I were the only beginners, we rode together, joking and chatting a half mile behind the experienced ones. I tried to befriend her and was careful not to be too flirtatious with Brad. This was Miya's intended husband for me and after a little fling in Gunnison in 2006, Brad and I had emailed back and forth. I figured the occasional email would keep him on the back burner. I did not realize that when I saw him a year later, those feelings would resurface.

I thought back to Valentine's Day when Brad had sent me a dozen roses. The gesture—greatly appreciated—completely scared me. I had been only used to boys playing games with me. Flowers? An actual gentleman? Did they exist? I wasn't prepared for a "yes" answer. So I stopped it and didn't allow the fling to trickle over into reality. No doubt Brad had room to grow, just like we all had, but his gentle, genuine way overcompensated for any lack of confidence or emotional strength.

When I returned to the winery from mountain biking, my cousins Marcy and Shelly bombarded me, clothing me in a funky, wild hat and ball gown gloves. Our very own wedding shower-tea party for all the Jacobs/Brontman/Must women! Leave it up to my crazy cousinsto utilize all luggage space with party decorations and costumes, instead of clothes for the weekend. Sitting on the patio in the back of their hotel room, facing the river, which outlined the winery, we celebrated what it meant to be women in our family: the freedom, the ridiculousness, the honesty, and the unconditional love. Balloons wearing shower caps, markered with Picasso faces, streamers, miniature brownies and ginger snaps, mismatched antique teacups from Great Aunt Sally, noisemakers and a "Happy Shower" banner with Miya's name scratched on it decorated the scene. Nothing was proportional, nothing matched. The perfect must-have tea party (pun-intended). Absurdity was part of our genetic makeup.

We toasted to continuing a tradition of pre-wedding tea parties for each of us and for our kids and their kids and their kids forever. "It'll be our tradition. And, each one must be better and more ridiculous than the last!" It was our finest hour.

Getting dressed for the wedding ceremony was also an ordeal. Shuffling six bridesmaids and Miya into two showers and then the make-up artist's station in two hour's time took skill. I helped release a little pressure…or at least I thought I had. While I was adamant about not wearing any makeup or getting my hair done up, everyone else was annoyed. I figured shaving my legs, running my fingers through my hair, and tossing on my bridesmaid dress and stilettos was more than enough.

The dresses: Miya's search for the perfect bridesmaid's dress was tortuous. Having to choreograph buying dresses for people in six different sizes in six different locations globally was difficult enough. Adding Miya, her sort of bad fashion sense, and a three-month deadline into the equation made such a feat nearly impossible. Tackling online catalog after online catalog, department store after department store in both NYC and LA, Miya was relentless. I sat on the phone with her while at school for weeks, receiving countless emails with website address links, looking at her "maybes." Nothing really turned either one of us on.

Finally, while in New York for her bachelorette party, Miya and Margo (her maid of honor and childhood best friend) found it. Miya thought it was gorgeous; I thought it looked like an Easter egg. I did my best to keep my mouth shut, not wanting to hurt her feelings, but mostly just so she'd stop the shopping. Mom agreed, and we'd laugh on the phone about it. It turned out that when the six of us were standing up at the ceremony, we did look beautiful, Easter-egg dresses and all.

Before the ceremony, all the sisters congregated in Mom and Dad's room for photos. While the wedding photographer set Miya up on a chair in her elegant off-white, lace gown, her hair tied up, Emma, Kacee, and I surrounded her, looking up. These photos were some of my favorites. Second, of course, to the one of Miya, Kacee, and I posing nude on the back porch of our hotel room with our butts facing the camera, a photowhich was later framed and displayed on Mom's bathroom counter. (A photo that Emma, being the "conservative one," would not be part of under any circumstances!)

We surrounded Miya and Matthew—bridesmaids to the left side of the chuppah, groomsmen, wearing light grey dress suits and flip-flops, to the right. The service faced the river with mountains in the background framing the ten or so rows of chairs, the stage and chuppah. As Caren led the service, Matthew and Miya exchanged their vows in rhymed, Dr. Seuss-like meter. It was 3 p.m., the sun was out, and we were handing over our sister, who stood there gleaming and poised.

After an hour of photos, drinks, and appetizers, the party began indoors. Linda, a very close family friend, had decorated a dozen tables with sage green table cloths and white flowers. Huge 50x60sepia portraits of Miya and Matthew hung on the walls.

Steve, Matthew's best man and business partner, first toasted the newlyweds, telling about last New Year's Eve in Chicago when they got engaged. Then, we projected the video slideshow Miya had put together of photos and video clips. Next, Matthew and Miya danced alone. Miya looked like an angel, smiling uncontrollably, kissing her husband, her world as full as she ever wanted it: family and friends surrounding her and her new life. And finally, as John Denver's "Sunshine on my Shoulders" played, Dad danced with her.

The night was perfect. We danced and danced. Mom ran back to her room to change into a spandex outfit and I changed into my favorite, summery white dress so I was also comfortable and rid of the Easter egg. We hopped around, sang, twirled, exuberance spilling from every cell of our bodies. I was so proud of all of us, finally getting along without any drama or bickering. We were all on a high.

The greatest moment of the night was when we four girls, plus Sammi and Becca, both like sisters, were dancing in a circle around Dad. He was clapping his hands, every bone, extra layer of fat, nose and ear hair smiling. He was with his little girls. After a few minutes, he needed a break and retired to a chair just to the side of the dance floor alone. I looked over at him as I jiggled and shook from side to side, watching him slouch in the chair, hands in his lap, grinning…I have never seen him look so happy and joyous. Mostly because Dad finally believed the doctors were wrong. There wouldn't be hospitals in her future, only a loving husband and lots of babies.

Chapter Six

Miya never missed a beat. If one of us was having a problem, she was right there to negotiate a solution. Such was the case, in May 2007, when I had to break the news to Dad I was leaving in a week for Rwanda. Miya and Matthew were in town that weekend and so they joined me in the sunporch directly after dinner to go through my "agenda" for Dad. Miya sat across from me, helping to plead my case. "What a great opportunity, Beiners! Right, Dad? I mean, it's fully paid for, nothing from your pocket, and when else would she be going to Africa? You know what, can I go with you? You think that guy would pay for me, too?"

Going to Africa had always seemed an impossible feat. A place enchanted, bubbling with richness, history and culture, but also instability and destruction. I knew my parents would die if I ever traveled there, especially alone. (Traveling throughout Europe and Southeast Asia was hard enough on Dad.) I learned about the cradle of civilization in school, about the slave trade and genocide. Yet as much as I was taught, the beauty, diversity and brute reality of Africa was still foreign to me. Therefore, when a vet from Baltimore offered to sponsor a journalism internship with the Mountain Gorilla Veterinary Project (MGVP) in Rwanda, I couldn't pass up the opportunity, despite Dad's (and everyone else's) uncertainty. Rwanda was so undiscovered, mysterious, and most of all, off-limits to me. I absolutely had to go.

MGVP is an organization of veterinarians dedicated to the preservation of the highly endangered mountain gorillas. In total, I hiked six different mornings, costing $375 each time.

This best described our fifth day of hiking:

The overcast sky had thrown a feathery blanket of fog over the hills, causing light to barely penetrate. This was our second time visiting this group. Today, they seemed to be hiking straight down the trail we hiked up. So, despite the haziness, it was an ideal situation.

Automatically I clicked, clicked, clicked my camera. But I soon stopped to just absorb the scene. To my right, the others in my group stood, photographing our subjects. A young male was crouched directly in front of me about ten meters away, engrossed by the voluptuous leafy branches fallen in an organized disarray. Bamboo trees stood in a maze-like clump to his left, so I watched his palms clench each bamboo trunk one by one, ripping them from the enlivened ground with no apparent effort. He stripped the outer bark like a corn's husk to reach the bamboo's marrow. Rain droplets that had collected on the leaves and branches surrounding him were tossed onto his body, giving his hair a glisten and shimmer.

I then zoomed in on his hands—deep grey, plump, slightly swollen and rubbery looking. As he gripped the branches and leaves, devouring them without interruption, he finally glanced up and we locked eyes. I didn't remember if I sat there mesmerized for ten seconds or ten minutes. His eyes scanned my whole presence from the clothes I was wearing to how I was kneeling, penetrating straight into my soul and intentions. There was something so familiar in his gaze. A homey-ness and understanding. The same feeling I have whenever I lock eyes with children. Like they know the mystery of the world and want you to recognize how simple everything actually is and could be. I felt entranced by his stare, by the dense underbrush surrounding me and him, and the knowledge that the rest of his family was scattered around our little camp of photographers. I glanced down at my hand clenching my camera, and realized that those ten meters from me to him translated to thousands of years of evolution.

The mountain gorillas symbolized hope. A hope that people would return to Rwanda and fall in love with the country and its people as I did. That the communities would revitalize each other, ridding themselves of the segregated conceptions of the past. In a country where I assumed I should not mention itshistory, it seemed at every other street corner a sign stood, bearing words of warning against genocide and the need to reunite as one. Every time I asked about someone's story and how the genocide affectedhim or her, he or she would get quiet and reserved, voice quivering from years of hurt. But the local would willingly narrate the horror seen—parents and siblings murdered by machetes for all to witness. MGVP's mission helps much more than just the mountain gorillas. It had become part of Rwanda's mission to become whole again.

My experience interning for and traveling with MGVP particularly affected me after Miya's death. Every individual within the Rwandan community was a survivor. Being able to move on and forgive like these people was something almost incomprehensible for me. Especially when it may have been their next-door neighbor who had hacked their parents to death in front of them, leaving them orphaned. Such forgiveness seemed impossible. Therefore, since the Rwandans seemed to have successfully restored their lives and impossibility had become their reality, it was inspirational for me. This could never have been if people did not forgive as they had, if grudges were kept, and if the Tutsi/Hutu distinction was preserved.

In most instances, I seem to forgive too easily. If I am supposed to be mad at someone, I forget more times than not and my initial reaction is excitement when seeing that friend. But when it came to Matthew I struggled to apply such forgiveness toward him. So much of me considered any effort to reconcile with him and his actions as an injustice toward Miya. I felt doing that would be accepting her suicide.

I felt guilty though that if the Rwandans had the capacity to forgive, shouldn't I? Shouldn't it have been as easy as the gorillas wanted us to realize? That life is simple: eat, sleep and make babies.Maybe the missing link, and what I needed to understand, was that they were not forgetting. That Rwandans might have forgiven on the surface as a means for survival, but they never forgot.

Maybe that was just a front and inside they were just as bitter as I was toward Matthew for the way he treated my sister.

Journal Entry, August 26, 2007:

>*It was nice out w/ all of us at the dinner table. Miya stole the floor. She needed our opinion about what to do about Matthew. I had not yet connected their issues with him being abusive—but he is. He recoils from her touch, despises how needy she is. She was crying, Kacee was acting like the all-knowing healer, Emma was methodical/business-like about the issue, etc.*

>*"It is what it is," Miya kept acknowledging. Yet, the truth is that it shouldn't be this way 3 months after one's wedding. Matthew will NOT really change. It may have seemed as though he had in the spring after India—but really it was just a honeymoon, stash the skeleton under the bed stage. All Miya wants is to be unconditionally and suffocatingly loved. Period. I feel bad—I felt like she is trapped. Mom advised to stop calling him—give each other space, but the truth is that separation is going to have to happen every 3 months when Matthew acts this way. Matthew also complains that our family will poorly affect their children so he isn't ready for Miya to get pregnant. Plus, how can they have kids when Matthew reacts so poorly to Miya—he will definitely speak to his children the same way.*

The way Matthew treated Miya was not novel. In fact, his behavior was well documented.The best example: his most recent ex-girlfriend, Paige. I had met her while visiting Gunnison in winter 2006at the ski lodge in Crested Butte. While Miya was busy doing her thing, Brad had taken me snowboarding that afternoon.

Miya joined us in the afternoon at the lodge for hot chocolate and filled me in with "how crazy Paige was, blah, blah, blah, blah, blah." Claims spoken as though directly from Matthew's lips. I listened to the story of how Matthew got a police-ordered restraint against Paige after she punched him in a bar. What Miya did not yet know was that Paige had only hit Matthew after he shoved her down during their argument. Why a grown man would find it necessary to file a restraining order against a woman was questionable.

There was also supposedly an episode while they were dating when Matthew had punched the wall next to Paige's head. She cried so hard out of fear, veins popping, she gave herself a black eye, which she admitted to

Mom at Miya's memorial service. No one believed that he didn't hit her. Matthew had tried to play her off as crazy and violent in order to save his own reputation for being hotheaded and abusive. This was exactly what he did to Miya.

Paige's story was significant because it proved Matthew's behavior toward Miya was how he typically treated women, causing them to feel belittled and powerless. As Miya became more aware of Matthew's abusive behavior, she sought reassurance and compassion in Paige, hoping to unveil the cloak Matthew had draped over her eyes and to better understand who Matthew really was…as well as be reassured it wasn't her being crazy, but Matthew being Matthew.

Miya's Journal Entry, October 26, 2007:

> *I am scared shitless. Honestly, Paige is right. He can be so mean & push away. He does it when he is threatened. If we are to salvage, I must do work w/o him & just show him w/ actions. Truth, I love him. Are we different? Yes, but it's totally doable. It hurts what he does to deal. Remember, Miya, it isn't about you. Just do your work. Eat well, practice yoga, work, be a good friend, & figure out how to be more positive.*

At Miya's memorial service, Paige explained to us, "I was where Miya was two years ago," except for two things. One, Paige wasn't married to him and therefore wasn't as "locked in." Two, Paige wasn't Miya, which meant she wasn't as extreme in her thoughts and did act with boundaries.

As newlyweds, Matthew again started in with wanting Miya to wean herself off the meds. He considered medication weak, as he did when they were dating in 2006.

Miya's Journal Entry, October 29, 2007:

> *Zoloft—well, I feel it. I definitely am still scared that Matt has some plan. Getting paranoid. I hate it. My mind is crazy. What is real is that he loves me but has pulled away. He probably doesn't believe this will work. I know it will. I just need to prove it. Detachment or not being attached is hard. But I need to focus on getting myself stable and working on my reactions. I want to make him happy. I'm so worried he doesn't want to be associated w/ someone on medication. Maybe he is disappointed in me. I don't want to let my mind take over. My mantra: Trust—inner strength, inner strength.*

If her insecurity about their relationship (especially after their wedding) and his faithfulness didn't make her feel insecure enough, the shock to her chemical balance beam sure as hell didn't help either! When Miya was off her meds, you knew. Reactions were completely dramatized. Everything was an issue.

Miya was calling Dad for financial aid in order to purchase the proper medication, since Matthew refused to pay for insurance, which would have covered it. Matthew allowed her to take the generic brand, which never worked for Miya.

By this time Caren was no longer acting as Miya's therapist.

Email from Caren to Sabrina:

When I became a friend in name (though of course there was still an aspect of the client/therapist relationship, as there was a parent/child relationship), I was no longer bound by the client/therapist privilege. It is certainly unorthodox to take on a previous client as a friend, and I'm sure that things could get a bit murky if put to the test, but it does not breach any ethics that I am aware of, and certainly in a small town like this, that sort of thing is bound to happen.

Regardless, all my comments and observations I have shared with you were during that time when we were no longer in a therapeutic relationship and thus I am not bound by that confidentiality rule.

Again, I think the circumstances are unusual here. If Miya were alive today I certainly would not be sharing any of this information with you because I would be morally obliged to keep the confidences of my friend. Instead, she is NOT here today and I share this information in an effort to help you- her family- her friends- try to make sense of this tragedy and understand it in a way that helps allow all of us to begin to accept our world as it has been permanently altered by Miya's loss.

Leading up to the wedding and until her death, Miya was working with Caren as friends to figure out why she was the way she was. Why did she have to feel loved? Why did she always have to make an issue out of something? Was it she that was tearing their marriage apart? What was wrong with her?

Just as I believe you are what you eat, I also consider what you think and tell yourself on a daily basis affects your overall well-being. If you told yourself you're beautiful and intelligent and kind and empathetic, you'd exude those qualities and trust in your ability to be the best you could be to yourself and everyone around you. Telling yourself you're sick and insane and unloved and annoying and suffocating, you'd become exactly that. Miya was not. But she convinced herself she was since people, such as Matthew, judged her in those ways. Yet that may also have been the reason why she worked so rigorously to fight Matthew's diagnoses and judgments.

My biggest regret is encouraging and convincing Miya to stay and work it out in Gunnison. "You can't just run home every time something in your marriage isn't working out, Miy," I'd say. "If you actually want this marriage to work you need to deal with these issues now. It can't be three months of happiness, then three months of misery, then run home and escape, then have Matthew crawl back to you, then be great again once you move back, and then the cycle starts all over."

I sent her there. Told her to suck it up and deal with it. I didn't want her marriage to be miserable forever. I wanted the absolute best for her. I wanted her fantasy to come true. Such advice seemed most logical to me but I never realized how truly horrible he was to her. I wish I had taken one step back from my "busy and important" college life and dealt with her marriage the way it should have been dealt with. I wish I had realized how very sad Miya was.

Not only did I regret my lack of attention the last few months of her life, but I wished I could have gone back to so many conversations and prodded her for more specifics. When she'd call me and tell me Matthew would yell at her if she ate cereal in bed because he was annoyed by her chomping, or wouldn't allow her to speak on her cell phone in his presence, forcing her to retreat to the basement and whisper, or wouldn't allow her to work for the Gunnison Directory any longer when they got married, even though she was their most successful saleswoman, I wish I would've said more than, "That's ridiculous. Do it if you want." I wish I would have connected that to the bigger picture. I told her, "Why would you want to be with someone who makes you feel like you have to tiptoe around and try your best not to annoy him?" But I just didn't recognize how torn up she was. Enough to kill herself.

I definitely also didn't know that Miya would walk around the house naked, trying to get Matthew to look at her…without success. Just to look at her and want her like a newlywed husband should want his 28-year-old, gorgeous, yoga-body-sculptedwife. Not be disgusted by her and look passed her as if she didn't exist.

I didn't know that Miya would cook and serve elaborate lunches for every staff member. Yet Matthew wouldn't speak to her while she was there. She wanted to please in every way possible. If one thing didn't work, she'd explore five other avenues. But Gunnison was small and the number of avenues was limited. She had been shut down and felt abandoned so many other times in her life that such treatment was too much.

When things got even rougher, Miya had supposedly called Ben, her ex-fiancee, and asked him, "Am I this way? Am I annoying? Am I difficult? Do I try to make an issue out of nothing? Is this all my fault?"

Ben replied, "Well, yes. You are all over the place. But that's why I loved you. You were never annoying."

Email from Miya to Matthew, September 7, 2007:

Matt,

I understand you are busy today, and I don't want to make tonight about last night. I really want to enjoy each other tonight so I thought I would email you my feelings. I just want you to know that I don't think you are this abusive and horrible person- I do however feel you sometimes act in abusive and angry ways. I still think this is linked to intense feelings of anxiety and irritation in a specific moment and that is probably what happened last night. You were probably anxious that the house was out of sorts, that I was doing work downstairs still, you were hungry and then when you cut yourself—it put you over the edge and you reacted. I can understand, yet at the same time WE need to figure out how to deal with this.

Last night, I was really upset because I feel you are unwilling to recognize this as unhealthy behavior and in all seriousness explosive behavior is not ok when we have kids. So last night I thought that until we address this and you face this anxiety I will not get pregnant and have kids with you. I feel that it would be irresponsible and selfish of me to bring a child/children into an environment where their parents have issues like this. Honey- I know that I have my issues—what concerns me is that you are so reluctant to admit and face yours.

It is up to you to research or do whatever you need to do to work through this. I will be gone for a while, so you have time to figure this out. I will not have babies with you until you address this, I am just trying to set a strong boundary here. I love you no matter what.

My respect, my love,
Miya

I often replayed a sun porch discussion with my parents five months after Miya's death. Watching my 64-year-old father cry, defeated, as he spoke about his deceased daughter was possibly the most excruciatingly painful and difficult thing I ever experienced. A man who stood over six feet tall, strong and thick physically, but emotionally wrecked. As the muted Detroit Pistons' 50th season anniversary celebration game flashed across the television, and Mom retired to their bedroom, I regained Dad's attention and continued to drill him about the reasons for Miya's death and failed marriage. "Do you think Miya would've married Matthew if she hadn't been Bipolar?" and "Do you think she therefore would've seen how dark and mean he is?" Questions that continuously tumbled through my mind.

"I shouldn't have let her move back out there," he cried. Regrets. Regrets. Regrets. *If only... If I hadn't...* Those would always haunt you, even though you *knew* it was not your fault. But it always was...or at least you thought so. Regrets for Dad about the number of times he hung up on Miya, as she called 80 times a day, nagging him about this and that. He would cut her short, screen those calls. *If only* he had been more sensitive to her needs, listened to her, really heard her...this all wouldn't have happened. Those may have been the most destructive, plaguing, recurring thoughts he could have. People always say: "No regrets." But how could he not have regrets when he was *supposed* to be his little girl's savior, her protector, the all-knowing one of what was and was not in her best interest?

As disconnected as Dad seemed at times, he would surprise me quite often. Introspective statements of truth occasionally stopped me in my tracks. That evening he asserted, "Miya wouldn't have had that need to save him if she weren't Bipolar. People try to balance things out. She had her problems and she picked someone with his own. It's the old story of misery loves company."

Was he right? Would Miya have "seen" Matthew for who he was if she wasn't struggling with her own demons and issues? I couldn't answer that, and I probably never will have the answer I want. What would such an answer really accomplish? Would it allow me to come to terms with my sister's death? Would I have something to blame for her death?

Maybe Dad was right. Maybe Miya was attracted to Matthew because she thought she could fix him, could devote all her energy to someone else who was "sick." Wanting to know, as Caren noted, *Why is he so abusive? Why does he have such a horrible temper? What happened in his childhood?* Miya would pine over these questions and issues and really believed that she could change him.

Kacee once said, "There's a darkness in Matthew. And at one point she also had that darkness." The difference though was that Miya overcame those dark tendencies. She had too much love to dwell on such darkness and allow it to detract from her goodness. Matthew, however, never faced his issues. And so they had been marinating for over 32 years. Miya's eagerness to deal with her issues and not allow them to consume her without a fight was possibly her best quality, encouraging us all to learn from that.

Email from Caren to Sabrina:

When she met Matthew, she wanted to iron out some issues that she felt were hindering their connection, so we met 2 or 3 times, the three of us, and had informal, therapeutic conversations. Obviously there was nothing much therapeutic about them because Matt thought I was "on Miya's side" and nothing useful, as far as I could see, was coming of our conversations. In fact, things did not seem to be going well at all, so I told them they needed couples counseling and Miya said they would see someone in Crested Butte who Matt liked.

Even though Miya was able to convince Matthew to meet with Caren as a friend in the spring of 2007, Caren explained, "He never let me in from day one. Any time I tried to push a little, he'd explode." When I prodded Caren to describe his explosions, Caren stated: "It was scary. It was intimidating. It was overpowering. I was frustrated…and Miya would be sitting in the chair, knees nestled to her chest, crying. Matthew uses body language. He says the most horrible things to you."

He rejected and regretted those informal talk sessions with Caren because he felt ganged up on, the odd man out, which very well could have been the case considering Miya and Caren's relationship and therapy history. The aspiration to work through their issues was well directed. However, primarily because of Matthew's nature of needing control, discussing such issues with Caren present (even though not acting as a therapist, but only as a friend) was not the success Miya had hoped it would be. So they stopped.

Email from Caren to Sabrina:

Nothing came of that then because, if I remember correctly, that was when Miya was going to India with you and that of course was when, on NYE, Matthew surprised everyone by asking Miya to marry him.

From that day until the day they married, things appeared to be great. The issues seemed to disappear and they seemed to be so happy that when they asked me to "officiate" at their wedding, I felt confident that I was doing the right thing. And for some time after, it all WAS good.

It had seemed Matthew's solo bike trip had transformed him into a new man while Miya was in Southeast Asia. It hadn't though. Only his external layer had been wind-swept. His internals were still soiled with abuse and anger. By the second week into their honeymoon, he returned to the real Matthew.

What Matthew didn't realize was that with Miya it was black and white. She would have felt secure, if he would have only hugged her and embraced her. Instead he became a statue, cold and stiff, reciprocating no emotion.

This was what Kacee witnessed when she met the two of them at the tail end of their honeymoon. They had been biking in Sicily, while Kacee was working on an organic farm in Italy. When Miya and Matthew showed up three hours late to the train station in Rome, Kacee was infuriated. Miya kept changing plans, inconsistent.

But what Kacee did not realize was that their lateness and inconsideration was because of Matthew. Miya was tiptoeing around each and every childish request and demand. "No! I will not eat there. I don't want to do that. I don't want to go then. You deal with and return these train tickets, Miya. They're too expensive." Miya was embarrassed. Who wouldn't be? She thought she had married a 32-year-old man. Matthew was a six-year-old little boy who stood with his arms crossed, pouting the whole time. Pushed to her limit, Kacee left Miya after only 24 hours—Matthew had refused to board the train to see a bike race (an event organized by Kacee's Italian boyfriend just for Matthew, since he was obsessed with biking.)

Email from Caren to Sabrina:

> When they returned to Gunnison, I'm pretty sure is when they started seeing that guy in Crested Butte for marriage counseling. And Miya and I spent many hours, taking walks, sitting around, just talking about things and trying to figure out how to make things right. So it was around that time that I began to go back to the old diagnosis that she had gotten so many years before of Borderline Personality Disorder (BPD).
>
> You are right that when Miya was young, there was the belief that a child really couldn't be diagnosed as Bipolar (nor with BPD either, actually), but it was clear to most everyone that her symptoms were congruent with such a diagnosis. And if she were a child today, there is no doubt in my mind that she would have that diagnosis. But what is interesting about that is because children were not previously given such a diagnosis; there are no long-term studies that look at what an adult with childhood bipolar disorder looks like. We don't know if the disorder continues, changes, disappears, etc. My feeling is that it had definitely remitted in Miya. She hadn't been on lithium or any other meds for bipolar disorder for several years and her mood swings and impulsive behavior and relationship problems were, as an adult, much more indicative of BPD. And we'll never know for sure if in fact that diagnosis was accurate the first time around, and in truth, I was not so much concerned about her "having a diagnosis" as that we were appropriately treating the symptoms and as far as we both could tell, she manifested enough symptoms of BPD to make it worthwhile to try treating it as such. (symptoms of BPD: frantic efforts to avoid real or imagined abandonment; patterns of unstable interpersonal relationships characterized by alternating extremes of idealization and devaluation; unstable self-image, impulsivity; mood instability; chronic feelings of emptiness, and several others, but do you recognize someone in those symptoms?
>
> I knew she hated it, but it made so much sense, and we decided that we would, together, as FRIENDS, not as therapist/client, learn about a fairly new therapy used in BPD: Dialectical Behavioral Therapy (DBT) that was proving to be extremely helpful for others with that diagnosis. I ordered a book and a workbook and we were very excited about really doing some good work.

Caren had outlined BPD for me: "It's a life-long, basically untreatable personality disorder. So intrinsic to one's basic core personality that it affects every move. You function in the world with an impaired personality. There's no pill for it, no particular brain chemical shown to be at fault or absent. With Bipolar, when you suffer from a mood disorder your moods are affected, as opposed to a personality disorder where every aspect of your functioning is affected—not just your moods.

"It's like an orange. Look at a normal person, maybe a bit brown on the outside, but looks pretty normal. Take an orange for someone who suffers from depression and the skin will appear damaged, but the insides remain healthy. You can peel off the damaged part and the orange will be perfectly fine. Now take an orange for someone that's BPD. Not only is the skin look rotten, but the inside is also rotten through and through. It affects everything. You can't get rid of the damaged part. There would be nothing left. Life is chaotic, makes you impulsive, makes you introspective to the extreme…life becomes difficult, and that was Miya—life was difficult for her." Miya's shifts in emotions were definitely characteristic of bipolar disorder, but her lack of boundaries seemed to be more definitive, a characteristic of BPD.

Some explain Borderline Personality Disorder as being like Swiss cheese. There are holes, gaps that help to explain why and how Miya was unable to suppress certain impulses. "Her frustration tolerance was minimal," Whitaker had told me. It was torture for Miya to think of her reaction and thought patterns. So Miya openly allowed them to just run straight through those open gaps.

I had never considered BPD as a diagnosis until the spring of 2008. I had always been certain: *Miya's Bipolar.* In fact, I was a bit shocked. *Miya was narcissistic?* It was a question Miya worried over as well.

Miya's Email to Caren, November 5, 2007:

Caren,

    Lots of clarity this weekend. This is what I wrote on Saturday morning before going to the Thai temple:

    In many ways, I feel that an aspect of my personality mirrors that which is described about BPD, but I don't believe it is all me. I believe that because I am & do experience things at a physiological level so emotionally—that all the trauma and the ways in which I developed in order to deal with the emotions caused a layer of my self that is dysfunctional. I recognize that when I am dealing with my feelings and not running these personality characteristics aren't so obvious or in control. Although, when the same emotions that were so huge for me as a child are triggered and I am not mindful, the BPD type of personality works as a defensive block to that which is too intense. The intensity is not self-created, and when I run, I run into people around me and that intensity causes them to pull away, which in return wounds me more. (I don't think, wow, am I doing something that I need to be aware of? No, I am only working from a feeling state.)

What I understand about the brain is the emotions and the memories and experiences that are attached to the emotions do not have a sense of time—meaning that my brain doesn't recognize that what I am feeling may not be happening because the cognitive part of my mind isn't working. The emotions are in overdrive. This intensity causes destruction, the constant bubbling and oversensitivity of my emotional state on a regular basis along with the emotional trauma I experienced in childhood causes me to have issues and what it seems like to people on the outside— unjustified emotions causing the chaos—but to me on the inside the emotions are so overwhelming, extremely difficult to sit with.

From an outsider's perspective, these emotional outbursts are unjustified and cause chaos for no good reason (which is why Matt thinks I am addicted and need chaos). But to me, on the inside the emotions are so overwhelming and extremely difficult to deal with. Not sure if this is borderline—but I am sure that many of the ways in which I manage my internal world looks similar to the life of someone who struggles with BPD.

I think too I have a lot of sadness & I found people don't want to be around someone sad. I think I am a calmer person than what I put off. I think I get exhausted by my performances.

So this weekend, I learned this mediation technique called divide and conquer. It's great. It takes an experience, say Anxiety:

> **stomach is in knots*
> **mind is obsessing over a thought*
> **feeling worried*

And it divides them up. Stomach in knots, you think- well that's not comfortable- but I can handle that- I can breath through that. Mind obsessing- well- the mind likes to act like a broken record, but I have experienced this before and can deal with it.

It's pulling the huge clump of overwhelming experiences into pieces that are easier to manage. I did it this morning, I will continue to practice.

The week before Miya's death she and Caren had a great conversation. Caren told me: "We were working in her workbook. She was going to get herself healthy and work through it all. And then Matthew knocked her over her head with that bombshell that he wanted a divorce."

Email from Caren to Sabrina:

Then I went in to Denver to spend the week with my grandson and then it was November 14 and it was over...

The first time I read Miya's journals was in the police station after her memorial service. That experience was draining, yet not as intense as it was nine months later when the head Gunnison detective sent me copies of four of her journals I had requested. Her words were an invitation to me; I was able to know exactly what my sister was thinking leading up to her death.

Sabrina's Journal Entry, September 5, 2008:

Am I ready for this? No. Ready to be over-consumed with Miya's sadness? Entry after entry in her journal. I remember how painful it was to read through them with Kacee and Emma the Tuesday after the memorial service. I wish I could believe that it was only so very sad because it was so raw—her death. But, I'm afraid it still is so sad. Almost ten months later. Just like I was scared to meet with Whitaker and Caren and be disenchanted and know Miya on a different level, I am scared now to dive into Miya's truest thoughts and feelings. I feel sadness because I sense hers.

…

Definitely not ready. Tearful gasps, holding my breath, and then gasping. Constant blame. Miya blaming herself, her thoughts racing, never able to quiet her mind, yet having clear thoughts as the 14th approached that Matthew will never change.

I think what was most difficult to read and absorb was Miya's words: She knew it. Knew it would never work. Matthew would never and could never unconditionally love her. Always would push her away. Knew divorce was lingering and that terrified her. But, even though you can write or say something, it does not mean you will not be affected by it when it becomes reality. Better yet, I think you write or say things often to try to convince yourself you'd be okay. Prepare yourself for it. Or, maybe think that if it is written or said it won't come true.

Miya's Journal, October 31, 2007:

It's interesting—the fear feels endless, overtaking me. I feel restricted to breathe. I believe I want something healthy—Matt is not co-dependent—but for me, it's got me. I feel like running, hiding, doing anything to not be consumed by the pain inside. The pain I felt on solo, as a child in the corner of my bedroom, in the hall at school. I am worried I am just this way, a way that causes problems, then I will lose Matt. Dipping into this, I feel debilitated, I am consumed with it—It is all over me. The hurt & pain runs deep. I freeze up inside—I will do anything to not have this there, to keep him here—to not leave—to manipulate the world around me so it feels safe and I get what I need. The thing is I cause myself problems when I do that.

My insides are like lava. It's dangerous to try to handle them, so I have to work the world around me. But it never works. I fail. I cause problems,

I upset people, I go too far, I am inappropriate, unaware and pushy. It's as though I have a crying child inside and the internal nourishment is too hot and so I go outside and try to make it work for me. I sell, I convince, but the baby won't stop—nothing satisfies it but the inside nourishment which isn't able to. I am running around w/ adult knowledge. I get, do what feels good or make things happen w/ the belief I will feel fulfilled and the fire inside will be put out. I run frantically around, searching for the perfect water to stop the fire when all I have to do is stop moving, drop, roll and it would be gone. What am I without the fire?

Miya's Journal, November 1, 2007:

I fear some anger b/c I am scared. It's 2 in the morning and Matt is sleeping on the couch. I do feel unsafe. He is saying divorce. I am trying to not focus on that. He needs to tell me he's out and his feelings. Do I think we need separation? No. I will try anything.

I am laying here in bed. I am scared to death. I feel like I am going to be left. I feel so anxious. Matt keeps blaming me for his unhappiness and for my issues causing harm to our relationship.

Fuck. I need to focus on my own healing.

I am terrified that I am damaged, that I can't work things out fast enough. He said yesterday that he will be 33 soon and wants to have kids—I feel so much pressure. My head is spinning. He is right—I do always have an issue. How can I change this pattern?

I notice the minute I am uncomfortable, I do things that exacerbate it. Talking to Mom makes it worse. Truth is, I know why and all the times I try these feelings, I run, and my running causes the issue. Then I can blame the issue for my unhappiness and not myself. The loneliness—no it's not that—but I think I associate these feelings with being alone, left, abandoned. It's a strong emotion—it's probably something many people feel—but what triggers it is different for everyone. I believe I get angry now when I get hurt. Maybe I feel angry.

I need to change my patterns, I need to change my thoughts or my obsession with my thoughts. I tend to sulk. I need to learn new ways to react to these emotions—not escape—and not obsession. I am committed to doing everything it takes to get myself healed and to bring my part of our marriage to a place that is a healthy track.

I need to write—I need to talk therapy—I need to verbally express myself. Undoing takes time. I don't want to live in crisis—so what causes me to? What keeps me from a serene feeling? I think I always need to connect and be validated. I need to learn to stand on my own two feet and clear out all the junk that keeps me out of balance.

Later that same day:

I just realized how much I am affected by other people's moods, especially Matt's. I feel so much fear, instability—I definitely based my stability on others—I think maybe that is why I am draining. I lean too much. I have been like this as long as I remember. What I am writing resonates. It's true. I can't rely on myself b/c I either quit something or can't get along. My mom said something once—she said, despite everything, her friends love her— how can I figure out how to stop whatever it is that turns people off, which makes it hard for me to get along? Maybe my parents were right, but the stability to deal with this wasn't there. I didn't have the self-esteem to then face what isn't easy to hear. I did fall apart & I still do now. Maybe Matt's right. I have a whole world of fakeness in order to survive—my real self is lost inside. I am scared to lose him, so scared I don't deserve for him to stick around—I am terrified.

OK—the more I say that, the worse the feelings are. It feels almost safer to create the issue that I fear may happen—then chance it—what is that about? Most people do need to be forced to face this stuff. I must create so much chaos outside b/c it is what lives in me—Matt is the opposite. He worked so hard to not let any chaos in at all.

Miya's Journal, November 4, 2007:

Got done this morning w/ the meditation retreat at Wat Budda…Thai temple. I got a lot of ideas and learned many new ways of dealing w/ my issues. Right now, I feel itchy everywhere, maybe just dry skin. I have a knot in my stomach. I can't escape this anxiety & fear that Matthew is going to leave me. I tried to breathe through it this morning. Maybe I have an agenda for it to pass. When I give it too much energy, it multiplies easily. For now I am going to recognize it as tightness in my solar plexus—that's it— nothing more. Divide and conquer! The temple feels like a place I can go—talk & be w/ whatever pain or feelings are present and have that be ok. More importantly, I want to begin to feel my body as a temple—a safe haven. I am exhausted—long day—ready to sleep soon. I am really happy to see Matt. Today we were talking about enlightenment to see our path to know. I knew Ben wasn't right—I know & know Matt is the one to walk, learn, grow & spend my life with. I want a sign—I want something—right now to reassure me. Maybe things don't work that way but I could use it right about now. Anyway time to be here in bed.

Miya's Journal, November 6, 2007:

It's 4 in the AM—I just woke up from a terrible dream. I was in Las Vegas—was with someone else, running around, never looked at my plane ticket—until I saw that I was suppose to leave at 2:30 pm. It was 2:15. I rushed and finally called Matthew and his phone was off. He was on the flight home. I let him down. I was on the next flight—the attendant was giving another gentleman a package. I overheard. It was suppose to be for us—it was an engaged couple—he was in one seat & she another. 2 empty seats—suppose to be ours together. Matthew took the 2:30. I was on the 4:18. But it felt like the seats across the aisle were suppose to be us together. I thought for a moment I was on the right plane and looked all over for Matthew. He wasn't there. Then the guy next to me told me it was the 4:18 flight. I did miss the 2:30. The plane was driving on a road—up and down—steep w/ traffic lights—I saw down the road—snow-packed street & said I hope they know we can't drive on that.

    I opened the package. Matt had left it for me. I read the note—it said something about the pilots going faster b/c I am on board to get me home sooner. That he wants to stay in touch, email is the best. That I have "by accident" missed too many flights and he was breaking up with me. I got to the connecting city—and he was in Burger King line. I said hi & sat down at table to finish reading. All of a sudden everything was closed. He was really nice—acting like what his letter said was "can't wait to see you." We were going to be on the next flight home together, he had a longer delay, that me being there now wasn't enough, damage was done. Then all a sudden he was shopping, or had all this stuff. We were somewhere else, he was showing me many ties—some were green—the bright green I love of our wedding—he was nonchalantly asking me what I thought and telling me which he thought helped him to look single.

Miya's Journal, November 8, 2007:

    Right now, I can't sleep, I am going to divide and conquer this state as best I can.

Miya's Journal, November 10, 2007:

    Really upset this morning, almost resentful. I know the anger is based on hurt and rejection, and I know he wants to make himself feel better for pushing me away—but he needs to realize for 3 weeks I have done nothing but create a peaceful environment and he still chooses to push me away—these are his issues. I feel I want to make him pay. I notice I do this when I get hurt by pulling away—but in Matt's case it makes him happier—which leaves me resentful. I am going to try something new. I am going to try to allow these hurt feelings to surface & release them.

Miya's Journal, November 11, 2007:

    I feel like I want to crawl out of my skin—<u>anything is better than this.</u>

    Foundation. Feel unsteady. The workshop, I believe, went well. Not feeling really good though. My anxiety is through the roof. I feel like he is going to just leave me—it's not about being ok—It's about hurting like this enough *in my life—I don't want to be hurt again. Last year hurt so bad. I feel he is doing it all over again—I feel so disconnected—he has cut me off in our first year of marriage where he is suppose to want to have me around. I feel I am trying so hard—doing my work and he keeps bailing on me—I need him not to bail. I need him to be here—to stay connected—even when it's hard. Like in yoga—not zoning out when the sensation is intense but staying with it and riding the wave with me.*

I am not running. I actually feel as though I am pretty balanced in the middle of all this—it's just very uncomfortable.

It's really hard for me to understand. My life has been very smooth. I'm making money, taking care of myself and the house and dogs and wanting to love him and he just continues to push me away.

It feels good to sit still. I have been running around the last two days, trying to prepare for today—It's done and that feels good.

Miya's Journal, November 11, 2007:

What's really interesting is that if Matthew could say—forget it, I love you, let's just be happy—and not push me away and keep me at a distance, and not talk to me like I am his child—then despite my ups & downs I am working on regulating even more—I could let everything go. I think I keep my anger as a defensive—in reality I want to let down my guard, be able to take a deep breath and be myself w/o monitoring everything I do—I am tired.

Miya's Journal, November 13, 2007:

It is so clear this marriage isn't going to work. Matthew is so unforgiving, stuck and distant that I will spend my whole life chasing him. I feel like I can't win. The truth is I keep telling myself that if I change, if I do something different then it will be better, but he will always find something to be angry at, or be uninterested in me. He changed for a while, then the reality of how he struggles in close relationships once they get too close to him is clear. I know I am not perfect, but I also know I can work through conflicts—I have done it before—but I can't do it all on my own.

I have convinced myself that I this and I that—and although yes I still have too many issues, insecurities, etc…I find the stiffness of this marriage drowning my real self—and my ability to freely be me. I don't want to be married to someone who doesn't want me—I am sick of not feeling wanted—I understand I have partially created that dynamic in the past, but now it is clear that Matthew is done.

Chapter Seven

During the first year after Miya died, I flew to Gunnison three times. The day after to pick up her body, then the first week in December for her memorial service organized by friends, and finally for three days in May to pack up and ship her personal belongings back to Detroit.

When it happened, Kacee, 24 years old at the time, was traveling in Australia, and Emma, 26, was studying in Madrid. Only I was around to accompany my parents to Gunnison. If I hadn't been there and experienced it first-hand, I never would have believed what went on in those first 24 hours.

When we landed at the Gunnison airport, Matthew was not there to greet us. He even had his parents, who were, to our surprise, on the 30-passenger connecting flight from Denver, picked up by a friend and driven to the condo. He couldn't face us. It was a sneak peak into the real Matthew. He closed himself off from us, just as he did to Miya, and it was the first time I really understood how he could make you feel: helpless and vulnerable.

We drove directly from the airport to the police station, but there was no red carpet laid out for us. Instead, the three of us were forced to wait over an hour in the conference room for the head investigator, Detective Dan Thompson, to arrive. He filled us in with as many of the specifics as he legally could. That included showing us Miya's suicide note, which Matthew had not yet seen, nor knew about supposedly.

Her words verified my initial assumption. He did this to her. He defeated her.

Miya's Suicide Note:

I did this before—I am so very sorry, I can't do these feelings again. I opened up and gave my most vulnerable part—I am in too much pain. It will be easier. I will not be thrown away again. I can't go through another 2 years, I really went for it this time & I am too wounded this time. I'm sorry, Mom and Dad. Too many years more this pain.
Matt I loved you unconditionally. (This was written down the side of the blank computer paper, as more of an afterthought.)

Two hours after Thompson arrived, Matt walked in, an attorney at his side. Thompson led him and his parents—Nancy and Jack—into the main office area to have a moment to read over the suicide note before joining us in the conference room. About 20 minutes later, they walked into the conference room, Matt sinking into the chair at the head of the long table, not once looking at us, his parents standing on either side of him. Thompson left us alone in the room with only Caren as a mediating force. The lawyer waited outside.

Journal Entry, November 16, 2007:

> *I'm so angry at Matt. I can't believe he actually got a lawyer. Why? It was our Miya. He was her husband—why a lawyer? What did he have to hide? He knew it was his fault. She left a note...it pretty much said: "I couldn't do it all over again—it was too painful." He killed her. It would've been so easy to make her happy—he pushed her so far over the edge.*

Mom looked at Matt and stated firmly, yet compassionately, "Matt, all we want is to take Miya home. We want to get her things, take her home, and bury her next to Grandpa Billy. We want to fly out tomorrow and not have to ever come back here."

Matt agreed, "Yes, I want her to be next to Grandpa Billy," but he then began to state his concerns. He wanted to make sure he could have a memorial service in Gunni—his way of playing up the role of the grieving, innocent husband.

"Yes, of course, you can do whatever you'd like," we answered. His requests and concerns seemed ridiculous. Why wouldn't we let him do those things?

But he expressed no compassion, no remorse, no sympathy, nothing.

I was waiting for the moment, any moment, when I could allow myself to just explode. And I did.

Journal Entry, November 16, 2007:

> *I snapped and screamed, "You fucking killed her!" I meant it—sort of thought about it earlier—so much of me felt guilty. His mother lunged at me. "Don't you ever say that! Ever. It was his wife!" And Matt burrowed his head into his arms on the table—the saddest look in his eyes—the saddest for an outsider—a look of guilt and fear of us. He knew. He feared us. Knew it was him. I left the room, with Dad yelling after me, "Why would you say that?" Mom, I know, silently thanking me for saying it aloud.*

I had to say it; I wanted him to know that I knew he did this to Miya. Her suicide note said it all. I could imagine it as a complete moment of weakness, feeling as though there was no other way out, the humiliation and disappointment of a failed marriage. Being bipolar, everything my sister felt, did, and said was done with the greatest intensity and love. Therefore, once Matt told her he wanted a divorce the night before, she considered herself to be the greatest failure.

I left the room immediately, heading into the courtroom across the hall. Brad and Steve, Matt's business partners and close friends of Miya, were there, along with other police officers and one of Matt's childhood friends who had flown in that afternoon.

I melted into Brad's embrace, crying, repeating, "He did this. He killed her."

But he argued, "No, he didn't. It's no one's fault." I didn't have the energy to fight his words. The two of us retired to a pair of chairs and sat, holding hands.

Ten minutes later, Dad and Mom came out, having finished the meeting, and we left to see Miya's body at the coroner's office directly across the street from the police station. The three of us were led through an office area and into a back room, where Miya was laid out on a table.

I watched Mom stroke Miya's cold, naked body, encased in a linen cloth, tracing her fingertips down Miya's left arm, to her hip bone, down her leg, rubbing her feet, then comparing hands. Mom's hands, gloved with tenderly, smooth skin, were larger than Miya's rough and calloused hands. That was Dad's gift to Miya, as well as to me. But Miya's hands were worse; hers were tougher. Or so I thought.

The only thing I considered beneficial about Miya's hands was her great, intuitive, massaging touch. Other than that, I always thought Miya got screwed with the worst degree of Dad's dry hands. Would've always thought this unless those poorly circulated, strong, rough hands would have been the reason she were still alive. If only she had changed her mind mid-fall. Right after she knocked the wooden chair out from under her feet, right when she began hanging, right when her legs were probably kicking, her tears cut short due to fear, her hands ripping at the rope to loosen its hold on her neck.

However, her hands didn't come in handy. She didn't take advantage of Dad's "gift." They were clenched into tight fists. So clenched, it was nearly impossible to pry them open to remove her jewelry. Just about as tense as her locked jaw with her discolored tongue wedged between her lips. Clenched as if to say, "So there! This is what you did to me, Matthew."

There was no turning back for her. Maybe when she finally crossed over, yes. But not during the process. Were her hands clenched out of anger? Resentment? Shock? Did she regret it? It was hard for me to think she didn't regret her impulsive decision right when the rope snapped taut. Hard for me not to wish she hadn't...because that would mean she was ready to leave me behind.

For a week after she died, I barely slept—two, maybe three hours a night. The night of November 15 was only the start of it.

Journal Entry, November 16, 2007:

I don't know if it was a good idea to see Miya last night. I am terrified by the thought of her tongue half out of her mouth, her neck a deep red, across her chest stitched up where they did an autopsy. Part of me wanted to hide, part wanted to hug her. I was terrified that her eyes would all a sudden open.

We pried her hands open, clenched so tightly—so much pain.

Her OM necklace, her pearl earrings (the ones she gave to all of the girls at her wedding), her tan OM bracelet, her wedding ring, her other ring. We'll divide all of them up.

I want to take the time to write but I just want to get it down, graze over it—hope to wake up.

**

This morning, Mom and I drove to Brad's place and hiked the trails above Gunni with Henley and Billy [Miya's dogs] and Boone [Brad's dog]. I felt so energized, racing the dogs along the trails—I couldn't cry when I was running then—I was too happy—releasing all the pain.

On the trail I asked Brad to promise to make sure Matthew was nice to Henley and he just said, "Matt loves Henley; he'll take great care of him." But then later that morning, as Matthew and his parents screened our calls, Brad wouldn't answer either. Yes, I understand the position he's in, but come on, you know exactly the situation and how Matthew is. At least pick up—don't give me some bullshit answer on the phone in Denver airport to my question of "Where were you today? Why didn't you answer?" and say, "I was everywhere today. I was busy. Sorry."

Around 10 a.m., after hiking, Mom, Dad, and I waited in our hotel room for Matthew or his parents to return our dozens of phone calls. But they didn't. We felt pressed for time because our flight back to Detroit was leaving at 3 p.m. Mom was enraged. We just wanted Miya's things.

When Mom finally got hold of Detective Thompson at 12:30 p.m., we were told that instead of allowing us to go into the condo (which was still on lock-down for the investigation) and take one outfit for the funeral in Detroit, Matthew had decided that Miya's friend Ashley, who worked for Matthew's company, would be the only one allowed in.

Mom screamed at Thompson, "Do you have children? How would you feel if this was happening to you? We are the only ones who would know what *my* daughter would want to wear, not a friend!" Thompson hung up.

With Matthew, it was all about control, all about deciding when and where something would be done, what and how it could be done.

Journal Entry, November 16, 2007:

How could Matthew not let Mom in to be with Miya's things? What an insensitive prick! I wanted so badly to just drive over there, tear down the door and grab whatever I needed of hers. I needed her notes/drawings/letters. We needed her journals.

I sat with Ashley telling her to find hats, sweaters, yoga clothes, jackets, bags—everything she could stuff into suitcases, as much as she would be allowed to take. I felt bad for her—stuck in the middle between me and Matthew.

It was like we were the criminals. Why were we being pushed to the side? What was so secretive? Why was everyone on Matthew's side and not giving the family proper consideration?

While I was on the phone with Ashley, I acknowledged, "I know this is difficult, Ashley. I realize you're in the middle of it and I'm so sorry. I'm assuming he's standing right there?" Her silence was my answer.

Journal Entry, November 16, 2007:

Matthew was saying he needed to first go through her things and work through it. I couldn't believe he actually played off his pain—he had 7 months of grieving time. He killed her. He killed her. He took her from us. Our perfect six.

Fifteen minutes after I hung up with Lizzie, Detective Thompson and his partner arrived in the lobby of our hotel, along with Ashley, carrying two bags. I thanked the girls, unzipped and unloaded the bags directly onto the lobby floor, and began to unfold a piece of my sister's life—a photo of her and Grandpa Billy;a photo of me as a two-year-old, dressed in high heels, a pink hat and bathing suit; her wedding shower dress; yoga spandex; her North Face vest; and her knit, Lululemon hat, my favorite. I sank further toward the floor, frustration so overwhelming. All I could think was: *How is this really happening right now?* My eyes by that point were in pain, my neck and head banging, my temples throbbing.

Afterward, we stopped back into the Firebrand, Mom's favorite eatery off Main Street. While I sipped a smoothie and Mom ate her sandwich, Caren called to warn us that Matthew was demanding Miya's wedding ring, which we had removed from her finger at the coroner's the night before. I was shocked, yet thrilled, because finally we had something that he wanted. It never occurred to us that taking the ring would be an issue. It was now our collateral.

We hurried to the airport in fear that Matthew would send the police to confiscate it. We did not know then, when Matthew had called the detective to demand the ring, Thompson basically laughed at him. Sending policemen to the airport for a wedding ring was not happening.

At the airport it became apparent that Miya had touched everyone in Gunnison. Even the women at the United Airline desk loved her. When we checked in, they made sure we knew Matthew "wasn't their favorite employee" when he had worked at the airport a few years before. The attendants opened up to us, and we opened up to them. It was the first time in the past 24 hours that we finally felt someone in Gunni was on our side, that someone understood there was more to Miya's death than what appeared to be a sick, mentally-ill wife and a grieving husband. They shuttled us past security and made sure, even if Matthew showed up for the ring, he could not have it.

Journal Entry, November 16, 2007:
> *Mom and Dad are a mess. I think we all are cried out—or at least a constant mess. It's so hard to see Dad's eyes, red, puffy, circles imprinted, his body shaking, Mom's face buried in her hands, mouthing: Why? So sad and lonely. I'm so happy I came to Gunni for them mostly. They wouldn't have been able to hold it together.*

Chapter Eight

Miya's body was on our flight from Gunnison back to Detroit. That was comforting, yet, at the same time, because she was below us in the dark, cold and alone, it was terrible. That was always her worst fear.

I was eager to land in Detroit, pull into the garage at the Big House, open the back door and have the dogs bombard me, yelping and shaking their tushies—Rosie, Ellie and Gracie. When we pulled into the driveway, a handful of cars were there, even though it was 1 a.m. Everyone waiting for us to arrive. Part of me wanted them to be gone, to disappear, let us be. Part was grateful for the warmth and security in the house.

Journal Entry, November 17, 2007:

I barely slept last night—up from 1 a.m. on—working on her eulogy. The whole house has been prepared by friends—stocked with food, cleaned, etc. They're so good to us.

All of Detroit knows. My phone has been ringing off the hook all morning. I don't know if I'm ready to be home. Ready to be home alone. Not for the funeral. I know it'll be huge. I just hope I can keep myself together while speaking.

I want my eulogy to be perfect for her, my best work. And, I feel like I nailed it this time.

After I walked into the house, I retreated to my bedroom upstairs. As terrified as I was of Miya popping out in the dark while in the hotel room in Gunnison, I was more terrified in the Big House. The long, poorly lit hallways, ample hiding spots behind every door and under every bed frame. I needed company. And definitely didn't want to burden Mom or Dad with my needs that late. At 1:15 a.m. I called my best friend Lauren and asked her to come over.

As I waited for her to arrive, I did anything I could to work on replacing that horrific image of Miya, which was replaying like a broken record over and over in my head. I hurried back downstairs into Mom's closet and snagged the only copy of Miya and Matthew's Wedding DVD on her shelf. Then, retracing my steps, hurrying and running from one shadow to the next, I returned to my bedroom. Not wanting *it* to get me.

Hunched over on my bed, I sat cross-legged, watching scenes of her wedding weekend flash across my computer's screen. I wanted so badly to reach in and strangle Matt, but couldn't. Not just because I physically couldn't, but also couldn't emotionally. I'd catch myself smiling, unable to replace my joyful emotions from seven months ago with my newly found three-day anger.

Watching clips of Matt tickle my sister with joy whenever he feigned a loving kiss or hug. Tricking her and me. Miya smiling and smiling. Looking so deeply into his eyes during a candid shot as Matt headed out for thebike ride the morning of their wedding and also as they danced alone on the dance floor. Another shot of Dad and Miya, dancing.

And then there it was. What hit me hardest: Miya and I outside our hotel rooms in the dusted parking lot of the Moab winery. Together, Miya in yoga clothes, me, wrapped in a towel, too lazy to throw clothes on after showering. As she tried to pick me up, cradling me sideways, I quickly slipped from her grip and laughed, while Miya shouted, "You're too heavy!" Thinking I was still six years old and her little sister.

Freeze. Rewind. Replay. Freeze. Rewind. Replay. Again. And again.And again.Tears streaming down. It was the first time in days that time finally stood still.

Lauren arrived in the middle of this screening. Sitting on the end of my bed, mainly speechless and quiet, with an occasional, "I'm so sorry, Sabrina." Allowing me to unload my thoughts, as I gradually curled up smaller and smaller into a ball and passed out, Lauren snuggling next to me.

The next morning I joined Mom at the Sports Club to swim, and then at the trail to walk the dogs. We both needed release, and Mom needed me there as a safeguard. I should have stitched a sign to my shirt: "Don't bother me, don't speak to me, don't even say you're so sorry; nothing. Act like nothing is different." We didn't want pitying eyes following us from our lockers to the pool into the showers out the door to our car. The Jewish rumor mill already had released our family's stats on Friday. So by Saturday all of Detroit knew. But it wasn't real just yet. Gunnison felt like one bad nightmare. So I assumed, since I had only slept a total of six hours in the past three days and could easily be hallucinating, that I was still sleeping. Neither one of us was ready to be awakened.

Later that Saturday, Mom forced the funeral home cosmetician to unfix Miya. She wanted him to remove all the makeup caked onto her cheeks and smeared across her lips, which he had applied the day before so she was more "presentable." Mom wanted her exposed, to broadcast what she did to herself. Not hide it and act as though we were ashamed of her. But only for a few minutes, in order to take a photograph. A photograph that Mom very well might have considered her most important work ever. Important, but also morbid and vengefully inspired. Miya, just as I saw her in Gunnison at the coroner's, and just as Matthew saw her upon finding her hanging in their basement. Not candy-coated, as she would be for everyone else the next day, looking at her in the open casket at the funeral service.

There were only a few other things I imagined would be more horrifying than the sight of walking downstairs, finding your wife hanging, seeing the effects of such an act on her body, and having that memory and sight forever branded in your mind. Seeing your beloved sister dead on a coroner's table with her tongue clenched between her lips was second to that.

People originally excused Matthew's decision not to visit Miya's body before she was flown to Detroit. Was his decision not to say goodbye because seeing her again would have been too painful? Or, was it maybe because he couldn't look at her knowing that he drove her toward her suicide? That even though he might not have physically wrapped that rope around her neck, he definitely played a part in her decision?

Mom was not going to send him the photo within a week. No, she'd sit on it…for seven months, a year, five years. She didn't know yet when the time would come, if at all. She just wanted it on file and available to her if and when everything did eventually dissipate, and Mom still wanted to capitalize on the opportunity, despite everyone (except me) being completely against such an action.

If she did decide to go through with it, she would send it, sealed in an envelope and addressed to Matthew. Stamped with Miya's personalized stamp of a photo of her in the yoga pose of Upward Dog, and signed, *This is what you did to my daughter.*

Emma had arrived early Friday evening from Madrid and Kacee's plane was landing around 10 p.m. that Saturday night. Having flown for two straight days from Australia, Kacee was completely in the dark. She did not know any of the specifics—how Miya killed herself, how Matthew was acting, how we were not allowed into the condo, how Gunnison had basically excommunicated us. She told me once she arrived that she wouldn't allow herself to even consciously process that Miya was dead.

She had been in a library in Melbourne when she found out. She just knew something was wrong. Unable to access her email, she frantically tried to get hold of Mom or Dad. Since their phones did not get reception in Gunnison, Kacee instead called Katie, one of her best girlfriends and a sister-like figure for Miya. Upon hearing Miya died, she collapsed onto the library's tile floor, screaming and screaming.

Loaded into Mom's suburban, with my cousin Jeffrey driving, Mom, Dad, Emma and I drove to the airport to pick Kacee up. As a family. Hair braided in pigtails, wearing her army green khakis and grey button down sweater, she was surrounded by us. The five of us stood, ignoring the fellow travelers weaving in and around us. We were absorbed in each other's confusion and tears, hoping whoever was to our right or left would soak it all up and be that comforting force we each so badly needed. Age didn't separate us at that moment. Mom and Dad needed to be cradled just as badly as I did.

I sat all the way in the back of the car afterward, feeling so empty, holding hands with Kacee. We drove directly to the funeral home. Its director, David, met us there despite the time of day. Sitting on the lounge chairs in the main lobby, Mom, Dad and I filled Kacee in and prepared her for what she was about to see.

Beyond the main service hall and into the backroom, Miya was there. Not like I had seen her; makeup again contaminated her face, her mouth was locked shut, her lips pursed, as though silencing her. It was no longer Miya.

I watched Kacee hyperventilating, Emma hugging her, Mom desperately trying to remove the makeup, unveiling the cloth covering Miya's head in order to stroke her long, healthy brown hair she had worked so hard to grow out, Dad hovering in the corner, trying to hide his face. I watched emotionless, wondering what was wrong with me because I wasn't crying. Nothing left in me.

Jeffrey and David waited patiently in the lobby for us. And after about 15 minutes, we got back into the suburban and headed home.

Some of Kacee's girlfriends from college and others from high school were waiting at the house, having jumped on flights as soon as they heard the news. We joined them in the library.

Emma and Kacee then began attacking my eulogy. I didn't realize what I was writing when I had started. I simply opened my journal on the flight from Baltimore and began jotting down stories. I didn't want Miya to slip away from me. Our stories kept her alive. As they began to flow more freely, I opened up my computer and let my fingers go.

My sisters were enraged that I had written a eulogy. They wanted something read which we all could stand up and read. From a "we" perspective, not an "I." I sat that Saturday night in the library fully exposed. Emma, with pen in hand, tearing my eulogy to shreds.Kacee backing her with equal frustration. Mom stood in the hallway, countering their objections, saying, "No, I want Sabrina to read this. This is from Sabrina. You can both write your own."

I felt alienated. My sisters were making me question my motive for writing a eulogy, as though it was a selfish act on my part. But I wouldn't concede.

By about 3 a.m. a ceasefire took hold and everyone drizzled out of the room toward bed, taking over any spot in the house they could find for some rest. Kacee and I didn't move though. I sat, lying with my head in her lap on the green leather couch, as she lightly stroked my hair and massaged me. Letting our up and down relationship come to a steady spot for the first time in three years. I was homesick for her comfort and allowed myself to feel protected by her. She was unable to sleep, and even though my eyes kept fluttering shut, I tried to resist as long as I could. I didn't want to lose this connection with her. Wanted it to last forever and have her comfort me and tell me it would all be okay again.

The morning of Miya's funeral I swam with Mom and Kacee. Mom doing her laps, Kacee and I acting like five-year-olds as we competed in relay races and made faces underwater as Mom swam past. It felt like Miya was also in the pool, playing along.

We then headed back to the Big House to meet and carpool Miya's four friendsBrad, Ashley, Daniel and Stacy (who had flown in from Gunnison for the funeral) to the Yoga Center. The backroom of the studio was reserved for our family and friends. A class was held in memory of Miya. We all felt her presence. I collapsed into the Child's Pose at one point, and Emma scooted from her mat over to mine, cradling me in her arms, followed by Kacee and Mom, and then all of my Mom's girlfriends. It was one united glob of love, swaying back and forth, perpetuated by each other's breath.

Back at the house, I showered, tried to eat something and sat at the kitchen table, attempting to finish the eulogy. As I added four star-shaped stickers in four different colors to symbolically represent the four girls to the eulogy copy I would place in Miya's coffin, I started to have an anxiety attack. I felt alone and overwhelmed. Waiting for the limo to arrive and drive us as a family to the funeral home. Miya's funeral. It was a thought so overpowering I couldn't catch my breath. So I wrote.

In the limousine, the previous night's scene in the library continued. Emma argued with Mom, "Why should Sabrina be allowed to read a eulogy that is not written from all of us?" I had accepted some of her editing suggestions, but I refused to rewrite it. Shame was tearing me up inside as she and Kacee made me question my intention and purpose in writing something for Miya.

Unable to fight their criticisms any longer, I retreated toward the front entrance doors of the funeral home, tucked away, hovering in the corner. Watching hundreds of people arrive, everyone so uncertain how to act, dressed in their best black attire, I was trying not to completely fall apart. I wanted and needed my sisters' support so badly. My eulogy was for us. Not for everyone else packed into the service hall. I tried my best to center and remind myself that Miya would want me to read it.

I continued to practice the eulogy, shying away from people coming up to me. I just wanted to be alone. At Jewish funerals, people line up, waiting one-by-one to comfort the family in the backroom. Miya's casket was open so many people also walked into the viewing room. After I composed myself, I walked in as well, having to fight the hoards of people cramming the doorway. Faces flooded my mind with memories. Every person wanting to be *that* person who could console me. It was too exhausting, too real.

I leaned over her casket, rubbing her cheeks, placing the extra eulogy copy at her side, wanting to hold her hand that was hidden underneath the white cloth wrapped around her body, dripping drops of lavender oil that we bought together in Mysore onto the white cloth, kissing her cheek, and then tracing her lips with my fingertips. Cold, stiff, a bit rubbery, motionless.

The funeral service was beautiful. Hundreds of people, every pew filled, forcing many to stand in the main lobby. Unexpectedly, Miya's friends from Gunnison were the first to speak. Not having asked our permission, we were all surprised. At the time, still skeptical about whom we could and could not trust, I was frustrated. But I enjoyed what they wrote, Ashley speaking on their behalf, reminiscing about Miya and what her friendship meant to them collectively. Since Matthew did not attend the funeral, it was wonderful that they shared their memories. Gunnison was such a big part of Miya's being.

I was next. When I stepped up to the podium, I gazed out at the crowd of people—took it all in—and began to paint a picture of Miya's life for everyone there while Kacee and Emma stood behind me for support and unity.

My Eulogy for Miya :

She'd suffocate you. With love. With hugs. With plans. With changed plans. With changing outfits. And with more changed plans. But mostly with love. Unconditional love.

All Miya ever wanted was someone to hug her back. She and Mom were even supposedly kicked out of mother-toddler class just because she hugged the other kids too much. She always excused herself for how loving she was, as though it was her downfall...

When I was young, she'd creep into my room, scoop me up and burrow me underneath her covers, forcing me to snuggle with her. Butt naked.

Her windows were always wide open in the middle of February. I'd be so uncomfortable, nestled into the contours of her body, so hot and sticky, her blankets stuffy. But, it was just so cold, so I was left with no alternative other than to stick it out and fall back to sleep. I hated it.

It had always been a constant battle with Miya over the thermometer. Up, down, up, down, up, down. There's no equilibrium in the Must household...

We are the world's best ticklers, all of us—Monni, Miya, Emma, Kacee and Sabrina—the five little women. If there's a genetic code for ticklers, it originated in the Jacobs/Brontman families. Mom understandably educated us on the magnificence of the tickle chain, lining up one-by-one while watching

TV, or waiting at the doctor's, or lounging in bed together, tickling backs, arms, legs, anything you could convince the other to touch—it's "The Must Tickle." The original soul train.

Some may think that our nudity and openness is a bit too much; I think it's just right…

I used to hate how she wouldn't order anything to eat and then say, "Oh, that looks good, can I just have a bite?"

"No," I'd say.

"Just one bite?"

"No."

"Just one."

"Fine, here, just take half."

"No, I don't want half, I just want a bite."

"No, take half. You'll ask me in five minutes for another bite and that will just annoy me."

"Umm…ok, fine."

She'd eat hers and then finish mine…

I already miss those incessant phone calls, her "You're my little Beeeeaaaaannnn Dip's!" and "Hi, Boopers!" and, most of all, those 3 a.m. smothering, naked snuggle sessions.

I wish I could cash in and take back every time I was annoyed by her and told her to stop kissing me or poking me for just one more of our morning conversations. Or to get one of her famous, colorful, self-made birthday cards with her beautifully ugly handwriting. Or to hear her annoying "dog talk" to Henley and Billy, "Stinky #1 and Stinky #2." Or to have her hop into the shower with me at the Big House, hogging all the water, as though she didn't realize our shower was only two-by-two feet wide. Or to enjoy how she'd bellow: "Grannnndpppaaa Billyyy!" Or to leave her voicemail messages when "Running Just as Fast As We Can" came on. Or to hear her call Kacee "Dimples". Or to listen to her and Emma joke about their "Remember when…" anecdotes when Kacee would "remember" and then they would say, "It never happened!" Or to watch her characteristic hand motions, twisting and turning in mid-air while she spoke. Or for her to give me airplane rides on her feet. Or to hear her chant: "Miya Must, Must, Must increase her bust!" Or to hear her sing and encourage: "Sabrina, please stop singing, now, now, now!" if I was singing in the car and annoying everyone. Or to have her magically rub my leg cramps out. Or to hear her tell me how much she loves me and misses me. Or, most of all, to spend just one more night, suffocating in her sheets, just to feel her breathing.

After the service, many people who didn't know our family or Miya very well told me they understood what it meant to be a Must and who Miya was.

Journal Entry, November 18, 2007:

After reading the first paragraph, I was fine. I loved standing up there—leaning up against the podium, taking my time. I was falling in love with each and every story all over again, reliving every memory of Miya.

Kacee then took my place at the podium and spoke.

Journal Entry, November 18, 2007:

Kacee's eulogy had a very different tone—very personal and spoke more about Miya as a loving soul who helped her during a really rough time a year ago. When Kacee had flown out to Gunni for two weeks in October of 2006, she rediscovered the beauty of living through Miya. They hiked with the dogs, swam in Western's indoor pool, biked around town, practiced yoga at the Yoga Room studio and cooked. It was a time for Kacee that will always be invaluable. A memory and experience that now represents Kacee's biggest regret—her inability to help Miya when she most needed it.

Mom and Dad then approached the podium to say a few words; Emma, Kacee and I remained standing. We all sat back down and Rabbi Cohen delivered the final eulogy. The night preceding a Jewish funeral service, family and close friends gather at the home to speak about their loved one—telling stories and describing what type of person he or she was. It's a way to honor that person and also to give the rabbi additional material with which to work for the sermon. Despite being in his late fifties, Rabbi Cohen was known for being hip, easy-going and charismatic. He was also known to be long-winded. Mom didn't want him speaking for an hour. She wanted my words and stories to be how we'd honor Miya's life, complimented by anything the rest of our family would read. That was the plan. Somehow, between 9 p.m. Saturday night and 1 p.m. Sunday afternoon, the rabbi forgot to factor in Mom's demand into his speech. He did everything Mom asked him not to do.

We had always belonged to Temple Beth Ami. If I had to be associated with a synagogue in Detroit, I'd want it to be Beth Ami, based solely on the fact that it is the most reform temple in the area. That meant showing up for services at best once every two years was not considered utterly sacrilegious. It might not be the norm or preferred attendance pattern for all its members…but at least, when it came to the Musts, it wasn't looked down upon.

All four of us were Bat Mitzvahed there. Since Rabbi Cohen had not spent much time with Miya since she was 13, he spoke mainly about her as a child and teenager. As the story goes, in the middle of Miya's shaftorah, the rabbi corrected her when she had butchered a Hebrew word. Miya stopped mid-sentence and declared, "I know!" pissed off and confident. His credentials as a learned rabbi gave him no credibility in Miya's world. She was capable and wanted everyone to know it. He told the story with humor.

But then he began to talk about Miya as sick and broken, reading and referencing a poem titled "Broken Glass." That although the glass was beautiful, the cracks got in the way of seeing the whole picture. That Miya went through life broken.

I wanted to scream. I was literally holding onto the edge of the wooden bench, in order to hold myself back from jumping up and forcing Cohen to shut up. Mom reacted in the same manner. I was appalled. It was all lies. Lies that everyone at the service would assume were true. Miya was not broken, just heartbroken. I wanted everyone to know that it was just a case of spousal abuse—a husband who made the most loving person I've ever known feel unwanted, unwholesome and, most of all, unloved.

After our Gunnison trip, I wanted nothing to do with Matthew. Not showing up at the funeral seemed almost appropriate and consistent with how he was acting anyway. I had already divorced myself from ever using the word "husband" to describe him after our police station meeting, but since Miya was still legally his wife, I also couldn't write off his absence as, *Oh, it's just Matthew.*

For everyone else, it was confusing. I'd hear people, who knew very little about what had happened in Gunnison and what their marriage was like, murmuring, "Wait. Her husband isn't here? What husband of a seven-month marriage, whose wife just hung herself, would not attend her funeral?" Did he love her that little? Did he want her erased from his life so badly that attending her funeral was too much? Was it past his self-proclaimed expiration date for how long Miya and her death could affect him?

After the service, a procession of 100 or so cars drove to the cemetery. Congregated around the grave, as the rabbi whispered his final prayers over her body, her coffin was lowered deeper and deeper into the earth. An unfinished, plain pine coffin for an unfinished life, as Dad explained upon choosing it a few days earlier.

I remembered being numb, I later realized as an emotional defense, worrying about the gusts of mid-November wind against my bare legs and my heels digging into the soil. Acknowledging anything but what was really happening, that there was no turning back, no practical joke. She would be sealed in there forever.

Journal Entry, November 20, 2007:
> *I've been in a daze the past week. Yesterday I stepped outside for the first time at 7 p.m. Maybe it has a bit to do with my period, some because I'm*

home, some because of Miya, but all I've wanted to do is eat, sleep and lounge around.

A lot of me doesn't feel like recreating these past 6 days of Shiva, etc. I couldn't deal with everyone repeatedly asking me: "When are you going back to school? What are your plans once you're done?" Or, even worse, cornering me and telling me how they were very sorry for 10 minutes, as though their words would be most comforting. Nope. I learned quickly how to say automatically: "No, please don't start asking me. I don't know." Annoyed, frustrated that they wouldn't just leave me alone.

Chapter Nine

We knew what we needed to do as soon as the funeral and shiva were over. We needed to hire an attorney. We needed to hire a private investigator. We needed to know exactly what went on the night she died. We needed to know if Matthew really was having an affair with another woman, as every attorney with whom we spoke suggested after reading the last email communication between Miya and Matthew. We needed to see if there was a case to be built against Matthew and start digging for answers immediately.

There were so many questions about Miya's death.

1. Where did Miya get the rope? (She had sold all of her climbing equipment the previous summer.)
2. What happened between 2 p.m. and 8:30 p.m. on November 14?
3. Why would Matthew and his parents NOT call to say "sorry," or even ask to come to the funeral?
4. Her phone log. We wanted to know for sure with whom and when she spoke during November 14.
5. Where were the crime scene photos?
6. Where were the items she was wearing?
7. Was there a video from the police station? (Documentation of how Matthew acted in the conference room.)
8. How far was the chair pushed away from her body?
9. What did the coroner's report say?
…And on and on and on.

We were so completely in the dark as to how this happened and played out that we were considering all possibilities, asking every question, elementary and complicated. The version that Matthew had given the police was not completely consistent with what the police thought might have happened. There was enough reason to think that Matthew had lied about what he found and when he found it.

He claimed that he came home after work at 5 p.m., didn't turn on the lights, went directly upstairs to their bedroom, played with the dogs who were gated upstairs, changed clothes, and left to meet a buddy for dinner, not having heard Miya in the house. Then he returned home at about 8 p.m., walked down the stairs to find Miya hanging, and ran next door to their off-duty police officer neighbor, screaming for help.

What didn't make sense was the specific detail of "not turning any lights on." Sunset on November 14 was at 4:48p.m. It would have been almost impossible to maneuver around their condo without lights. And, on top of that, why? It's Gunnison. It gets dark.

The truth was that if Matthew wanted to avoid Miya, the last place he should have gone was home. If Miya was upset with you or wanted to talk to you about an issue, you didn't want to be within a mile radius of her, let alone in the same condo.

When Matthew stopped at home at 5 p.m., Miya's car was in the driveway, her bike was leaning against the porch stairwell, the dogs were home. She would absolutely have heard Matthew come into the house, even if she was in the basement working. The dogs would have been barking. There was no way that the two of them did not see, speak, interact or fight with each other when Matthew initially came home that evening.

In addition, why would Matthew have walked downstairs at 8 p.m. if he needed his personal space and did not want to face Miya? In order to see her hanging, simply opening up the basement door and looking down the stairs would not do. He had to physically walk down the staircase in that condo. Plus, to see the rope inconspicuously laced around the banister peg, he would've had to know to look for it. It was easily overlooked (as I realized when reviewing the police photos months later).

He knew something was wrong. Most likely because they had a huge blowout before he left to have dinner with his buddy. She might have threatened suicide; he might have disregarded it, provoking, "I don't care. Do what you want!" He left her there, knowing that his wife was not okay, knowing that she was bipolar and had a history of suicidal attempts. As her husband, Matthew had an obligation to her. Whether he had just asked for a divorce the night before or not, he was still her husband, she was still his wife.

The police kept Miya's file as an "open case," as we might have expected, which meant the cause of death was not officially determined. Any and every possibility was being considered. Like us, they had unanswered questions and wanted Matthew to slip up and disclose something.

Initially, Thompson remained neutral and maintained a very professional relationship with both Matthew and our family. He had not wanted to jump to any conclusions. But, as time went on and Matthew still refused to let us into his world, Thompson's opinion became a bit more one-sided, as did the rest of the community's in Gunnison. Matthew had shown his true colors one night in front of Thompson, exploding, his temper raging, just as he would with Miya. It all began to make sense.

Our search for an attorney was another issue and much more difficult than expected. We tried for the high profile ones, but none of them thought we had a case. They didn't realize winning or losing was not our main concern in a civil or criminal lawsuit. The only thing that mattered to us was finding out the truth and making sure Matthew could never treat another woman like this again.

We began compiling information, creating a document detailing specifics about Miya's last day alive. It included notes on everyone to whom she spoke, saw, emailed and called that day, and tried to fill in the time gaps, which still were foggy.

Journal Entry, November 27, 2007:

I'm supposedly the last one to have spoken with her. If that is true, had she decided that she wanted to kill herself by that time? Is that the significance of "I love you so much, Beiners. So much. Do you know that? I love you so much."? Kacee asked me if she had sounded crazy by that time on the phone. And, in a way she did. She was in a rush to get off. I assumed late for her yoga class. But, what if she simply made up her mind right then when she was talking with me about how upset she was and angry at him?

We have also discussed how uncommon it is for a woman to hang herself. It is a very violent act. Men hang themselves, shoot themselves. Women use pills, slit their wrists. However, Emma brought up a valid point. Miya did take a bottle of Tylenol when she was 16. It did not worked quickly enough and she got scared and rushed into Mom and Dad's bedroom to tell them. She would have ruled out that option. Hanging is violent; she wanted obviously to make a statement to Matthew.

It seemed strange to everyone that she had written such a short note. It's Miya. Nothing is unstated. We are surprised she never addressed her sisters in it. We are surprised she wouldn't have written each of us a note. Maybe she didn't want to change her mind.

We also wanted to get better acquainted with everyone associated with Miya and Matthew and every incident of abuse between Matthew and Miya, as well as between Matthew and former girlfriends, especially Paige.

Thoroughly combing MySpace, we studied and tracked people's profiles on a daily basis. We got to know all their "friends" through cyberspace to judge which friends were and were not trustworthy, and as a means to search for the "new woman."

MySpace was only the start of it. Emails were also an enormous source of information. I sifted through and forwarded every email she had sent or received from Matthew since mid-September. Accessing her Hotmail account (her longest standing email account) was not as successful. I tried hacking into it for three weeks. Attempting to change the password by answering the secret question of "name of your favorite dog." Sammy, Sadie, Henley, Liza, and Sonny Boy. Every different spelling for every different past dog of ours. Eventually, Hotmail finally refused to allow me any more attempts.

I guess desperation causes someone to do really illogical things, and I was desperate; we all were. We didn't want Matthew signing in and changing the password. We didn't want him hiding or destroying the email exchanges that most likely did not show him in the best light.

Fortunately, Gmail offered quite a bit. There was enough there to show the way in which Miya and Matthew interacted, and how much she invested in their marriage, apologizing over and over for how she felt, what she did, and excusing him for his blowups.

My parents didn't pay for Grade-A educations at Johns Hopkins, Northwestern and Cal-Berkeley for nothing; we finally got our money's worth. If Gunnison wouldn't openly give us the answers we needed, we would do the investigating ourselves.

What we found was that Miya had kept a lot from us. Secrets about their marriage and her ever-present sadness were painstakingly documented in her journals. (Journals that the police were still holding as evidence. Thompson assumed Matthew would destroy them upon release because her writing would expose their marriage for what it really was, so the detective kept them as a safeguard.) Maybe Miya kept the truth from us because she knew we would not have allowed such a marriage to continue and would have forced her to move home—no ifs, ands or buts. There would have been no room for "working it out" or "saving Matt."

Emma was the prime mastermind behind our investigative document, her meticulous note-taking skills our most effective weapon. It was our very own simulated game of Clue—the only way we could emotionally numb ourselves from the harsh reality of Miya's pain. We'd remind each other while brainstorming possible scenarios of what really happened that this was not "real." "Where was the butler while Mrs. White was shot in the ballroom?" became "Where was Matthew while Miya hung herself in the basement?" Day by day, it grew and grew, eventually to 40 typed pages, the web of unanswered uncertainties gradually threaded and woven.

Journal Entry, December 1, 2007:

We're on the flight to Denver—the five of us and Uncle Robert. Emma, Kacee and I lay in bed the Tuesday after the funeral and came to the decision we needed to be at the memorial service this Sunday, December 2. Mom woke up the next morning and had reached the same conclusion. We were planning on taking an entourage of people—wanted to demonstrate our strong support base. But the attorneys/investigators we have spoken with warned against that since we want Matthew to get very comfortable, so when we start searching for answers he's caught off guard. We have to be very relaxed and calm—we cannot react to Matt, yelling or slandering him publicly. I simply want him to have to stand in front of us at the memorial and act like the grieving husband.

Ashley is like Matt's puppet. She called me last night to "see how we were" and if we are coming down. She already knew we were, which we found out this morning in a phone message from David at the funeral home. She had called him to get the "Broken Glass" poem Rabbi Cohen read at the funeral.

She obviously was calling on behalf of Matthew. Mom said on the phone today she doesn't feel like Miya's helping us. I'm only hoping she comes through with Rebecca. I need answers. I want to hear what happened, want her to play those hours like a film for Rebecca and let us know the truth.

Rebecca Rosen is a medium, a messenger of light who connects with the spirit world. As she states on her website, she acts "as a conduit to help you reconnect with your loved ones who have crossed over into spirit form. The spirit's intention was to let you know they have made the journey and to communicate their true essence and love." She asserts, "My job is not to question or judge the information that comes through, but simply to deliver the messages." She sees images, hears voices, sees light. It is hokey stuff. Hokey stuff that, after experiencing it, is hard to consider not real.

The spirit world is not tangible, and maybe that is why people don't typically believe and have a hard time accepting that the dead are always with us, watching over us. But there have been way too many "coincidences" over the years for me to write it off as that. Way too many dimes strategically placed and discovered at key moments—dimes which Rebecca had noted in past readings as being Grandpa Billy's sign left for us so we knew he was around. Never pennies or nickels or quarters, only dimes. A dime under Miya's graduation cake in Gunnison in 2002, so Miya knew Grandpa was there celebrating with and proud of her. Or a dime that fell into my lap that morning while writing in my journal at LaGuardia Airport in August 2007 on my way home to say goodbye to Great Aunt Ruth (Grandpa's oldest sister, with whom I was very close) before she died. I noted the time, wondering: *Ok, why did that happen?* It wasn't until I arrived in Detroit when Dad handed me a box of tissues and told me Aunt Ruth had died right around 9 a.m. I knew before I *really* knew.

Such coincidences weren't that at all, but purposeful messages from our unforgotten loved ones. Purposeful words left so we know that they are still with us.

Journal Entry, December 20, 2007:

I want people to experience Rebecca. Want them to open themselves up to the spirit world. I bet their grandparents and loved ones try to contact them, yet they just don't know to look for it. It's a new way to consider God even for a religious person—to question if hell/heaven really are what they are taught, or simply an existence for all people? Seems more plausible that they are simply an energy/light existence that doesn't discriminate. "God" doesn't judge or exempt people.

We weren't rookies. Rebecca had read for us a few times before. First, for Mom when her best girlfriendCindy died in 2001. Then, for me, Miya, Kacee, and Mom after Grandpa died in 2002. (Never for Dad or Emma though; they had always been skeptical and didn't buy it.) Rebecca was working in Royal Oak, Michigan before she moved to Denver. Mom had even photographed her for her website in the past. To say the least, Rebecca knew us.

However, she had no idea what had happened in the past two weeks. Why had she, on November 14, emailed Mom while we were in the Denver airport on our way to Gunnison the first time, inviting, "When you are ready to talk, call me"?

I could have potentially regurgitated every word spoken during the hour and twenty minute reading, but I decided to not. Instead, I wanted to hone in on a few specifics that gave more details surrounding Miya and Matthew's history, the infidelity, and events of November 14, in addition to things Rebecca said that demonstrated the utter reality of the spirit world. The specifics that Rebecca picked up were mind-boggling.

The week leading up to our reading with Rebecca, Emma persistently stated, "The only way I'll believe any of this hoo-ha is if she mentions yellow sunflowers. She can't just say flowers or yellow flowers. She has to say 'yellow sunflowers.' Miya, have her do that." Sure enough, in the middle of the reading that Saturday afternoon, Rebecca announced out of the blue, "Oh, and yellow sunflowers!" In unison, everyone looked at Emma and started to laugh and smile. "See!" we gestured.

Our whole family loved sunflowers. I requested that sunflowers be displayed at the funeral by her coffin and we routinely placed fake sunflowers at her grave. They're something she loved, something we loved together. The chance that Rebecca would have mentioned sunflowers and have them hold such meaning to us was more than highly unlikely…it was impossible.

During the reading, Rebecca again acknowledged our dime-finding tradition, yet added that now it will be a penny and dime combination, "something about the number 11." The significance: Miya's birthday was October 11, and it would represent Grandpa Billy and Miya together (who had always shared an unbreakable bond).

A few days after the reading, when Mom and Dad flew home, Emma, Kacee, and I met with Detective Thompson. Rebecca had directed us toward most of our leads. When we told Thompson that Rebecca kept stressing the importance of the bathroom, saying she could see Miya looking in the mirror, hysterically crying, rocking back and forth, contemplating what to do, Thompson replied, "Well, that's interesting. We found tons of used, crunched up tissue on the bathroom counter."

During the reading, I asked Rebecca whom we could and could not trust in Gunnison. My biggest uncertainty was Brad. Rebecca said we absolutely could trust him, and added that Miya was saying Brad's name and holding up a cell phone. None of us understood the cell phone connection at first, not until the night of December 2 while having dinner after the memorial service. When we told Brad what Rebecca had said, his face turned Casper-white. Gradually, he began to open up, explaining that every night since Miya died, he had been dreaming that she was calling and calling him, but he couldn't hear anything. It all made sense then—it was Miya's sign for Brad so he knew she was around him all the time.

When we asked Rebecca why Miya hung herself, automatically she answered, "Anger. Resentment."

"Did she threaten suicide?" Dad continued.

"Yes. I can see him walking out of the house, throwing up his arms and just saying, 'Whatever. Do it; I don't care!'"

Rebecca explained Miya's decision as a "moment of weakness. She was pushed into a corner, or at least she felt that way."

She clued in on Matthew's infidelity, directing us: "Go to Chicago," considering that city as a possible location where Matthew's new woman would be living. Rebecca claimed that she "doesn't feel like he's telling the truth. Like he's hiding something…She's zipping her lips, like he's not going to be an open book…I feel like he was cheating. Go to Chicago, something about a girl there"? She was right. Not only did Matthew grow up in Chicago and his parents still lived there, but in Fall 2006 he also was involved in an online relationship with a girl in Chicago. Our family knew that, since it was the catalyst for Miya and Matthew's month-long break up. What Miya seemed to have forgotten to mention to us was that he had continued contact well past the engagement and wedding with this girl—Julie.

Chapter Ten

Mom, Dad and I had never wanted to step foot in that town again. We didn't want to revisit our hell. Things had changed over the past week, though, so we were preparing ourselves for the memorial service trip as best we could. We arrived at midnight from Denver, driving the five hours in our rented SUV.

There was really no service on Sunday, December 2. It was more like Miya's memorial day. A morning yoga class followed by a dog walk through town, and then an afternoon service with a candlelight vigil.

After having breakfast at the Firebrand, of course, enjoying Miya's favorite muffins in her honor, we joined thirty or so others in the student unionon Western's campus. In one cohesive circle, all our mats faced the center with a mini-Miya shrine (a small framed photo of her) in the middle. Everyone was free to flow as they wished with her music playing for an hour.

Next, people gathered off Tomichi Street for the dog walk, but Henley and Billy, the honorees, were a no-show. Matthew would not allow it, would not allow us to even see them. While everyone held their leashes, our hands were empty. One more blow to us—unable to be with Miya's "children."

The memorial service was not as large as I had expected. I assumed the whole town was going to show up. I think people may have felt out of place, awkward and confused by what was polite and appropriate. The service was much longer, though, than I anticipated. For three hours, people stood at the podium, one after the next, sharing their Miya stories; many of which our family had never heard. For example, how Miya used to shower Henley and Billy in the locker room at Western's pool. She would turn on every shower head and toss a tennis ball against the wall to entice the dogs to run through the water to get clean. Everyone laughed. It was such an outrageous thing to do in a public facility; it was something totally Miya.

After the memorial, we realized we had more work to do in Gunnison. The town seemed to be opening up to us; we couldn't leave now. As Matthew cut more and more ties and people began to understand the truth and abusiveness of their marriage, the town welcomed our family in as their own. So we stayed—Emma, Kacee, and I. Mom and Dad returned home on the scheduled flight, encouraging us to have three days of sisterly bonding.

We knew Miya was right there with us. We tried to be patient and allow things to unfold. Our agenda included meeting and hiring an attorney, trying to get more of Miya's personal belongings, and spending more time with her friends. But we ran into roadblocks along the way. With Gunni sunshine came the occasional snowstorm.

Journal Entry, December 3, 2007:

I had a long conversation with Brad last night. I snuggled up next to him, which felt safe and comforting. We eventually moved to Caren's office for privacy and so Brad would feel comfortable speaking. We spoke about how and why people tip toe around Matthew, more about what the medium said, suggested Matthew's infidelity, how Brad should deal with balancing the two sides. We left around 11:30 p.m. and when he and I hugged I felt confident he would always be there for us.

I had assumed Brad would welcome us in, being the support Miya would have hoped for. But the next morning, after seeing Brad at the café, our hope was deflated.

Journal Entry, December 3, 2007:

He said he wanted to talk and we agreed to meet in our room at the Holiday Inn. He wouldn't sit on the bed, sat in the sofa armchair, computer sack over his shoulder, hat on—he glanced from each of us to his hands. He has decided he needs to separate himself from this whole situation. He cannot be in the middle trying to mediate any longer. He is thinking of returning home to Carolina and grieving with his family.

We were expecting to play him the CD recording from Rebecca's reading. He objected automatically. He couldn't handle it.

I sat silently—mad/frustrated—but mostly sad. He knows the good thing to do is side with us—or at least force Matthew to do the right thing—if that's even possible.

We all feel so lost right now. Gunnison is shutting us out again. Matthew's lying, people seem to open up and then the next day shut down and close us out again. I keep playing the past 2 years over and over. How could I let her be with him? I should've instead pushed her to come home, not stay in Gunnison and work through their issues. Why didn't I understand how much pain she was in? Mom/Dad wanted her home. I realized if she actually thought her marriage would work, she couldn't escape to Detroit and leave like she had for Thailand/India and then come back with him crawling back to her. What a way to live! 3 months wonderful, 7 miserable, 2 apart!

I left the hotel room five minutes after Brad, escaping to the hotel lobby, collapsing onto the leather couch, writing and crying. On the stereo speakers, "Let It Be" by the Beatles played, but that was the last thing I felt like doing.

Journal Entry, December 5, 2007:

> *It was a really bad day on Monday when Brad came over to tell us he needed to remove himself because he felt stuck between two sides. Emma said, "It's not between choosing sides; it's about right vs. wrong."*
>
> *I don't know when I'm going to write him an email—but probably by next week once we're away from Gunni and are able to give him some space. And, honestly, a lot of me just wants to see him. As much as Miya pushed the idea of marriage to Brad on me and I laughed at the idea, I was intrigued by it. I always have liked knowing that Brad had a crush on me—and I always had a small crush on him. Like it would be my back up plan and a way to really start a life with Miya—even if I got nervous that she would've driven me crazy.*

On Tuesday morning we stopped into Ashley's house to pick up a few boxes of Miya's things—CDs, photos, books. I assumed she was going to pull a "Brad" and say she also needed to separate herself from us. Instead, Ashley confided in us.

Journal Entry, December 6, 2007:

> *It felt so nice to hear Ashley acknowledge how crazy Matthew is. Last Saturday night, 10 people had been over someone's house, friends and family, and once we called to ask to take Billy and Henley for a walk, he scuffed, "I'm not going to the dog walk for the memorial day." Everyone fell silent. So, finally Ashley stood up and said, "Just let them see the dogs for an hour."*
>
> *Matthew exploded. Ashley covered her eyes with her hands and left the room, listening to him rage, "Fuck this, shit, fuck" all over the place. "They'll never see those dogs again!" he screamed, over and over again in an incoherent shouting rage.*
>
> *Ashley told us she finally realized how crazy and mean he is and what Miya must have gone through. She has not spoken with him since. She wanted to ignore any negativity before and only dwell on the positive memories of their relationship. Due to her involvement in the business...?Or just because it was easier that way...? I don't know. But, finally, people are seeing his true colors.*

The attorneys with whom we originally spoke were the ones who first suspected Matthew's infidelity. After reading the last email correspondence between Matthew and Miya on the morning of November 14, each attorney independently concluded that he was absolutely having an affair. This was a week before we even spoke with Rebecca, who confirmed it by describing the physical characteristics of Julie.

Matthew's email to Miya, November 14, 2007: (Written Wednesday morning after telling Miya he wanted a divorce at counseling the night before.)

> *I would like to talk when we can be civil to each other. We need to figure out about living arrangements for now. I am leaving on friday to moab until sunday night.*

Miya's Email in Response (an hour later):

> *I can see on your face how sure you are about this- the hurt for me is tremendous, especially knowing that you are unwilling to do the work for me and think you can figure stuff out and offer that to someone else- yes that is probably what hurts the most.*
>
> *I am struggling right now- as I know you are inside (although I can't see it). I do love you and when I put my pain aside at moments feel so sorry I can't ease that for you. Lets take a few days or so and then talk- maybe we should think about talking next tuesday with Neal present since you seem to feel safe there, what do you think?*
> *With Love,*
> *Miya*

Both attorneys picked up on Miya's "offer that to someone else" statement. Mom had always told us: men only leave women when they have another on the back burner.

I knew nothing of it. Miya left out those details about continuing to email and call and text Julie whenever we had spoken since her engagement...almost an entire year. By the fall of 2007, she would openly admit that their marriage was dysfunctional, a change from her usual affirmation of "it's supposed to be this difficult your first year of marriage."

Miya told me that Matthew would tell her whenever someone asked him how married life was: "I say it's fine. But it's a lie. I'm playing the part, but inside I'm miserable." He'd use such words to dig his fists into her side, kneading and kneading until all her bones were broken.

By June 2007 there was no room for understanding. Matthew and Miya were now married. She would not accept anything less than complete loyalty, love and truthfulness. She was infuriated and heartbroken that Matthew was continuing to go behind her back. Somehow she still had faith in Matthew and the love they shared for each other.

No wonder Miya went to such an extreme to try to please him. She had to compete with another woman. Miya's biggest insecurity was her fear of being alone and abandoned. She considered marriage to be the ultimate seal of lasting love and companionship, her blanket of security, something that would never fray. However, their vows didn't secure anything. For

Matthew, he was probably crossing his fingers at the ceremony, playing along with their Dr. Seuss' rhymes.

I also had figured out what I wanted to say to Brad.

Email to Brad:

I am speaking from my heart, so this can't be wrong. I think the reason I am so disappointed in you is because Miya worked so hard with you to stand strong and be confident. When you know what's right, be strong with those intentions. Yes, Miya taught compassion and forgiveness, but most of all right and wrong. You know how horrible Matt was to her. Why protect someone like that? Why would Gunnison take the role of the grieving family? Why should we wait while friends sift through her things? We felt so shut out of Gunnison—why would it ever be right for Matt's mom to pack up her things? Why wouldn't we be allowed in the house? Why wouldn't it be the family's job to decide what we want from her personal things? Why would we be given copies of her CDs and not the originals? It's as though we're in a horror movie. This small town wouldn't embrace us at first. Doesn't anyone think it's strange that her friends are taking the role of the family, the ones most pained by her death? Our family was her life, her 1st love. Everything else came 2nd. Period.

It wasn't until the memorial service that we learned Miya had actually known about Matthew and Julie's continuing affair. If I hadn't butted in on Mom's conversation with Julie during the short reception after the service and asked her name, since Mom had not realized it was she, none of us would have known Julie came.

"Julie," she replied. "I'm a friend of Matt's from Chicago." Rebecca's words from the day before stung my heart. *This is her, this is her.* I yanked on Emma's sleeve, since she was speaking to someone behind me, and when she joined us, we conversed more.

I believed Julie approached Mom and introduced herself at Miya's memorial service because she felt guilty. Same guilt that encouraged her to claim, "You know, Miya thought there was something going on between me and Matt, but there wasn't. She even called me in July and yelled at me, but I kept telling her nothing was going on." If those accusations were not true, though, could you ever imagine flying halfway across the country, from Chicago to Gunnison, for your ex-online-boyfriend's wife's memorial service, which had supposedly ended a year before?

The truth is that the last time Miya spoke with Julie was not in early July as Julie told us at the memorial service. It was in early November, two weeks before Miya killed herself.

Julie finally came clean to Emma a few weeks after the memorial service. For two hours on the phone Julie rambled on about the history of her phone conversations with Miya. When Miya called, Julie supposedly screamed at her on the phone, while Miya listened silently. There was no fight left in her. She was defeated. Couldn't continue making those weekly calls and text messages, pleading with Julie to leave her husband alone and stay out of their marriage. Julie told Emma on the phone, "I said the most terrible things to her. After a while I heard a dial tone. She just hung up."

Not only was it difficult to convince an attorney that we had a case, but it was difficult to convince an attorney that Matthew was abusive and not some quiet, non-reactive man. On Wednesday, December 5, the three of us had lunch with an attorney based in Crested Butte, the ski-resort which was a 30-minute drive north of Gunnison.

Journal Entry, December 6, 2007:

Thought it was a joke at first. Dressed in a long-sleeve T-shirt, wiping off his sweat from his forehead with his sleeve since he just came from the gym. Completely unprofessional. He was appalled by Matthew's actions— wondered how/why these two ever got married…exactly! But, Emma got the feeling we were having to prove to him what we were claiming. He disbelieved that Dad did not demand on the phone that 1st Thursday—"We are going to take this house, those assets, that car and this other house." I told the attorney that would've been impossible since Dad couldn't even walk 5 feet without sobbing.

After our meeting, we packed up a few boxes of Miya's things to be shipped to Detroit. While Kac/Emma went to buy plastic bags, I opened up her oldest journal—brown leather bound w/ an imprint of a leaf. There were notes from Mom + Dad from 1995—about how proud they are of her—how much she had grown and matured. Dad's note about what a hard time he had in his 20's—how sad/lost he was. Mom wrote about naming Miya after Debbie, and that she filled that gap for her. The next page had a card from me—writing about how much I missed her—how I was listening to Enya and Enigma in her room. I remember that night in her bedroom. The lights were off, Enigma was blasting on her stereo and I think a couple of candles were lit. I was sad about something—and Miya was trying to console me.

I keep reminding myself that I will never see Miya again, never skip down the street with her, never be able to call for advice about how to get a boyfriend. It hits me, but then it doesn't.

I did this before - I am so very sorry, I can't do these feelings again, I opened up and gave my most vulnerable part-I am in too much pain. It will be easier. I will not be thrown away again. I can't go through another 2 years, I really went for it this time & I am too wounded this time.

I'm sorry Mom & Dad

too many years
More this
pain.

M. I loved you
unconditionally.

Chapter Eleven

I looked forward to driving the eight hours back to Baltimore, to escape to my apartment away from the mess. I couldn't take the emotional stress any longer. Day in and day out, there was no escape: Gunnison, the funeral, shiva, Gunnison, and then just reality. The dream effect was wearing off. "All" of us were now home, but every light wasn't being left on, you couldn't hear her shuffling around at 6 a.m., wanting to swim or bike, the cabinet doors in the kitchen weren't all ajar, all your favorite clothes weren't suddenly lost, and the thermometer upstairs wasn't turned down to 60 degrees. Miya wasn't wreaking havoc.

I was returning to Baltimore to pack up my apartment. I had only to take my final two written exams in order to graduate early. Knowing this the morning of November 15 on my way to the airport to fly to Gunnison, I was relieved that I wouldn't have to stress about school while at home and in Colorado. Instead, I knew I could focus all my energy on what was more important—life.

I relived the past couple of weeks, listening to Miya's music as I drove Mom's Suburban back to Baltimore. It also gave me a chance to call Grandma Maggie for the first time in eight years.

I knew I had to eventually call her. I had written so many un-sent letters to her, so many times I wanted to call and just say "hello" so she knew what she was missing. But part of me felt guilty about reaching out too much, since I knew how it pained Mom to think that any of us would make ourselves vulnerable to Grandma. Miya had been one of the few who maintained a relationship with her over the years. Never wanting to speak to Mom about visits or phone calls, Miya did it quietly. So while driving back to Hopkins, I called—for me, as well as on behalf of Miya.

Grandma's voice had not changed one bit. She cried on the phone to me, about how sorry she was and how much she had loved Miya. "You girls need to be there for Mom and Dad," she said, empathy in her voice, since she knew what it was like to lose a child. She also reminded me how much Miya loved me, and how every time Grandma spoke to her Miya would tell her how very proud she was of me and the woman I was becoming, how I was her favorite.

I knew I had to take everything she said with a grain of salt. But, genuine or not, it was nice to "feel" that love for which I had so desperately been homesick. I had tried to prepare myself for who would answer—which Grandma Maggie would I get. The clear-and-compassionate-for-a-moment Maggie or the scary Maggie. Luckily, I got her good side.

I realized how very much I had missed her. Until I was a teenager, Grandma was my favorite. Grandpa almost consciously put her in the spotlight to balance out her craziness. Sleepovers at their apartment with all my sisters were always a blast, lounging in bed, naked, watching TV, while she tried to convince one of us to "Do my nails, clean my ears, make me up!" She loved beauty nights. Never wanting to disappoint her, I complied, although I hated cleaning her ears.

In the years after Grandpa's death, having closed off any communication between herself and the remaining links, she alienated herself from everyone—life-long friends and all of her family. I felt sad for her, a feeling I didn't know if I could justify since she alone was the cause of her own isolation.

After calling, I didn't hear from Grandma until two or three months after Miya's death, when she wrote an obituary message. It was just one more blow to my reality. "Miya Jo, I miss you so," she wrote. I miss you so? Miss you forever? *Is she really gone,* I wondered. I couldn't decide whether I was more upset about having to read an obituary about my own sister, or that Mom might see it, or by the thought that Grandma submitted it to the *Detroit Jewish News* only for sympathy and to vent against Mom. Who did she do this for?

Packing up my apartment, sorting through three and a half years of school papers, bills, photos and books, sifting the must-keeps from the has-to-gos, and reorganizing all of my "Sabrina piles" was therapeutic. It was a way for me to clean out the clutter. Clear out and clarify my life. Regain some control, while everything else seemed to be fraying at the seams. As I continued to play Miya's music from her burned yoga mixes, rediscovered letters and pictures flooded the room with memories. Miya's face and handwriting continuously popped up.

Journal Entry, December 16, 2007:

I wonder what Miya thinks of how I go about my days? Is she judging me? Is she proud? I wish she could observe and give me tips. Does she look down on my behavior? Maybe she'd be proud of me, seeing my interactions with friends at school.

I sat crying in the corner of my apartment Friday night while packing up—saw a note Jenny from Koh Tao wrote when she sent the DVD of our scuba diving movie. I go through periods of forgetting about it, can't stop thinking about her, and crying uncontrollably about her. Maybe spectrum of emotions because I am so removed from it while here in Baltimore.

It was nice to have my best friend Ben who lived four floors below join me occasionally on those lonely nights. Ben would lounge and relax on my bed, as my Koh-replacement, sipping his much-loved wine. Nice to just have someone around. But, it was just as nice to be completely alone at times. Exposed to every raw emotion and memory.

I drove back to Detroit on December 21 with Sara, my best childhood friend from Sylvan Lake who was in her last year of college in Virginia. I filled her in with all the events of the past three weeks, prefaced by the CD of Rebecca's reading. I knew while she was home my time with her had an expiration date since she had to fly back for the spring semester. I couldn't remember the last time the two of us had eight hours of straight alone time, followed by two weeks of playtime, so I took full advantage of it. Very few people could make me feel as calm and grounded as Sara could. Not ready to be home and face reality yet, I absorbed myself in her presence.

Journal entry, December 24, 2007:

The family's upset at me—I have not been around too much since I've been home. I think being away from the house is easier for me—keeping busy and with friends helps me forget. It's painful for me, like right now, to be lying in bed and thinking of Miya. Plus, I am constantly stressed about being around Kacee and Emma.

Sitting in the kitchen with Mom while she writes thank you notes, listening to Miya's CDs. I started crying, leaning over the chair—told Mom I was sorry for not being around—said it's hard for me to be around here…It's been nice to sit here alone with her.

From December through February, until probate was completed in order to allocate Miya's assets, we were at a standstill. We still were not given any of Miya's personal belongings. Somehow Matthew's mother thought it was appropriate to box up Miya's things within 24-hours of her death. Out of sight, out of mind, I guess. On New Year's Day 2008, Mom sent a letter to Nancy, hoping to persuade her to let down a bit.

Nancy,

I ask you to read this letter in its entirety, so that you can understand what I have to say from my perspective. I struggle with trying to understand your actions since Miya died. I won't go through each and every point that I have found distasteful, insensitive, & unethical, but there are a couple things that stand out. Miya was your daughter-in-law, a woman who reached out to you & loved you. In return, you did not attend her funeral, send a card or call us—nothing. The fact that you were driving my daughter's car around Gunnison as though it was yours and packing up my daughter's personal belongings in order to put them in a place of storage that was inaccessible to me and my family is inconceivable. By not being able to go through my daughter's sentimental items, you stripped me of an important aspect in the grieving and closure process. I misjudged your character.

> *There is something called "karma." You have a daughter—can you imagine what it would be like for you? Can you imagine David's mother packing up Melinda's things without you being allowed in the space where she was and understand how her last hours were spent? It is little bits of Miya being taken away and it makes me feel like I'm losing her over and over again. This creates so much pain that no letter can express adequately.*

> *There is an expression "Time heals." For us, it has gotten worse with each passing day—not having Miya & becoming increasingly aware of the injustice before and after her death.*

> *I can be reached by email, phone, or mail.*
> *Monni*

While Matthew tried to convince everyone that he "needed to have time to go through everything," he actually wanted absolutely nothing to do with her. He was frustrated when people came to redeem money for their pre-paid yoga classes with Miya. Frustrated that he had to deal with all the loose strings of her finances. Frustrated he had to pay for his wife's funeral.

I think Matthew assumed we were going to go after the house Miya had purchased with her trust money two years before. But all we wanted were her personal things—her clothes, books, journals, bike, snowboard, dogs. Anything smelling of or reminding us of her. Matthew could have the house and all other property. Why would Dad have wanted to worry about a mortgage in Gunnison, Colorado anyway? He had enough to worry about in Detroit.

The only time Dad had spoken with Matthew post-November 14 was while in the Denver airport on our way to Gunnison the next day. Dad called to request Matthew please leave Miya's car at the Gunni airport with its keys under the mat, so we could have a vehicle while there. Dad had just bought her this car two months before. Upon hanging up the phone, we found out weeks later that Matthew had declared to friends, "They're going to take my house from me."

Dad had no energy to think about claiming property. In fact, if Matthew had acted in a different way, saying "I'm so sorry," giving a hug and allowing us to enter the condo and pack up Miya's things, nothing would have unfolded as it had. Instead, he acted guilty. The only reason we even wanted Miya's new car was simply because it was Miya's. It was never about the money, just about holding onto anything that was hers, since she was quickly slipping away from us. What was most frustrating was knowing that Matthew's mother and father were driving Miya's car, instead of us, whenever they visited. That, and the fact that every time we had been back since her death, we were forced to rent a car. How anyone could actually rationalize and justify such a thing was beyond me.

If we acted too quickly with an attorney and a private investigator, pulling the rug out from under Matthew and slamming him with a civil suit for wrongful death, we knew we would never get all her belongings and the dogs. We knew he'd become defensive and shut us out even more. We knew that the boxes of Miya's things stacked high in a garage would remain there forever, be sold, or even worse, become tomorrow's trash. So we were patient and allowed things to calm down.

We remained in contact with Ashley throughout those months. She loved Miya and knew who Matthew really was, having finally seen his true colors the night before the memorial service. She stopped working for the Gunnison Directory soon after that, and broke off all communication with him. She admitted to us that she had always written off any problem in their marriage simply as Miya overreacting and just being "in-your-face Miya." Luckily, Ashley was the one caring for the dogs. We had at first questioned her loyalty to Miya, confused about why she agreed to go into the condo without our permission and picked out that one outfit for the funeral, and why she spoke at the funeral without ever asking. Once Matthew had exploded about the dog walk, though, she was completely on our side. She finally understood what Miya had lived with day in and day out and understood how someone could be driven to do what Miya had done.

Henley and Billy had always been our number one concern. They were an extension of Miya. To lose them would have been to lose her all over again. The third time Mom returned to Gunni after Miya died, it was primarily to be with the dogs. Kacee joined her during that visit. Matt was not in Gunni that weekend, having flown back to Chicago for his mother's 60th birthday party. With him away, Mom knew there would be no hurdles to jump or barricades to hide behind.

The dog whisperer, Lisa Mapes, was that weekend's main event. Just like Rebecca was alternative, this woman was as well. In Rebecca's reading, she had consistently returned to the closet, emphasizing that she "really thinks the hanging happened in her closet." It was definitely in the basement from the stairwell. Yet the closet was a vital part of the night's drama. Lisa explained that Matthew had locked Henley in the closet that evening, tormenting him, something which sent Miya into a rage, greatly angered.

Certain "he tortured the dogs," Lisa was overcome by the darkness surrounding Matthew's evil soul, sobbing that he was so dark, the darkest person with whom she had ever dealt. She had been crying during the session with Mom, Kacee and Ashley with the dogs present. Crying because she was experiencing Miya's sadness and Matthew's darkness all at once.

She warned them that the most detrimental thing for the dogs would be if Matthew was to have them. She said that Henley was deeply depressed and hated Matthew. If Matthew was to ever get custody, Henley would die from depression or attack him and be put to sleep. Billy, on the other hand, had the ability to see Miya's spirit. That was something Brad had confirmed for us. While the dogs were staying at his house in the first few weeks after Miya died, Billy would crawl into bed with him every night around 3 a.m., the time that Rebecca noted Miya would come and wake us up, too.

Despite having threatened, "They will never see those dogs again!" Matthew himself had not seen Henley or Billy even once since November 15. He never wanted anything to do with them. He was only being controlling out of spite. Therefore, when Matt received the funeral bill for $17,000 in January, he quickly let up. Dad and Mom would have willingly paid the bill if Matt had not acted the way he had. Instead, Dad sent the bill, figuring *If he wants to be in control, then take on every responsibility, including all finances.*

By the time I called Brad in February, things had quieted down.

Journal Entry, February 8, 2008:
>It's been over 2 months since I've heard anything from him. Left him a voice message: "It's me, Sabrina. Just calling to say hi. I hope you'll call me back. Don't know if you're in Gunni or home right now. Hope you're okay." He called back tonight (Friday) at 8:30 p.m. It was only about 5 mins. Told me heading to North Carolina on March 15 for the summer. Finishing up the phone book right now in Gunni. Just took Henley, Billy and Boone (his dog) skiing since the snow's at a record high this year.
>
>He sounded down so I told him to "Cheer up!" He apologized and said he just ran into Jack (Matt's dad) at Hartman's (assuming that's a hardware store or something in town). How awkward. Your son's ex-best friend who hasn't spoken with your son for almost 3 months b/c of the circumstances surrounding your son's "wife." Using quotes b/c I can't bare to think that Miya was Matt's wife and actually loved him. She loved the conception of him, I'm certain.
>
>I called Mom back since I hung up with her once I saw Brad was calling. Told her finally heard back from him after 2 emails + a call. She felt sad for him. Glad he's moving away and speculated that the reason Matt called our financial advisors to inquire about Miya's trust this past week was because Matthew's dad is in town.
>
>I checked my email after speaking with Brad. He had responded last night…it just took a while to process and get to my Inbox. "I can't tell you how wonderful it was to hear your voice tonight. It's late, I will give you a call tomorrow. Sleep tight."

I replied, "I just want you to know how much I love you. And you don't have to ever apologize for having been so distant. My pestering and persistence was merely to let you know that we are and will always be around whenever you were ready to talk. As much as we're going through this, I know you are too. I also want you to know that the initiative to write my book (or at least hope it turns out to be one) was greatly inspired by you. I can't wait to sit down with you and read parts of it to you. I wish I could fly out to Gunni next week mostly to see you. Talking on the phone tonight was like talking to a piece of Miya. If I wasn't sad enough, I'm sadder now, but also comforted. I've been coaching the girls' hockey team at Cranbrook. But once the season ends, first week of March I think, I don't really have any specific obligations since my only "work" is writing right now and babysitting. Hopefully, you can take the time to visit our family if you need a vacation from North Carolina. Or, if we ever get Miya's bike, maybe you'll go for a long bike trip with me. Sleep well, hope she comes in your dreams."

Is it wrong of me to hope to one day reconnect with Brad? Maybe b/c Miya loved him so much I feel pushed toward him. I can only imagine how lost he feels. And what hurts me most about him is that I know how sensitive he is. When we were hanging up the phone, I said, "I don't know what else to say or talk about." He said, "Yeah, probably smart if we hang up for now. I'll start to make a fool of myself. Baby steps for now." Fool of himself meaning confessing how much he wishes he could see me, or just in general talking about Miya/the situation? I don't really know.

Matthew's attorney from Gunnison called after the funeral bill was forwarded and told us Matthew was giving us custody of the dogs. In a frenzy, Mom went searching for a new house, a house essentially for the dogs because we were already over the county's legal limit of two dogs. Sure enough, she found it—a house with a green door that Rebecca spoke about in the reading. Directly up the street from the house being built in Sylvan, where the Cottage and Lake House originally stood. This new house would be for the sisters—me, Emma, and Kacee. It would be ours forever; a house that would promote Michigan visits. The newest version of Miya's Gunni Cabin, which we named the Kids' House.

It was agreed that Kacee would care for Henley and Billy and become their adopted mother. When Kacee visited Miya in October, 2006 they had reconnected as sisters. Miya in turn had flown Billy to Detroit during those lonely winter months to be Kacee's temporary companion. From then on, Miya knew Kacee could do it. When she asked Kacee in the spring of 2007, "If anything were to ever happen to me, I want you to care for the dogs," Kacee took a vow. By the week after Valentine's Day, the vow was finally fulfilled. Emma and Kacee flew into Gunnison, rented a car and drove cross-country back to Michigan, precious cargo and all.

When the four of them arrived a week later, I crawled into the rented Ford Explorer parked in the Big House's driveway. With the seats folded down, the dogs laid in the back. It had been the first time since November 15 that I had seen them, after running the trails above Miya's house. I cried, just as I had on the trails...and cried, and cried. Burrowing my face in their fur, as though suffocating myself would erase the nightmare and finally allow me to wake up. But I didn't, and I forced myself instead to stare into their all-knowing, sad eyes.

Chapter Twelve

A busy schedule was my main coping mechanism. I had always loved my schedules, my days jam-packed with minute-to-minute activity. Yoga, swimming, running, writing, eating, hanging out, napping, studying, exploring. Each activity fitting into self-manufactured time slots. Post November 14, my busyness was not just for pure enjoyment and feeling as productive as possible; it was for my survival. I amped up my usual constant stream of activity to help stay balanced. Stagnant time when I wasn't doing *something* was never a good idea—I would think too much, get too sad. Was I running from the stillness, which otherwise would allow the sadness to overcome me? I thought so. Was it the right and healthy means to cope? I didn't know. All I knew was that when I tried to do and act in a way others expected of me, I tumbled out of balance. When I acted in a way I knew was best for me in that moment, I remained centered and focused. So, at first, being busy worked just fine.

From a run, swim, or yoga in the morning, to subbing at Cranbrook, to a possible therapy session with Dr. Burch, straight to hockey or soccer practice, I'd end up writing in a café all night long before retiring to my bedroom in the Big House with Koh. Hours upon hours of punching the keyboard, writing. For me, for Miya, for our family...for every woman who ever felt that there was no way out, there was and always will be.

Coaching the Cranbrook girls' hockey team was my first *shtick*. By early January, I was on the ice everyday from 3:30 to 4:50 p.m. as one of two assistant coaches. The minimal season salary was nothing desirable, but the time on the ice with the girls was invaluable—a great release for me, an escape that was much needed. It was an opportunity for me to be a role model, show these girls what it meant to play on the Cranbrook hockey team and demand nothing less than pure hustle and heart, just as with my old teammates and past coaches. Fortunately, the hockey spark was still alive, even though none of the program's original superstars or coaches were there.

An added bonus was having a crush on my fellow assistant coach. There was almost nothing attractive about the kid. He had a missing tooth, wasn't the most motivated nor intelligent guy out there, just the stereotypical hockey jock. But he was around, something to spark excitement, someone with whom I could swoon and flirt. A distraction. Plus, the girls *loved* the idea of their female "hip" coach getting it on with their other male "hot" coach.

My girls were wonderful, other than a few dramatic tiffs and tuffs, which should be expected from a group of 21 teenagers. They laughed at all my idiosyncrasies (i.e. burping on demand) and absurd comments.

By mid-January, coaching opened up opportunities for my next profession as a substitute teacher. In fact, it seemed I became a "professional subber"—Latin, health, computer, physics, and English classes, as well as occasionally filling in at the Dean's Office desk. I was all over the place. Whenever faculty or administrative staff were sick or out of town, I'd be called. The best part of my days was running into my hockey girls in the dining hall, having them as students in the classroom, or when they'd visit my temporary classroom during their free periods.

Soon, I wasn't only my girls' main attraction, but also garnered the rest of the Cranbrook student body's attention. Most often, I was mistaken for a student (since I kinda looked 17 years old). I was known for religiously letting the kids out 20 minutes early as long as they got their work or labs done, allowing them to frequent the book store for snacks, and joining in on gossip, giving them advice whenever asked. I was no longer 22. I morphed into a high schooler, asking for their advice on my latest crush—when I should call him and what I should say.

I did switch hit, too. After I joined my students for the very limited selection of safe vegetarian options in the dining hall, I'd sit with my old teachers, now colleagues. At the teachers' tables, I'd even get their advice on how to play my new crush or how to deal with one of my overly hormonal hockey players. The women became my girlfriends, the men still made fun of me as they had four years prior. Despite their constant pleas, I still couldn't rid myself of their Mr. and Mrs. titles. Mr. Winter would never be John, Ms. Chun would never be Gail. It was just way too awkward!

Did my students love me because I was a 22-year-old, Cranbrook alum who could care less whether or not these monkeys were on time? Or, because I let them occasionally "help" each other on assignments with material they were never taught?

The only time I was thrown a bit off guard was when one of my 8th hour boys, who called me Sugar Lips, asked me on a date in a very confident manner. "You're the girl of my dreams. Let me take you out for a nice dinner. Please, Sabrina." If knowing he was only 15 and my student didn't discourage me enough, the metal in his mouth brought me to a halting stop. I thanked him for the offer, but respectfully declined.

This was the same boy who asked, "What do girls go for, Sabrina? The Genius or the Jock?" In between chuckles, I tried my best to hold my composure and replied: "Well, I think more of a combination. Not just one or the other." Just at that moment, my old chemistry teacher walked into the lab room, so I asked him his opinion. He agreed with me and then complimented me, his voice hinting at sarcasm.

"See, Sabrina, you're not only teaching these boys physics, but also coaching them in life skills." I giggled, nodding, while another one of my students innocently, yet seriously, requested:

"Can we just do the life lessons?"

I became obsessed with high schoolers. I felt like I could really talk to them and understand their insecurities. Knew what would and would not work in order to inspire them to be better and fuller, because I knew what worked for me. I could connect with them on a level that was influential, while reliving my teenage years all at the same time.

I loved being employed by Cranbrook for an even more basic reason: it legitimized being on campus constantly. Otherwise, I would've just been some creepy alum. As soon as I stepped onto the 360-acre meticulously groomed campus, I felt balanced and at home. I couldn't explain it. The place was simply magical. Every time I flew back from Baltimore or abroad, Cranbrook was my first to-do. Sitting in the Green Lobby or in the Dining Hall or in the Oriental Gardens or in the Cranbrook Commons Room; walking from the PAC parking lot through the Senior Hallway to the Dean's Office; playing all-school hide-n-go-seek or "Hit the Backboard, Baby" dodgeball in Ms. Mel's middle school gym class; running from the Lower Fields to Cranbrook House around Kingswood Lake and up Suicide Hill; visiting my 3rd grade teacher Mrs. Roche at Brookside, Mrs. Yeager and Ms. Holland at Kingswood, Mr. Watson and Mr. Pickett and Ms. Briske and Doc Rosenquist at Cranbrook, along with Chun, Schuette, Cox, Ladd, Fred and Snitz in the Math Office. Unforgettable campus, unforgettable teachers.

I had fallen in love with Cranbrook as a five-year-old in kindergarten. I was just as in love as an 18-year-old when I graduated. I was still in love as a 22-year-old college graduate. I hadn't tossed my textbooks and notes in the air at graduation, like in *Dazed and Confused*. Nope...I cried. I had worn my high school ring every single day since Junior Ring Ceremony. And I'd bet one day I'd even find myself on the Board of Trustees.

Journal Entry, January 3, 2008:

I'm having a rough afternoon. I came back from yoga, stopped on the side of the road to cry. I miss her so much—so mad at the world for letting this happen. I go on living, enjoying people's company—laughing and smiling—but then, mostly when alone, it hits me. Stood in her closet looking at her books and old photo albums—just so sad.

Dealing with our grief started as a family effort. That's where Dr. Burch came in; he was a start. The first Tuesday in January 2008, a month and a half after Miya's death, we started seeing him as a family. From then on, Tuesday nights were our nights. Dad in the recliner, Kacee in the chair, Mom, Emma, and I on the couch. We'd talk about Miya's role in the family, Dad's weight and how it affected all of us, since we needed him to be healthy and around as long as possible, about how Mom couldn't sit still, and how we lacked valuable family bonding time.

One family session stuck out particularly. On our fourth Tuesday, Mom mentioned a particularly down Friday and Saturday she had had a week before. Spoke about what set her off. A conversation Dad told her he had with his doctor. When his doctor asked how many kids he had, Dad told him three.

Back in Burch's office when Mom told us, I stared at Dad at first and then mostly the wall, saddened by his lack of sensitivity and openness to the fact that Miya was still around. My face morphed as it always did when I cry, my chin quivering, my eyes watering, body heating up. Finally, after Mom and Emma spoke, Burch asked me what I wanted to say. I shook my head "nothing," but then added, "Why would you say three, you have four?" It was times like those that pained me most. Our family was defined by the four Must girls, not the three. I will always have three sisters, saying two was just not possible.

Later that night, I climbed into Kacee's bed with her and Emma, I was the meat in the sandwich. *Sweet Home Alabama* was playing on the DVD player, as we three spooned each other—Emma, of course, taking up most of the bed. I was overcome with a warming thought that Miya was probably hovering over us, so happy we were all getting along. *How could we possibly fit one more in here?* I wondered.

Just at that moment, the volume to the television shut off. I knew it was Miya right away, playing with the electronics as Rebecca Rosen told us she did.

Two months into seeing Dr. Burch our family therapy became much more than that. It became my therapy; he became my therapist. Writing wasn't enough of a therapeutic outlet. I knew I couldn't do it all alone, drowning myself in my written words. On the surface, I wanted to work through difficulties due to moving back home, my relationships with Kacee and Emma, my dating status, or lack thereof, and the pain of losing Miya. But my weekly appointments gradually shed light upon many more issues—any and every issue from which I had always run. Even issues preceding Miya's death were exposed in large part because of Miya's death. Learning how to successfully live and just be at home and around my sisters opened me up to the way I approach such tasks.

I couldn't really define what some of my struggles were exactly. I only knew it was the thing that drove my need to rush, need to chase after something, my feeling of incompleteness. Burch was there to facilitate that search.

We formed a camaraderie. Shoeless on the couch, I'd sit as though I was chatting with a best friend, as comfortable as could be. I needed someone to hear me out, give me opinions and suggestions. A vocal therapy, not just my writing. It was nice to have a place to sit and cry, to be with someone. As opposed to alone in my bedroom, reviewing my day's written material or in my car listening to music.

I considered myself a truly blessed person: a great family, the opportunities I had growing up, the financial security my parents provided us girls. I'd find myself driving on breezy spring days, sun peering through my sunroof and uncontrollably smiling, complete satisfaction. But I realized that a person could not be as alive unless he or she experienced occasional downs with all those ups. I began to wonder whether our family was just plain and simple crazy or highly aware. We were taught not to numb ourselves from truth, emotion, and pure sensation, to instead just put it right out there. No need to hide, no need to be anything than what we were.

Maybe most people consciously numbed themselves so they would never have to face their issues and could just live, day in and day out, in their ignorance. Ignorance was bliss, right?

Such a struggle was necessary for me, because I did not want to wake up one day as a 54-year-old and realize how truly unhappy I was. I would rather face it and discover what was buried so deep in me, and what I expected must be buried so deep in other people.

I told myself that maybe Miya died in order to teach me, to guide me, and for Miya to be my angel and help me do the work myself and face the fear that she was unable to do and conquer herself.

I had had other therapists; it wasn't all new to me. What was new though was the way Burch knew me and our family. Not just by what I said, but by means of seeing us interact and hearing other people's versions of situations himself. In turn, that opportunity gave Burch an even greater perspective. I began to connect what happened to Miya and how she was as a person with how I was dealing with her suicide and all other relationships. I finally saw that the years of dirty towels—towels which I had used to wipe up the mess of fouled friendships—had quickly piled up after Miya died. I wasn't hiding them under my bed any longer. Instead, I was piling these towels in the middle of my room, forcing myself to stare at them and begin to clean them up. I couldn't bear the stench and clutter any longer. It was too exhausting; I was too exhausted.

Some people just got it. Knew instinctively how to be around and available and check in on me. Others, especially some of my closest friends from childhood, did not. It was a hard reality to stomach that many of my best friends weren't really the best any longer. I was struggling enough to deal with the death of my sister, as well as all the issues and realizations that arose from her suicide and the lack of her presence. I had to learn how to fix my problems without her.

I soon became bitter about the way my friends were. Compared them to Emma's, Kacee's, Mom's and Dad's friends who were very much present and around. I realized I had always been walked all over because I had never considered holding a grudge or being angry worth my energy. I figured: *So, you screwed up. Okay. No big deal, move on. Let's go hang out.* Easy as that. My friends always knew that I'd forgive them, so in a way their hurtful behavior would never destroy our friendship.

Many times I did call, reminding them I needed them around more and available. A mere two-minute phone call would have done it. "Just calling to see how you're doing. How's your day going? What you up to later?" A phone call simply to make sure I wasn't lying in bed, crying. But everything remained unchanged.

I didn't have enough strength to juggle my grief as well as my inconsistent, self-absorbed friends. Their usual routine of sketching out and checking out for five-month periods was not going to cut it this time. I wouldn't and couldn't forgive and forgive and forgive like I used to. I needed them to be the reliable ones. I became unwilling to put so much effort into deep-rooted friendships that should have caused anything but disappointments.

Living in Detroit presented enough obstacles for me concerning family relations. Adding unreliable friends into the chaotic mix was too much. Those "best" friends should've been within hugging distance and balancing out the absence of my other close friends from Baltimore and childhood who were living out of state at the time. But they weren't.

Chapter Thirteen

As soon as I began finagling around town as some sort of Renaissance woman with 15 job descriptions, my social life had become almost non-existent, or at least compared to the stereotypical 22-year-old woman's. Socially, it seemed I was limited exclusively to hanging out with high schoolers and my rocking dating life of nightly reservations with my Mac keyboard and hot cinnamon tea.

Writing, as always, was my most effective therapy and my primary social outlet. The Bean and Leaf in Royal Oak became my first favorite writing nook. This had a lot to do with loneliness; I felt extremely lonely living in Michigan and thought being in a busy coffee shop might temper that some. I yearned for a social life, one more fulfilling than I had at that point. Once in a while I would meet up with Emma at her boyfriend's apartment in Royal Oak or at a local bar or restaurant (which she went out of her way to include me in); or every couple weeks I'd engage in the typical Royal Oak party scene, dancing at Fifth Avenue to jiggle it into the wee hours of the night with a girlfriend or two. Those nights were not often, nor were they fulfilling for me. I wanted more.

As much as I did enjoy my time at the Bean and Leaf, I usually felt sadder being there. I'd leave around 11 p.m. and realize everyone else walking the street in pairs or groups were just heading out, not driving home to cry themselves to sleep.

I wanted something more. A fling to keep my mind off of all the stress in my life. That deep need was probably what drove me to finally sell out and sign up for JDate, an online Jewish dating service. On the surface, signing up and creating a profile was for entertainment purposes, humoring Dad, tricking him into believing that I really was interested in finding that "good Jewish boy" he so badly wanted at least one of his daughters to marry.

Not only did I think online dating sites were a complete mockery, but I also was cynical that a person could really find true love by means of a programmed Cyber Cupid. Love for $40 a month? Doubtful. Both of the men I agreed to meet were complete busts. One guy made me split the bill, even though he was the one who asked me out. (In theory, I liked the idea of being an equal, but in practice not so much.) The other guy was a 32-year-old who had coincidentally graduated from Cranbrook. But I couldn't get over thinking that while he was applying for college, I was in 3rd grade still wetting my bed.

Journal Entry, February 27, 2008:

It was nice to have a date at least. Felt really down on Saturday while leaving Royal Oak after writing all afternoon. Every person is out for dinner with friends. And I'm alone. I can't say how badly I wish I could just meet someone who'll become my playmate. Lauren is still non-existent, even though I spoke with her on the night of her 22nd birthday. E.g. supposed to hang out for the first time in a week and a half, but on Sunday calls me at 2 p.m. to say she's going down to Cleveland for the Cavs game spontaneously. It's a joke. My best friend and I live a mile apart and I speak or see her less than I did when in Thailand. She doesn't get it. She's too selfish. Why can't she put me first for anything?

She asked me while I drove home from Royal Oak last night at 10 p.m. if I could come over and visit. I had been up since 7 a.m., unpacking at our new house, then had practice and wrote all night. Because she wants to watch the Pistons' game with her family, I have to put off Koh even longer and get tired at her house. I can never imagine acting this way if she were in my position (concerning Miya). It's bullshit! Mostly upsetting because I really do value her friendship so much.

That was when I met Carter. He was two years older and working the floor for an automotive company before finishing up college. It was easy with him at first, very easy. And he filled that need so completely. I did not mean to fall so damn hard for the kid, but it just happened, in part because I needed that sort of companionship at the time.

We wasted no time and spent every spare moment with each other over the next three weeks.I knew from the start using Carter as an escape was taking the easy way out and even if not physically running away from home, running from things just the same. Quickly and unfortunately, before I knew it, things with Carter went sour.

Journal Entry, March 22, 2008:

Friday at Carter's house in Waterford. All my friends, who were supposed to come with me, cancelled last minute. So, I was alone at the party with all of Carter's friends. It was that stereotypical college house party—beer pong and flip cup, the spectators standing around watching as though the games were a live Pistons game. I spent much of the time in the living room, playing and watching Rockstar with Carter's friends whom I knew. I was tired, trying to make a good effort at having fun/engaging myself with his friends.

Carter made close to no effort to make me feel comfortable, too interested in drinking and flirting with the other women. Six or so of his university lax girls, whom he coaches, showed up around 11:30 p.m. I thought nothing of them, in terms of posing any sort of competition to me.

He and I were alone only two times. First, in his room before heading out on a beer run to Meijer. We laid on his bed, as he continuously admitted,

"I think you are so, so, so great. And I get nervous that you'll leave in the fall like you say you want to." Second, on the drive to Meijer. He was so ADD and giddy from the alcohol. He was cute, not annoying or angry though.

As soon as we got back at around 2 a.m., after watching him swig Crown Whiskey and some other dark liquor, I had enough and climbed into his bed with the heater by my side. Wasn't pissed by any means, just indifferent to staying up any longer. The lax girls kept opening the door, laughing, assuming there were people hooking up in the bedroom, not just me sleeping.

About an hour later, I rolled over and saw Carter pop his head out of the bathroom across the hallway from his bedroom. One of his lacrosse players was in there with him. I tried to convince myself that I had not seen what I had, that there was a logical, innocent reason that a drunk guy would be locked in a bathroom with a drunk girl. I went back to sleep.

Journal Entry, March 22, 2008:

Then 45 minutes later, the house fell silent, so I got up to just check that everyone was safe. Standing in the kitchen, I came across Carter in his living room with the lights out. I watched him for about 10 seconds, standing over a different girl than the bathroom one, groping her chest while she laid on her back on the couch. She was moaning.

I went directly back into the bedroom, threw on my jeans and headed out, passing Carter [by the back door]. "Where you going? Wait," he said.

I just told him, calmly, "Goodnight, Carter." I admitted, "I'm not mad at you, just disappointed in myself for allowing myself to get hurt again. Guy after guy, I get my heartbroken."

Started to drive away as he ran across his front lawn through the snow, opening my door as I drove. He told me, "She's a good friend. A good, good friend." That the girl on the couch is only 19 and is so insecure so he was trying to talk with her about confidence, etc. Not grope her.

I want so badly to believe him, but I'm NOT BLIND. In fact, I'm VERY INTUITIVE and PERCEPTIVE. I know that!

Somehow I gave into him and his cute ways. He was almost on the verge of crying. And I was also a bit choked up. He said, "You can leave. Drive away and never talk to me again. And I will have a broken heart like I always do with every other girl, since I'm too nice of a guy."

So, I went back inside. Passed out in his arms, naked. I'm a sucker for his cute smile and gentle words. His "Goodnight, sweethearts."

I wasn't able to follow through with my intention to stay true to myself. I was convinced Carter's behavior was a figment of my imagination, that he was really just talking with those girls, that he was the great, sincere guy he claimed he was, that his tears when he admitted how great he thought I was while lying in his bed earlier that night and later in my car were genuine. I plunged deeper.

The Friday night ordeal wasn't soon forgotten though. I allowed those insecurities and mixed messages to marinate. Three weeks into hanging out, after just having slept with him for the first time earlier that morning, he called it off.

In retrospect, I was right on and very clear about what was going on with Carter. It had some to do with his fear that I might wake up one day, four months down the road, and think he's not good enough for me. And it had some to do with my insecurity about that infamous Friday night. Most people, especially Burch, noted, "What girl wouldn't feel insecure about that? In fact, most girls would have and probably should have completely freaked out if that happened right in front of them, which somehow you never did."

Carter's timing, March 30, sure didn't help either. I was on overload. Not only was March 31st Miya's one-year wedding anniversary, but on April 3, 2008 I had to deliver a speech for over 300 people at the Kadima luncheon in Miya's honor. I had a lot on my plate. More than any 22-year-old I knew.

Chapter Fourteen

In the days and weeks following the funeral, donations and contributions had flown in at a rapid pace. Hundreds and hundreds of people honoring Miya's memory. Donations in support of Mt. Bachelor Academy, the Gunnison Animal Welfare Society (for which she volunteered and supported), and especially Kadima (a Jewish organization which provides care and facilities for people with psychiatric disabilities). Kadima decided to hold their annual fundraising luncheon in Miya's honor because of the unprecedented monetary support for their organization in Miya's name.

On April 3, 2008 at Shaarey Zedek Synagogue in Southfield, Michigan, over 300 women and Dad congregated for lunch. Kadima's website defined the organization as: "A Jewish mental health agency whose mission is to provide psychological services, residential options, supported employment and social activities on a non-sectarian basis."

About a month before the event, Mom decided I would speak on behalf of the family. I wanted to write a speech that would speak to Miya's character and emphasize the significance of Kadima as an organization, as well as cause anyone present at the luncheon, who did not know Miya personally, to relate.

In a pencil skirt, a tucked in white button-down shirt, and black stilettos, I delivered these words:

The theme of today's luncheon is in itself characteristic of my sister Miya. Not only did she have a healthy body, but she also had a healthy mind.

She definitely struggled though with her mental illness. Struggled to understand it, accept it and live with it. Doctors, hospitals and meds were constantly coming in and out of the picture for years. But as she transitioned into becoming a well-rounded woman, once she finally conquered its weaknesses, she became whole, balanced and accomplished.

After studying and graduating from Western State College in Gunnison, Colorado, she moved back to Detroit for two years to pursue, among many other things, yoga. She mastered the practice—in fact, she became it. As beneficial as she was for her students, speaking only truth and wisdom, her students and the practice itself became her grounding force.

No longer was she defined by her illness. No longer was she embarrassed by "what she was." Bipolar was a hurdle, not her track. She used what she had learned during therapy and from others that struggled as she had growing up to affect other people.

When Miya was young, doctors and psychiatrists routinely warned my parents that she would most likely be in a hospital for the rest of her life, since they considered her to be so severely Bipolar. Therefore, my parents assumed Miya would grow up dependant on an organization like Kadima, which helps care for individuals affected by psychiatric disabilities. Our family had always supported Kadima, but I think Miya's disposition gave us even more reason to embrace their cause, fueled by the assumption, and possibly fear, that Miya would be unable to care for herself as an adult.

The objective of this luncheon is to acknowledge and honor Kadima and their work, especially on behalf of those families that have and do take advantage of their services. My parents, though, were fortunate to have the resources to provide treatment for Miya. Not every family has such a blessing. Nothing was too costly or too time consuming or too impossible.

Whether at boarding school in Oregon or a hospital in White Plains, New York, Miya was forced to face her issues from the time she was eleven years old. She would not be "ill." She had too much life and too much love to limit her to any hospital. She was not even confined by inhibition.

Bipolar is typically seen as a negative, but for Miya it was what made her her. Even though she lived life in extremes, she learned how to redirect those characteristic "Bipolar tendencies" and make them positive influences, allowing her to live life to its fullest. When she felt joy, she felt pure and utter joy, for example. While most of us repress our emotions, Miya welcomed each and every one with just as much intensity as the last. This was what allowed her to be the caring, understanding, compassionate person she was, because she had felt each one of those emotions. People loved Miya unconditionally just as she loved everyone else unconditionally.

Did Miya conquer being Bipolar because Miya was Miya? Or, was it because of all her treatment, which taught her how to own her illness? I don't really know. But our family realizes that such a feat is very uncommon. Most people do not have the compassion for themselves nor others to face it head-on. It didn't make Miya better than anyone else who struggles with mental illness.

It only made preparing for the future easier, because she and we knew and hoped that she had it in her to become healthy in body and mind.

A year ago at her wedding, I was certain that it would no longer be the doctors, hospitals and meds in her future—only babies and a loving husband. She had cleared those hurdles; she was beyond them. Her suicide was the last thing we expected.

The outpouring of support from friends and family in the Detroit area, as well as from out of state, has been, to say the least, overwhelming and heart-felt.

To all of you that have embraced us, honored us and loved us, thank you, thank you, thank you. A thousand times over.

"A year ago at her wedding…" Speaking those words was what tripped me up and sent tears flooding my eyes. I lost my composure and the pain of those disappointments and thoughts overcame my body, sending my muscles into a quivering fit. Still, I felt I had represented Miya well. Felt like she was working through Emma's hands as she stood directly behind me, rubbing my shoulders, trying to relax me and encourage my breath to remain steady and even. The day was a beautiful tribute to her. I was proud of her. The same photograph that sat in the Big House's kitchen was displayed next to the podium. She was a guest at her own luncheon.

Journal Entry, April 14, 2008:

Burch today at 11:15 a.m. Filled him in on what happened with Carter and also told him about the letter which I wrote to Carter a week after he told me on the phone he was done with me. In the letter I had tried to detail my feelings and thoughts.

What Burch and I primarily spoke about was:

a) Why can't I get into a relationship?

b) Why does each fling fizzle so quickly?

c) Why do all these men somehow NOT want to date ME?

d) What am I doing wrong? Is it that I seem unattainable so once they do "get me," I'm no longer wanted?

Connect that with how I often forgive everyone else in my life. My girlfriends who are completely absent/sketch out on plans constantly.

Then, connect all of that finally with our family. How can I not forgive/forget the way Kacee treats me and brush it off? Just as she said to me at our last family therapy session, why Emma didn't consider me, only Kacee, as an option to help her sell her new organic cheese line at Dad's food show, was because she thinks I have no social skills. Can't relate to people.

Our family dynamic had been flipped upside down and tossed fifty meters in the opposite direction as soon as Miya died. Over 30 years in the making, we were who we were because of who each of us was individually and who the six of us were collectively. As would be the case in any family, personalities and bonds formed that dictated the degree and type of closeness between every different family member combination possible. Mom and I; Emma and Miya; Dad, Kacee and I; Emma, Kacee and Mom; and so on.

If being a cohesive unit wasn't stressed enough before November 14, after Miya's death it became Mom's mission. She'd plea with me, Emma and Kacee, "It's just the three of you left. You all have to band together. All you have is each other." Easier said than done, and Mom (and everyone else) knew this.

We were all thrown back into the mix, living at home at the same time for the first time in over a decade. "All of us," except, of course, Miya. It seemed whenever one of us had left home, lived on our own for an extended period and then returned, each one of us would regress to the way she was when she lived at home as a child and teenager, even though she was a college-educated, well-traveled adult.

During the funeral, shiva, and memorial service, and for the first few months after, we were each other's support system—or at least as supportive as we could be. Emma, Kacee, and I were trying to rediscover each other and who we had become as adults, along with re-teaching ourselves how to respect boundaries. Differentiating the adult sister as opposed to who we were growing up was often difficult.

Learning how to actually co-exist, since we were three very strong and distinct personalities, was therefore a bit of an art—one that I didn't know we'd ever fully interpret and master. As my friend Heidi affirmed, "You're all Must girls, but you're all very different."

We were dealing with the loss of our sister, a sister who fulfilled a different role for each of us. How I had to deal with losing Miya was completely different than how Kacee thought she should, and completely different from how Emma thought she should. The same was true for my parents. Miya's decision had forced us to put our lives and plans on hold. What we all soon realized was that life would never be the same. Emma would no longer be living in Spain, Kacee would no longer be traveling in Australia and then India and Thailand, and I would no longer be moving to South America. There was "before November 14" and "after November 14." A watershed that brought with it consequences both horrendous and wonderful, all at the same time.

I no longer had Miya, my only ally at times. However, I did recognize the upside: this eye-opening opportunity to explore my writing and hone my voice, as I worked to create something with which readers would connect. There was also the joy of working with high schoolers in every avenue I could find—such as substitute teacher and athletic coach— and also by May, 2008 was the opportunity to create something together as a family—the Holocaust Survivor Project.

More than that, though, as I worked to rebuild myself and family relationships, I finally allowed myself to begin to examine all my demons. To not only investigate why Miya was the way she was, but also why I was the way I was. It became a journey that had many peaks and crevasses, a rollercoaster ride with hidden tunnels and gut-wrenching dips. Living at my parents in such close proximity to my sisters, dealing with Miya's death, disappointing friendships, and the utter confusion about life post-graduation were more than ample ingredients with which to experiment.

How many times I wish I could have cashed in those upsides for just one more day with my downside.

I was not a saint. I knew I had my downfalls. As I wrote this, I realized there were two sides to the story. There always will be, possibly even more, depending on how many were privy to seeing the story and relationships between me and my sisters unfold and prosper…and sometimes wilt.

Post November 14, I became the odd man out. Up until that point, Miya had most often been the scapegoat for criticism for years. An easy target since she was "sick."

Miya's Journal Entry, March 26, 2006:

I'm not exactly sure what I want to say…I guess I still feel invisible. It's like being beaten up and then asked to understand, forgive and accept it…I don't want anyone to do me any favors in regards to try to comfort me. What I really want is to be apologized to. As hard as I try to forgive and to understand my sisters it's the last thing I want to do when the past for them is still so prevalent and they continue to shut me out b/c they say: "They are angry."

I can't empathize w/ them. A voice in my head says: "Are you kidding? You have no right to feel or think that way!" I feel still so much was done wrong to me. I guess I feel I have suffered and that they caused a lot of that suffering. I never have received any apologies, but I have given many. I guess what hurts is that they aren't accepting, like a gift given that is thrown back in your face.

I am still angry. I don't want to be. I still feel silenced. I still feel as though I am irrelevant and invisible. I need to get over this. Wish that I will one day be done w/ my work, years of hurt (especially during the 1st 20 years) doesn't just evaporate after 2 years of therapy. I am a good person, but some things are too powerful. Some wounds run too deep for me to be able to look beyond. Yet, I am still struggling to find my own bearings.

Again there is nothing worse than being invisible and ignored…Why am I the one in the family still judged and hated so harshly? There are the questions I ask in my head. These answers are what fuel my anger, fuel the fighting. How can I possibly not let them affect me, how can I be within the family, how can I not disappear and feel I have to yell to be heard?

I unwillingly and helplessly felt like I took on that role for months after Miya's death.

With each family role and position, there were positives and negatives—mine being the baby of the family. For example, as the youngest, I was definitely favored a good part of the time. As the middle children, I assumed Emma and Kacee felt pressure to reassert their value. Both of them were still bitter that Dad was around more for my athletics. I knew when Mom stuck up for me that they felt disadvantaged. I felt they still characterized me as a tomboyish 11-year-old. But I was not any longer.

I hadn't spent more than a week with Emma in over seven or so years, and my relationship with Kacee had been non-existent over the past two.

I didn't fit into that cookie-cutter drinking, smoking and boy-dating teenager. I just never understood the enjoyment of going out and getting smashed. I was never willing to not stay true to those intentions just to bond with Emma and Kacee in high school. I figured there were so many other ways to relate and get to know someone other than by means of partying. Especially since that was never my way of doing things with any of my other friends…or with Miya. Take me dancing, fine. But I was always a sucker for sports playdates, long walks, study buddies and such.

I assumed this was how Miya, Emma and Kacee had all sort of bonded through the years. Miya and Emma used to throw parties at the Cottage all winter long, about which Mom and Dad had no idea. By Emma's junior year at Cranbrook, while Miya was at Andover, they made the clutch discovery of the always-open sliding window just behind the 'fridge in the back of the Cottage. It was a two-person operation. After one propped up the other and shimmied through the foot wide window a mere five feet from the ground, the party would begin.

Not that Miya wasn't known to host these parties on her own. Such as the time when Cindy, Mom's best friend and Sylvan Lake neighbor, was patrolling the Point and raided the Cottage, writing down each and every kid's name as a scare tactic. Meanwhile, Miya fled back to the Big House and left all her friends to take the blame.Mom greeted her at the garage door, holding out her hand as Miya dropped the Cottage's keys into her palm.

Same was true of Emma and Kacee. Emma was a senior when Kacee was a freshman at Cranbrook. Kacee was more apt to partake in the stereotypical crazy high school antics, with Emma as the main orchestrator among her friends. Having been teammates together for three varsity sports that year—field hockey in the fall, ice hockey in the winter and lacrosse in the spring—there was ample time for bonding. Their schedules were almost identical. It seemed a natural progression for them to jump straight into the social scene together. I never did that with Emma or Kacee.

After Miya died, I felt that Emma tried desperately to take on the role of the oldest sister. It seemed she felt obligated and stressed when trying to replace that gap that Miya had once filled, (even if Miya herself believed she was the culprit in any and all family problems). Emma and Kacee, best friends from high school, had that history of closeness; Emma and I did not.

Truth was I grew up afraid of Emma. I remembered being terrified to even set foot in her bedroom, as though I was doing something wrong. I expected her to jump out at me, yelling and kicking me out, punching me. Had this fear even when I knew she was across the country at college. And, honestly, at 22, I still felt uneasy being in or near her room at the Big House.

Over the years, while Emma was either traveling in Southeast Asia or living in Los Angeles, we'd occasionally email. I'd shoot her a copy of my resume and ask her opinion. Or I would pitch her ideas about what I should do with my life. She's the business savvy one in the family, practical (in the professional sense of the word), so I always assumed I could count on her to give me the most rational opinion and educated research on the issue at hand. Most often she did.

We never *really* communicated though. I never called her about boys or friends or when I was down. I counted on Miya for that (and Kacee too when we were on good terms). To put it bluntly, Emma treated me like I was socially stunted. Before November 14, I could only recall two, maybe three, real conversations between us. I never had a chance to get to know her. At least in terms of knowing how fun, playful, witty, and compassionate a sister she really was. I only knew her critical and judgmental side. In order to survive living at home, I thought I had to guard myself against Emma's constant criticism. Criticisms for what Emma considered I wasn't: "normal."

When I was in elementary and middle schools, I kept to myself. I was so intense about life in those days, more concerned about doing what needed to be done to meet my goals in the classroom and on the athletic fields. Maybe this was why I was not as close with Emma and Kacee as I wished I could have been. I had wanted so many times during those months after Miya's death to shout, "I'm no longer ten years old!" But, honestly, I didn't think it would have helped much.

It broke my heart to even admit this about my own sister. I was limited to her conception of what the little baby in the family should say and do.

The first time Emma and I spoke on the phone after finding out about Miya, I was pleasantly surprised. I felt nostalgia pin my heart when I heard her tell me, "I can't wait to see you."

"Ditto. I love you," I said.

"I love you, too," she replied. I had never felt that sense of belonging and understanding from her. We both sensed it. Both wished we were no longer in our twenties, but one and three and five and seven years old, when things were much less complicated. When there might have been a chance to rewrite history and not be forced to deal with what really was.

I kept replaying Emma's words over and over. Would she not be as critical of me now? Would she intuitively know I would need as much support as possible in the upcoming months without Miya around? Would that influence Emma to let down a bit? Would she do this because she finally realized how impressionable and crushing her words used to be to my self-confidence and balance? I only hoped.

It didn't all come true. Reality was glossed over a bit. Everyone limited the degree to which they reacted or criticized one another for the first few weeks of being home. Emma was the one that stood behind me while I delivered my eulogy at the funeral and at the Kadima luncheon.

I appreciated Emma's support at those moments, but every issue didn't evaporate just because Miya died, despite Mom wanting that to happen. Instead, they seemed to intensify for me with geographical closeness.

Kacee was a whole other story.

The two of us were extremely close as kids. We slept in the same bed until I was ten years old, were mutually homesick at Camp Tamakwa, and would pee on the toilet at the same time. That closeness wore off as middle school approached.

By high school, we just didn't understand each other. It wasn't until the beginning of her first year at Northwestern, when she was removed from home and high school, that we finally reconnected on a level we hadn't experienced since childhood. She got me, or at least accepted me for being the way I was. She wasn't continuing to judge me as "odd," just because of my disinterest in drugs and alcohol. Instead, as Kacee created her own world at college and suffered through disappointing friendships and an end to her athletic career, she realized the unimportance of a party life and began to invest into spending time with me. We held that bond well into my sophomore year at Hopkins. Constant communication whenever she traveled, and phone call after phone call when she was in Evanston, especially when Kacee was struggling at school with friends.

The honeymoon ended by the summer of 2006 while I was studying in Prague. Email after email, phone call after phone call, nothing was returned. I was confused...hurt mostly, wondering what I did wrong. Just wanting to share my experiences and joys abroad with her. All I ever got back were a couple sporadic emails claiming I wasn't taking care of myself, the usual criticism from my family. Here I was, having the time of my life, and all I got back from my sister was a put-down. When I finally returned home in December from India, I realized it wasn't the oceans that had distanced us. It was just us. She completely disregarded me. I was extremely hurt and affected.

Over that next year or so, both of us would take the dive, making up and forgiving each other, talking about trying to get along better. I felt though whenever Kacee decided she wanted to turn it off, I was clipped again. Miya's wedding was the last time I could deal with it.

The point of recounting all this history was to understand the difficulty of trying to rekindle a relationship with Kacee after the 14. I had been knocked down so many times, I fully distrusted any attempt to make lasting amends would ever happen. I wasn't willing to put my heart on the line once more,but I had no choice. I was homesick for that love and support we had given one another years before.

Chapter Fifteen

Since hockey season had finished, and I was utterly heartbroken over the breakdown of my relationship with Carter in March, and I was not getting along with Kacee or Emma, I was eager to fill the void. I involved myself fully in the spring soccer season. A family friend and former coach offered me the coaching position at Marian, an all girls' Catholic high school. Originally, I was supposed to be the assistant coach for the Junior VarsityA team. Instead, I was demoted (although I considered it a promotion) to Junior Varsity B team as the head coach. My girls were my girls. How I wanted to coach them, train them, inspire them was completely up to me. In my team goals/rules handout at the beginning of the season, my number one rule, inspired by our hockey mantra, was: "Anything less than pure hustle and heart is not acceptable." I meant it. I realized I was working with the JVB team, but I soon learned when I expressed my confidence in their abilities, they delivered beautifully. That was the case every practice and game. With hockey, I was more like the girls' confidant, cheerleader, hangout buddy, mistaken more often than not for one of them. With soccer, I was also their head coach.

The 3 to 4:30 p.m. practice consisted of a just under two-mile run through the neighborhood, a little agility work, ball work, and some possession drills. I quickly became known as the "running coach." Five minutes into the run, my 21 girls would be scattered blocks down the street, some keeping up with our starting pace, others walking, others hunched with a stitch in their side. My vocal demands such as "Run! Run! Run!" or "Get on your horse!" were some of many things the girls used as material while doing their daily impersonations of me.

A few weeks into our season, I organized a team yoga night. Short Form Ashtanga at 4:30 p.m with one of my favorite teachers at the yoga studio, Raina. Raina was 37 years old, but she looked 27. She knew Miya well, having taken teacher training with her. In a way, I enjoyed going to her classes mostly because I felt as though she helped me fill the void of Miya. Massaging me while in child's pose if she noticed I was crying, making me laugh whenever I saw her, and talking to me about life and family dynamics after class.

Raina's no bullshit. She told it like it was. If she liked you, you'd know. If she didn't, she'd just ignore you and go about her business.I made sure we went to her class. I knew the girls would enjoy her. I knew her sarcastic, blunt, yet endearing manner lessened the "yoganess"for the girls. Raina led us through the series. Some of the girls were natural, some just okay, others horrible, but they all enjoyed it. The whole time, as I tried my best to absorb myself in my practice and not pay any attention to the shenanigans going on beside or in front of me, I felt Miya. I knew she would have been so pleased that I was doing this with and for them.

Because it was close to catholic school, I switched my writing location from the Bean and Leaf in Royal Oak to the Java Hut in Birmingham. When I began writing at Java Hut, the café was called the Mobile Lounge and its most attractive quality was the hummus platter. But once ownership flip-flopped after a couple month hiatus and the new and improved Java Hut reopened in early April, my hummus platter was nowhere to be seen. I was bummed.

I didn't disown the café completely for two reasons. After a dreadful, four-month, weather-imposed hibernation in Detroit, which caused dark circles to encase my eyes and my skin to become transparent, I was willing to overlook its decision to clip their menu's edges. I needed to get out. Downtown Birmingham is filled with upscale shops, restaurants and bars, complemented by various legal and financial offices. The perfect location with constant traffic of cars and walkers encouraged me to engage in an occasional ten-minute break to stroll in the sun and help rid me of my winter wounds.

This was where Sammi, Heidi and Fish would often meet me for a quick hang out. Sammi, the daughter of Mom's closest girlfriend, lived a mere seven blocks away. Heidi, another close friend, having graduated a year ahead of me at Cranbrook, lived a mile down Woodward. Fish, my 40-something-year-old lawyer and entrepreneur buddy, worked only a block from the cafe. If Sammi wasn't working, Heidi was in town, or Fish and I were on good terms and not arguing, I could always guarantee one of them would swing by for my entertainment. Getting a break from the punching and sipping with some real life connection was necessary to my sanity. Even without the hummus, Java Hut looked damn good!

Heidi was possibly my greatest support. She was back home through April, but then left for two months to work on an independent film in Minnesota (living at Josh Harnett's home of all places!). The distance did not affect our friendship. There was still constant communication between us even across state lines. While I could go one to four weeks without hearing a word from other friends, Heidi and I spoke at least once, if not twice, a day.

I wrote in cafes for a more fundamental reason than any other. Point blank, I couldn't write at the Big House. Even if I locked myself in my room with Koh, people still seemed to trickle in from the woodwork, and all I ever found myself doing was carving a permanent path into the carpet and wooden floor from my bedroom, down the stairs, straight to the fridge and pantry. A trip I seemed to take at least a dozen times. Somehow my stomach became a bottomless pit and all my time was wasted. This was why I missed my Baltimore apartment. There were no distractions and I could have as much invaluable bonding time with Koh as I wanted, spending whole days and nights writing. The Big House rarely offered that escape.

More than anything, Koh was my greatest grounding force while living in Detroit.

I never suffered from the infamous "traveler's depression" when I returned home from abroad. Did I miss living abroad? Did I miss jetting away every weekend to an exotic island or neighboring country? Absolutely! But I also enjoyed the excitement of returning home and seeing my friends and family after a long time away. It has been said that distance makes the heart grow fonder, and I had to agree. Plus, in my opinion, if I was truly happy, it should not have mattered where I lived, but simply what I was doing to ensure such happiness.

When I flew back from my seven-month study abroad extravaganza, I only spent a week at home in Michigan before quickly heading to Baltimore, eager to move into my new apartment and get settled in time for the spring semester. Four days after being back in Baltimore, I woke up one morning and impulsively thought, *I need to get a cat*. I was shocked by my urge. I hated cats. I was terrified of them. Mostly because of Frannie's cat.

Frannie was our most beloved caretaker when we were kids. Occasionally, the four of us would sleepover at her apartment. If I ever stepped on the floor, her psycho cat would chase and bite me. I was forced to shimmy from the bed to the couch, making my way onto counters, just to avoid the damn thing. He was evil. From that point on, I never understood cats, especially their sneaking around. Therefore, that morning in Baltimore, it was understandably a strange thought. Still, I acted on it, and rang a good friend of mine, who was a cat person.

That afternoon he accompanied me to the Maryland SPCA. I gazed into every cage, and I knew he was mine when I saw him, rubbing up against the metal, inviting visitors to test him out. He was so gentle, confident, and eye-catching. A deep, slick grey with yellowish eyes. Two days later, I returned to pick him up.

I fell asleep for the first three nights he was in the apartment with my down-comforter pulled over my head, huddled in its warmth and safety, terrified that he would tear me apart in the middle of the night. His quick, jabbing strides from one side of the room to the other, under and then over the bed, were foreign to me. I tried to convince myself he did not mean to scare me, but instead, entice me into a playing fit that always overcame him at 11 p.m. nightly.

I called him everything but Koh for the first three weeks: Chai, for *dee chai,* meaning good heart in Thai; Tux, short for tuxedo, because of the little white spot just under his chin; Suay, meaning *beautiful* in Thai; Sky; Orley…but nothing seemed to fit.

Koh…simple, sweet, perfect. It just made sense. "Koh" means *island* in Thai. At that time naming him Koh was a constant reminder of the bliss and beauty I found while playing on those southern beaches. It soon became a constant reminder of Miya and the joy we found there together.

Koh quickly became my grounding force at school. I planned my days around spending time with and caring for him. I would (and still do) feel guilty if I was gone all day long. All too often I'd hear someone say, "Sabrina, he's a cat! Cats like to be alone." But, I knew differently. Koh depended on my company. He would finagle his way into the deepest crevices of my room and closet drawers, nestled into my coziest sweatshirts. When he heard the elevator door shuffle open and my keys fumble, he'd stretched his cute little body across the room just in time to welcome me home.

Every night, especially cold ones, I'd find myself tucked away with him in our homey paradise. Only candlelight would illuminate the room, elegant streams of smoke burrowing from the flames, dancing and flirting with the darkness all around. Old bills, half-read books and receipts, a glass vase with dulled sunflowers, and Grandpa Billy's 3x5 portrait were scattered on the chest at the foot of my bed. My reclining wooden Buddha was on another nightstand, left palm cupping the side of his face, the glow from the candle projecting his full, serene, voluptuous body against the off-white wall.

The lighting in my apartment, sexy, yet reserved, enriched the furniture's wood, the cork floor tiles and the chocolate, silk curtain and bedspread. All were intensely contrasted against the deep red accent walls on the left and window sides of the apartment I painted myself. The curtain, which hung unconventionally from the ceiling by nails, seemed to lock us in, and lock out the world, the noise, the confusion, the judgment, the future.

While typing on my MacBook, I'd watch Koh wisp from wall to wall of the apartment, chasing shadows, trying his best to bait me and play along. Grinning and cooing for him, I'd retire my computer for a bit and flash the laser light here and there on the bed, giggling as he'd instinctively pounce on the little red dot. There was something endearing and comforting about those nights with Koh when I chose to stay in instead of meeting friends at the local, "classy," smoke-infused, campus pub hotspot, PJ's.

I found our space to be safe, especially my last semester at Hopkins. Whenever I thought about the end of school—December 17, my last exam day—I imagined a black, steep drop. The unknown. I often brainstormed plans to move somewhere in South America. "Go to law school," Dad would bark, or my personal favorite, "Move home and get a *real* job."

Koh's ability to ground me was even more electrifying back home after Miya died. Many times, the only reason I did go home and didn't escape into a friend's bed at night was because I knew Koh was waiting for me.

Journal Entry, December 24, 2007:

> *Koh's been walking around the kitchen. So soothing to see how comfortable he is in the house with Mom's dogs. I had him in the sun porch with me and Dad a bit ago and while standing by the closed door kissing him, telling him "I love you so much, you know that?" And it hit me I was saying Miya's last words to me. I miss her.*

Even if Koh wasn't as wonderful as he was, I knew Mom would have welcomed him into the house. But since Koh was, he became her new obsession. "Koh did this earlier that was SO cute! I bought him a new playhouse today and a new brand of food. Did you clean his litter box?" Everything was Koh-related, and any and every nickname I would use, she'd use: Boo-boo, Koh-man, Koh-ster. I think Babalou was the only one reserved solely for me. She'd even click her tongue like I did when I called him.

Mom would guilt trip me if I was gone all day. "You're not around enough for Koh," she'd criticize. Most of the time I couldn't help it, if I was working all day subbing or coaching—something she wouldn't accept. The rest of the time I could have spent the day with him writing in my room. But I knew that any attempt to get work done would turn out rarely productive.

Mom was sold on Koh. The trick was Dad.

Dad and I had a unique relationship. I was the only 22-year-old I knew who pleaded with her father on a nightly basis to tuck her in. "PLEASE, Dad. Come on! Just five minutes. I just want you to talk me to sleep. Haven't spent any time with you today. Please! You finally have me living at home and now will never spend time with me. What's up with that?" The guilt trip used to work wonders all the time; in recent years there seemed to be roughly a 25% success rate. I was certain it was due to the fact that Dad had gotten much lazier with every additional gray hair and extra pound. The trek up a flight of stairs was way too strenuous!

On the rare occasion he did make the arduous journey, I could almost guarantee exactly how the scene would play out. He would enter my bedroom, gracing me with a Broadway performance, belching: "I'm the Duke, Duke, Duke, Duke of Earl, Earl, Earl...I don't know the words, words, words, words..." as his arms flapped up and down, and his bare, calloused feet pounded my white carpet. (A performance which wasn't complete until he was on his way out 30 minutes later, halfway down the hallway declaring, "I'm the Duke of Poop!")

His grand exits sealed the deal and shouldn't be overlooked. My personal favorite was one evening in April when he mocked, "Sabs, you're a stud?" reading the inspirational sign written by a soccer teammate which was tacked onto the backside of my bedroom door. "Thought you were a bitch!" he'd comment with a grin, gazing back at me, his shoulders beginning to shake as they did when he laughed and considered himself hilarious.

That was his way of saying, *I love you*. He then proclaimed, "Goodnight, honey," and I exploded into a laughing fit.

Our banter had been well calculated over the years. I knew what would and would not fly, and the same with him. I was certain our relationship inspired the phrase "Daddy's Little Girl." His quickness to explode from Mom's or one of my sister's constant "Can I have money for..." or "I need you to pay for..." requests rarely fazed me. I just countered, "Dad, calm down. Why are you yelling at me? Calm down. Okay, breathe. Think about this rationally. Compare spending $10 for food on the $1,000 my girlfriends drop on make-up and alcohol. Be thankful I don't do that." This was how I learned to sweet-talk my way into anything.

For the first week Koh was living in the Big House, Dad had no idea. Koh was out of sight, out of mind. Never having lived with dogs, we took baby steps with Koh. First, he was confined to my bedroom. Then, the whole upstairs was his, Mom's dogs eagerly waiting at the bottom of the staircase, separated by a child protective gate, engaging in a staring contest. They just wanted to know what this creature was. By the second week, once Mom broke the news to Dad that Koh was "secretly" living in the house, Dad still had not realized.

He definitely objected, but his agitation quickly subsided, since I knew each and every way to convince him that something was a good idea or reasonable. In other words, I knew I had him completely tied around my pinky.

Koh became the Big House's main event, even if Dad tried to deny it.

How ever much I had feared cats before getting Koh, Dad's fear was ten-fold that. More often than not, if I answered Dad's "What're you up to tonight?" questions on the phone while lounging in bed with Koh in our apartment in Baltimore with "Just hanging out with Koh tonight," Dad would warn and torment, "If you ever bring that damn thing into the house, I'll suffocate it with a plastic bag!" He was joking, yet serious, leaning a bit more toward the latter.

He had always considered cats "filthy, sneaky little things." He tried to deny the fact that I even owned one. Before getting to the "warning and tormenting," it would take at least three minutes for Dad to acknowledge who Koh was. "What!? Koi? Who? Coo?" he'd stammer.

"My cat, Dad, I own a cat, remember?" I'd sarcastically, yet cutely counter. Even spelling it out for him, "Koh, K-O-H."

"Ohhh…Kohhhh."

It was even more absurd while I was in Baltimore in December finishing up school and Koh was in Detroit. Dad would call me, complaining, "He's just staring at me. Why's he doing that?" And, sometimes he'd threaten, "He's sneaking around…Gotta get a collar and bell on that thing…to stop his sneaking around," or "I'm going to buy a mouse and let it loose in the house. Let this thing hunt. That's what cats do, they're predators. They're dirty."

Then he'd summon Koh: "Koi, come here. Koi!" The first time I heard Koh's new name—Koi—I couldn't decide if I should laugh or yell at him. So I just asked, "Do you know what *koi* means, Dad?"

"No…well, yeah, like cool, slick…He's a slick cat…Sneaky little Pete."

"Well, yes. In English, koi means that. But in Thai, it means penis. You've been calling my cat Penis."

As much as he tried to reject his impulse to love him, Dad also obsessively talked about "the cat." People would insist, "He's a dog." And I openly agreed. He brought our family together in an unexplainable way, something so charming about his presence.

I wished I could have escaped with Koh, shut my bedroom door and locked myself in as I had in Baltimore. Even now with Emma living in Royal Oak with her boyfriend and Kacee at the Kids' House, I couldn't center myself and not feel rushed.

Journal Entry, April 28, 2008:

Still feeling lots of anxiety being at the house—and it's all about food. I hate that I am so pressured/overwhelmed to stuff myself when home. Every thought in my mind is: "I'm home. I have to eat. People are judging me if I'm not eating." But I do it in private so they still don't really know.

Chapter Sixteen

I hadn't been completely truthful. I was encouraging people to be open about their issues, and I wasn't being completely open with mine. In fact, it took me a year into writing until I was able to acknowledge and face this.

I would binge.

I was ashamed of it, hated it, disgusted by it. I feared becoming fat, unwanted, not perfect.

Miya suffered from and was tormented by an eating disorder for over a decade, and I felt obligated to detail her struggle. Yet I feared admitting to such a *disgusting* vice/habit/disorder. Originally, I had cartwheeled around what really was going on with me whenever I was down and dark throughout the year. But I knew my story was not complete until I addressed these issues, telling of my own suffering in its entirety, fully and honestly, just as I had in every other section of the book; I knew it was the missing piece. These issues were real, and more people than I realized had similar struggles.

I decided to painfully document the history behind my most shameful way of being, because I realized the value of this disclosure and how therapeutic being open about my shit was for me and could be for many others. Just as I wrote as a means to reach out about the grieving process, about living with someone who suffered with mental illness, and about abusive relationships, I hoped also it would resonate with anyone that had ever questioned his or her own worth physically, emotionally or intellectually.

I was brought up in a family where control was revered and indulging was not. When Miya died, everything felt as far from controlled as possible. My world crashed down at lightning speed. All my issues that I had once suppressed through control, surrounding my fear of not being perfect, surfaced in uncontrollable ways. I began dealing with my pain by acting out, trying to become free, and in a way punishing myself. Binging manifested that uncontrollability, that self-hatred, that fear of not being acceptable, and that anger toward Miya for doing what she did.

I realized there was a common theme of self-doubt in our family. A theme of not thinking you were good enough, smart enough, perfect enough. Any outsider would have thought our family was insane for such skewed beliefs, considering how successful we seemed to be as women and parents. Skewed or not, those beliefs were very much present.

I used food to either control those insecurities and physically perfect myself, or punish myself by giving in to those beliefs and physically manifesting them; because being fat was, of course, wrong and horrible. (Or at least that was what I was taught.) What made *recovering* so difficult was that I had to eat to live. I couldn't just wipe food out from my daily routine. I had to learn how to balance it and discover what worked best for *me*, not anyone else, practice neither abstinence nor overindulgence.

I had all these beliefs about my body and food: what was good, what was bad. Through the years, some of those beliefs were empowered, while others were suppressed. After Miya's death I tried to heal my wounds of self-doubt. But they were very deep, so it took time to explore them, examine them, and then begin to heal them. I was ashamed to write and include a chapter about the binging. I feared my friends' reactions upon reading about it, because I feared I would no longer be the Sabrina they thought I was. But just as fearful as I was, I was even more desperate to heal those wounds once and for all.

My journey of exploring who I was and why included healing my eating disorder. It was an eating disorder. Something that terrified me to even write down. Yet admitting to such a thing made it have less power, so I chose to empower myself and therefore took power away from it.

Miya never healed this. She hated herself for it. I was determined to do it for both of us.

Issues with food had a long family history, which naturally trickled down through the decades. Dad's parents were absent from his childhood, since they were tirelessly building the family business. As a child he would stay up late and eat, watching television with his older brother and sister, waiting for Papa and Grandma to return home as late as midnight. Food became his comfort. When the car rolled into the driveway, the three children would scurry into their beds, fearing their parents' reaction if they saw they had not gone to sleep. Dad was so lonely and desperate for his parents' love that food fulfilled the warmth he neededas a child. Because he also had to hide his late night bedtime feasts, food for Dad also became a secretive thing. Well into his 20s, late night binging was a time all for himself, when he could relive his loneliness and in a way muffle it, his food coma drowning out his emotions.

He had always suffered with depression. It seemed Dad had trudged through his entire life unhappy, which he himself would admit. His belief was life wasn't supposed to be easy. You work, make money, raise a family, die. That was it. He always wanted to be happier and healthier, having gone in and out of therapy at different points during his life, even once enrolling in the Hilton Head Health Institute (a.k.a. fat camp) for a six-week program. Being unhappy and unhealthy was all he knewthough, so in a way change and healing seemed to be impossible.

The pain of losing Miya drove him even deeper into his struggles. I had to watch Dad literally try to eat himself to death, angry if one of us criticized what he was doing or not doing, or suggested a way to be healthier. I remembered walking into the sun porch many times late at night throughout winter and spring 2008 to sit with Dad. With a kitchen hand towel sprawled across his lap as his tablemat, he'd sit, grasping the packet of cheese slices, or lobster meat sticks, or bin of nuts, or even a fruit bowl. I'd become annoyed because I knew he had eaten all day and even that one more piece of watermelon was just over the top and unnecessary.

I'd ask, "Seriously, Dad, are you starving? Stop eating!" I'd reach over the couch, trying to snag whatever it was he was hoarding, as he held it more tightly, swinging his other arm toward me to push my hand away. It was another way for us to banter. It was entertaining the way he would react, both of us giggling as he got red with frustration. But just as "entertaining" as the scene was, it was serious, deadly serious. He became a borderline diabetic, and I had never seen him look heavier. (But he was still Dad to me, still adorably huggable, not disgusting.) He considered himself to be a failure as a parent, and therefore a failure as a person. Of course, food was his only way to comfort himself as well as continue to destroy his self-worth.

When I would get angry with Dad if he was eating late at night or unhealthy foods, it was also done selfishly. I saw myself in him, which terrified me. I was working to heal my binging behavior, hoping I could and therefore not wake up one day as a married, working adult to realize I never had. Seeing Dad still behaving in this manner at 63 years old, 80 pounds overweight, I almost lost hope in myself. I saw it as unfair. I wanted him to be a parent, to set a good example, not one of hopelessness.

Mom was the opposite. Grandpa Billywas extremely regimented, an athlete who ate healthily before anyone knew what healthy eating was. Grandpa was Mom's role model and hero. Anything he did, she wanted to do. Therefore Mom took on Grandpa's eating and workout ways. She always had a big appetite, as did Grandpa, devouring entire chickens, loafs of bread, her favorite peanut butter bagels, her favorite chocolate sorbet or Junior Mint candy. Yet, she balanced that with exercise everyday—from swimming to walking the dogs to a yoga class. Her suggested medicine, if I was ever not feeling good or down, was to go exercise. "It'll make you feel better!" she'd say with a smile. I believed her, knew it was true to an extent. But what her workout schedules and advice also taught me was that not following such a regimen was bad. So her "it'll make you feel better" assertion continuously played in my head as a conscience for as long as I could remember. I would feel shameful if I hadn't worked out…and even more so if I had binged and hadn't worked out.

While Mom learned from Grandpa, Grandma Maggie on the other hand was everything Mom hated. Grandma ate unhealthily (or at least by Grandpa and Mom's standard). She loved sweets and chocolate. Her late night Baby Ruth candy bars were her vice. Mom soon learned eating late was like Grandma and therefore bad and horrible. She feared waking up one morning and becoming Grandma, crazy and mean. Control for Mom allowed her to grasp a better handle on reality and maneuver the world around her as she sought fit…the opposite of what she experienced as a child with Grandma as a mother.

I grew up joking and laughing about how Grandma would hide her candy binges from Grandpa. It cemented a belief in my mind: late night eating was bad. If I wanted to avoid being like crazy Grandma Maggie, I should NEVER eat late at night and hide my food.

Unfortunately, it wasn't all that easy. My only role model wasn't just Mom. Dad was the other factor. He was into extremes. He'd go on these kicks, diets which would limit him to only grilled chicken breast and grapefruit for a few months, or protein shakes in the morning, or walking on the treadmill or riding his bicycle outside every morning for a couple of weeks. He would try any and every method to reverse the effects of his binging behavior. The other fifty weeks of the year seemed to fast forward the effects. He once even joked, "Sabrin, did you hear? I'm writing a book, *The 1-Hour Diet*. Diet for an hour a day and the rest of the day you splurge!"

While nothing ever stuck for Dad, I watched Mom stick religiously to her workout regimen. That was why sticking to a regimen for me was so difficult. My being was constantly playing with a yo-yo and I would swing side to side, up and down with each tilt of the string.I learned that if I wanted to be like Mom—fit, controlled, socially and physically appealing—I must never be like Dad—binging, eating unhealthyfried or sweet foods, fat.

Whenever we would see an extremely overweight person in restaurants or stores, or walking down the street, Mom would comment, "Oh my God! How could you live like that? How could you let yourself become that way?" I learned from an early age: fat was bad, skinny was good. That mental tape played and played, imprinting itself in my psyche. Which inevitably translated into fat meant undisciplined, skinny meant controlled. Fat meant Dad, skinny meant Mom.

But there was more to Mom's words. Indirectly, she was beating Dad down. He was like *those* people (maybe not as extreme, but still unhealthy). She was teaching that criticizing a person who was fat was okay and binging was disgusting. When I began to act in that manner, my entire being hated it, felt like I was betraying Mom (in a very weird, screwed up way).

Over the years, Mom had even mentioned how her marriage suffered because Dad was so overweight. I associated his weight as the thing that caused my parents' unhappiness at times. I never wanted my physical appearance to be the reason my boyfriend or husband did not want to touch me and found fault in who I was.

There were so many times I'd tell Dad matter-of-factly, "You look good, Dad."

He'd rebuke, "No, I don't. I am fat. I look horrible," becoming even heavier, sadness and anger and shame draping over his body, his destructive mental tape on ahigher level of repetition.

I would follow up with, "No you don't, Dad. Don't say that…Well, do you at least feel good?"

"No, I feel like shit."

Miya, Emma, Kacee and I were the Must girls—open, uninhibited, athletic, free-spirited. Our family seemed to have no inhibitions, nudity was, and will always be, a must (no pun intended), and being athletic was genetic. But there was a contradiction in that way of being…which inevitably created stipulations. I was to be athletic, yet not too butch or muscular. I was to be open and touchy, yet could only be that way if I was physically appealing.

In high school, I won the most athletic award, being immortalized as the only girl in the history of Cranbrook's annual homecoming powderpuff competition between the Junior and Senior classes to kick a field goal: 27 yards with 30 seconds remaining to beat the Seniors 9 - 8. That claim to fame was just one of many climaxes to my long history of athletic participation since I was a kid.

I played with the boys in our neighborhood, during recess, and on organized teams. I never exactly wanted to be a boy. I just wanted to dress like one, play like one, and hang like one. I loved being a girl, don't get me wrong. But, I loved being the girl who could outplay all the boys; better yet, I loved being the only girl who was allowed to play with the boys. I never understood the ribbons and frills growing up. I never understood why you couldn't throw a perfect spiral (and I never will).

Since I could remember, I also had an outrageous sweet tooth. There was a time when I was home sick from elementary school soon after Halloween and I snuck into the pantry to raid my sisters' Halloween stashes. Mom was not at the house for a couple hours, only our Polish-speaking housekeeper shuffling through the hallways. I did so sneakily, yet freely. I ate everything: Crunch bars, Twix, Skittles, Tootsie Rolls…candy with and without milk. I enjoyed myself. There was a pleasure in doing something I was not supposed to be doing.

When my sisters realized all their candy was gone, they were enraged, especially since Mom was known to give at least 70% of our candy away to needy children. Their stashes were already not as hefty as they should have been. My parents surprisingly didn't punish me, only laughed.

There was also the time as a seven-year-old that Emma and Mom came into my bedroom at the Big House and jokingly inspected every corner and cabinet. They found wrappers and wrappers of Starbursts in one of my desk drawers, stuffed to the brim, making it impossible to close it securely. It became a family joke: *Remember when we found all the wrappers in Beiner's room?* Slowly though, hiding my sweet tooth became the norm. If not, I wouldn't have been able to eat what I really wanted.

Another staple was family meals. They became a competition: Who could eat the most?My standard Sunday meal at Mom's favorite restaurant, Sunny's Café, was a scooped plain bagel with Feta and sliced tomato on top, two bowls of Frosted Flakes, a tuna melt with cheddar on pita bread, and hash browns. Or, my standard meal at my favorite Italian joint, Paparazzi, was an entire loaf of bread, an entire pizza-size bruschetta, and a filet mignon with sautéed mushrooms and roasted potatoes. The amount of food was outrageous. I did it because not only was it tasty, but because I received praise for eating the large amount of food.

Looking back, they were all mixed messages.

Come freshman year of high school, I decided to test my milk allergy. Finally allowed to eat ice cream (even if it gave me a stomach ache afterwards), my day wasn't complete until I had my dessert. I'd call Dad on his way back from the office and plead for him to pick up my favorite flavor, mint chocolate chip, from the grocery store. Any brand would do. I'd sit in his armchair in the library, watching television, decompressing from school and my sports' practices and games. I quickly associated comfort with eating something that was once off-limits.

By winter of freshman year, I remembered being in Mom's bedroom, looking at myself in the mirror in the dressing area, looking at my stomach.

Until that point, I had never really examined myself in a mirror. I never did my hair, put make-up on, or complained about this or that body part not being perfect. That night, I noticed the slight bulge in my stomach, which had always been perfectly flat and muscular. I grabbed my hips, asking, "Are these love handles?"

"Well, you could lose five pounds or so, I guess," Mom told me. Kacee was sprawled across mom's bed, listening, and her face reacted silently; she didn't want her baby sister worrying about that.

It was at that moment I looked at myself differently than I ever had. I wished for perfection. I wished for Mom's approval. What I didn't realize was that those changes in my body were normal. My hormones were all over the chart, my body was exploring a new way to operate and look. What I looked like when I was 11 was not what I should have looked like when I was 15 and not what I should have looked like at 22. Getting a bit curvier, then possibly leaner, then possibly taller was all part of my body's own discovery.

I had heard the girls at school talking about (and hating) their love handles, but never knew what a love handle was. I thought that they were a good thing, something appealing, love—who wouldn't want that to be part of their body? But Mom was saying "five pounds," so a tape was created claiming, "Love handles bad! Any bulge in my stomach bad! Ugly! Not perfect!"

I transformed my evening ice cream ritual from one of pure enjoyment to one of shame. "Do you really need all that ice cream?" Mom began asking. I knew she didn't mean to make me crazy about it, but I dealt with things in extremes since that was all I knew. It was hard to cut down from three bowls to one bowl, which would have seemed most logical; instead I stopped eating it all together.

I also remembered serving myself a hefty portion of Costco apple pie after one of our many family barbecues in Sylvan Lake that summer, and a family friend pinching my stomach, joking, "Oh, Beiners, getting a little tummy there!" I ran out of the house, escaping into my bedroom at the Cottage, crying myself to sleep. I never wanted someone to make me feel so imperfect again. I tried my best from then on to always try to be as healthy and physically appealing as possible.

But finding that balance was difficult throughout the rest of high school and college. I would maintain a healthy routine of working out and eating healthy for a period, but then once or twice a month I would fall off the deep end into a binge. A lot of the time those binges were leading up to my period, so my body craved certain foods that were not necessarily "healthy." I never defined it as a binge. Honestly, I didn't know what the word really meant until after Miya's death.

Over the years, Miya was the one with whom I was most open about my insecurities, or at least as open as I would allow myself to be. The first time I got a glimpse into Miya's eating disorder was at age 13, during a family trip to Miraval, a spa and resort in Arizona. I came out of the locker room by the pool, and Miya was already in her bathing suit. Her legs looked like chicken legs, skin and bones, (even more skinny than they naturally were). I wondered, *What happened to Miya?* No one ever discussed with me what was really going on with her. I only picked up on a few murmurs or glares, or Emma's angry, threatening, concerned words toward Mom and Miya.

Secretly, later that night at dinner, I followed Miya to the bathroom after she excused herself from the table halfway through the meal. Standing just outside of the bathroom, ear to the door, I did not hear any purging groans, so I was relieved. The next day Miya actually left Miraval a day early, worn down and exhausted from the family's criticisms. I felt bad and was terribly confused.

I never once purged. That, for me, was too unhealthy. There was something inherently wrong about it. Plus, I knew that if I ever purged, that one time would forever scar me and it would unfortunately become my drug of choice to re-balance myself, or simply rid me of the shit in my body. I never tested that forbidden fruit out of fear.

I recalled being a sophomore in high school, standing in the boiler room in the basement of the Big House where an extra storage freezer was kept for pies and leftover birthday cakes. Miya was neck deep in her own eating disorder at this time. She and I stood with a cardboard box from Panera on the counter, breaking off chunks of frozen brownie cake with our fingers. When she said, "Look at us!It's so nice to bond over eating cake and be okay with it!" it felt like her way of proving she could eat that "bad" food, and a way for her to make sure I was still allowing myself such a pleasure. Miya never wanted her littlest sister to suffer and be as obsessive as she knew she was.

During the winter months at college, when I babysat for local Baltimorean families, I'd raid the family's 'fridge and pantry of anything sweet and yummy. I'd wake up the following morning by 7 a.m., eager to begin my day in a similar way. I already felt like shit, and so I craved anything that could pick my energy level back up. I would jet downstairs, across St. Paul Street, kitty-corner to my sophomore year apartment, buying cookies and candy and fruit…anything sugary. I wouldn't workout during those slumps, even more exhausted than I naturally was from hours and hours of class and studying.

As far back as I could recall, when I did feel balanced, I was on top of the world, as confident as could be in my body and mind. As soon as my awkward high school years were over, I did come into my own. My body naturally became a bit leaner and more feminine, my hair continued to grow even longer down my back. Having worked hard to really trust and learn what my body needed and how much, I was very aware of which foods made me feel most energetic. Plus, I was a vegetarian for almost five years for moral, environmental, and health reasons, so what I would eat when I was not on a binge was naturally healthy. While most kids grew up snacking on Lunchables, the four of us were used to sharing a jar of pickles or half of a watermelon with Dad, and having Mom feed us chickpeas out of a can as a snack. It was hard not to have certain taste buds that craved those types of foods. Therefore, when I respected my body, I felt alive. When I had overeaten, acted in a way I believed was shameful, my body felt like it was literally falling apart and I would drop into a dark, deep space.

I'd wake up, feeling like crap, unable to move and sometimes even open my eyes, angered and drained for two reasons. First, because I knew it would take me an entire day or two days to recover, and secondly, because my mind was so angry about what I had done. I would not only focus on the food, but on everything that was unsteady in my life. I would beat myself up, thinking, *You're not doing enough in your life. I hate this side of you. You are a waste!* I didn't disdain my whole being, only the part that was willing to be conquered by this cycle. Somehow though, my mind and body would trick me into doing it again and again.

The issue had become my very own elephant in the living room. I knew it was there, wanted to deny it was there, looked at and touched it every so often, but did so secretly, so no one else would know how I was behaving. I could never let other people know how un-perfect I was, because I couldn't really admit these things to myself. Since this cycle occurred much more rarely throughout college, healing it was only somewhat of a priority. When Miya died, it became a one-, two, three-times-a-week ordeal, and because it limited me in so many ways, day after day, the need to heal it was much more urgent.

It wasn't a given that if I had eaten a certain amount or type of food I would dip automatically into this space. I defined "binge" more by the state of mind I was in, or by what degree I was almost obsessed with getting more and more to eat, or by how the food had affected my body. I was known to need a constant stream of snacks. This was how I got the reputation with my hockey and soccer players for eating all the time. "Look at Beins! She's still eating!" and then they would all laugh. I laughed with them, because some of the time I did find it funny, since in that moment my body felt fine. I also wanted to set an example for these kids of not restricting, of not playing into the Hollywood body image. It was afterwards, though, when the energy rush passed, I would crash and become frustrated with myself and it would start again.

I was a petite, physically fit, lean woman, weighing around 115 lbs. (Truthfully, I didn't know my actual weight, because I purposefully never weighed myself. I never wanted to consider myself healthy based on a number, but instead by how my physical and emotional bodies felt. That would have been just one more thing about which to obsess.) I would ask and remind myself: *Why should I be so worried about gaining weight when people are actually overweight? I am genetically programmed to be skinny and will never really have to worry about my weight if I eat in moderation.*

As Kacee often said, I too felt as if I was living in a circus fun house during a binge. One minute I'd be standing in front of the "body shrinkage" mirror, another minute I'd be standing in front of the "elongation mirror," another minute I'd be standing in front of the "normal mirror," and yet minute day I'd be back where I started off. My self-perception was detrimentally flawed. I couldn't see myself. Couldn't see what my 5'4" petite frame really looked like.

Only I could notice slight changes in my body. More often than not during the entire year after Miya died, people would comment, "You look like you lost weight!" I was baffled, because all I had been doing was eating and lounging, day after day.

Exercise at times became something I disdained. I wouldn't exercise, because I wanted to rebel and punish myself, my way of making a statement against the way I was brought up. I rather have sat on the couch, writing and editing, playing with Koh, eating and eating and eating and eating. I was using food to subconsciously fight and rebel against my life falling out of control. I would miss Miya more than ever when I was in that space, pissed off at her for leaving me and not doing anything to magically erase this darkness from my psyche…a darkness from which she herself suffered.

Journal Entry, April 29, 2008:

SO MUCH ANGER.

Why? Why do I do this to myself? Over and over? Hate it. Hate cravings. Woke up yelling and literally punching the bed at 4 a.m.—"Fuck! I hate this! Fucking hate it!"

So much self-hatred.

This sadness is also so overwhelming. I can't get myself up out of bed. I know this doesn't serve me, but there's comfort in sitting and doing everything that Mom hates about Dad.

Why do I still feel like rebelling against that control or balance?

The only person I feel would understand is Miya. Why can't she be here to talk to me—for even three minutes? I need her. I'm so ashamed of how I'm living.

Chapter Seventeen

I primarily wanted to meet with Whitaker in April 2008 because I needed to know her honest and professional opinion on three key uncertainties of mine: Was Miya indeed Bipolar? Or did she have Borderline Personality Disorder? And most importantly, would she have still killed herself if she wasn't mentally ill but the circumstances were exactly the same?

I needed to know what or whom I could blame for her suicide, as well as how to excuse and forgive my sister for doing what she did (to herself, to me, and to us as a family). To put it simply, I needed to know that Miya didn't kill herself just because she was had a mental illness. I needed to have the ammunition to fight off the judgmental, falsely informed, speculating acquaintances and strangers who continued to look at our tragedy from an outsider's view and say, "Oh, it's a classic case. Obviously, she was just off her meds." I needed to learn how to guard myself after a letter to a local newspaper triggered a depressive spiral for me.

Journal Entry, April 29, 2008:

I had a couple of great days this week. But something happened yesterday evening that set me off. Walking into the house and having Dad tell me about the article in the Detroit Jewish News*, the letter some woman wrote about how Miya did NOT own her illness, that the lack of care for bi-polar patients in Michigan "failed her."*

Dad was enraged. How could someone justify publishing a letter of such magnitude without the family's permission? Completely inappropriate! It's not this woman's place to decide how and what influenced Miya's death.

A local woman had submitted the letter soon after the Kadima luncheon. The printed words smacked me across my face and then punched me in my stomach. The words were utterly insensitive. She did not know my sister, knew nothing of Miya's past, her hardships, her triumphs, or the details of her death.

A mother of a mentally, psychiatrically challenged teenager herself, this woman was publicizing her frustration about the lack of state funding for the treatment of Bipolar patients, which probably was the case. But she was using Miya's suicide as her platform. The headline read "Society Let Miya Down." Really? Wasn't it her husband who devastated her and made her feel conquered as an individual? Moreover, there was never any public funding used or sought after to provide Miya treatment. My parents always took the weight of that burden, attacked it with a personal vengeance. Yes, maybe such a suicide for someone who was Bipolar would be the cause of a lack of availability of funds for such treatment and research, but for Miya it was not the case.

Reading the letter at the kitchen table, staring at the photo of Miya from her wedding, smiling at me, I was thrown into a downward spiral for the next two days. Until Mom returned home after her annual girls' week get-away in Florida and was able to re-inflate my punctured airbag.

In response, Emma submitted a letter on behalf of our family. She reminded people that Miya was extremely successful, having "graduated college, owned a couple of businesses, got married and was a wonderful mother to two dogs." Emma affirmed that the woman's letter was completely inappropriate, reiterating Miya's life as one that "continues to teach all who knew her how to embrace life passionately, face obstacles courageously and, of course, love unconditionally." The Jewish News never published it.

What did all that do? Part of me knew Emma, Ms. Argumentative herself, would competently write something that spoke to the truth of who Miya really was. But another part of me wanted to stop the fighting and justifying. I wanted to let people think what they wanted to think. I even believed close friends of mine did not accept my assertion that Miya's mental illness wasn't the only factor in her death. Should I have continued to fight to win their approval and support? And would that have actually helped me find peace?

Mother's Day arrived, and I had only been back to Miya's grave twice since the funeral. Once by myself and another time with Mom, Emma, and Kacee, leaving sunflowers and clay seal ornaments from her bedroom at the Big House for her.

I drove down Woodward Avenue at least three times per week and planned to make that turn onto 14 Mile Road every time. Planned to spend time lying next to her gravesite on Grandpa's left, with Debbie's on Grandpa's right. A Miya Jo/Debbie Jo sandwich. But I never made it. Planned to work through my sorrow with her as close as I could ever be to her now. But I never did it. Six feet under was too far away for me.

Since I had always wanted to buy a star, had always been enthralled with the universe, its vastness, the unknown, I figured I would buy one for my gift to Mom. I had always believed if I purchased a star, I'd be one step closer to that infinite and ultimate truth.

"Star light, star bright, first star I see tonight, I wish I may, I wish I might, first star I see tonight." This prayer was my usual custom whenever I gazed up into the night's sky. Naming a star for Mom seemed only appropriate.

I searched "how to buy a star" on the internet, clicked on NameAStarLive.com, named it "My Radiant Miya," and added a message:

> *For Mom, Not only is Miya the oxygen you breathe, weaving between and laughing with you, now she'll be your guiding light whenever you're in darkness. I love you. Thank you for being my grounding force. From Your Beiners.*

It was a thought inspired by the *Lovely Bones*. After purchasing it ($29.90, shipping and certificate included), three days later a golden star stamped certificate was on our kitchen table. At least I could wish on a star I knew would hear and hopefully answer me.

Mom had been dreading this particular Sunday for weeks. She simply wanted to fall asleep Saturday night and wake up Monday morning, skipping over it completely. Not have every television commercial, newspaper ad, store cashier, neighbor, friend, and family member wish her a "happy" day, since she didn't feel too happy or fulfilled as a mother. That wasn't an option though. Therefore, we, including all her girlfriends, wanted to make sure she was kept busy.

Emma organized the entire day's schedule a week in advance, email after email, obsessively editing the plan. The final cut: 8:15 a.m. yoga, 10:00 a.m. dog walk/swim at the lake, 11:00 a.m. shower time, 12:00 p.m. lunch, 2:30 p.m. cemetery visit, 4:00 p.m. Holocaust project meeting, 5:00 - 7:30 p.m. dinner.

Journal Entry, May 11, 2008:

> *Emma's snapping branches off the flowering lilac trees close to the gravesites. Waving and whipping the branch back and forth so the loose petals will lie across the top of the graves. Honoring their bodies. Sharing some spring cheer with them…despite the miserable rainy, cold weather today. In rolled up, oversized grey sweatpants, 3 sizes too big brown winter boots, she looks like a homeless person. But she's out there. Getting wet. Trying to do her duty as the "oldest." Then she retires to her car, having driven separately from Mom and me.*

> *Mom crouching under her umbrella. I watch it shake up and down, side to side. Know, without even standing next to her watching, that she is hysterically crying. Bending over her daughter's grave. And for what?*

> *I remain in the passenger seat of the Suburban. Sheltered from the cold and rain. Soothed somewhat by the windshield wipers annoyingly screeching across the glass. And I think, I need my own windshield wipers to turn on and off every day. I definitely cry enough for my downpours to be cleaned and tended to.*

> *Dad stayed home. In his typical lounging position on the couch in the sunroom porch. TV blasting, an original Indiana Jones flashing across the screen. He's snoring. Heavy breaths. "Want to come, Dad?" "No." A simple*

answer to a complicated question. Want to come to the cemetery to bless your daughter's grave? Are you ready to stare reality straight in its eyes? No.

It'll be 6 months in three days. 6 months. May 14. Wow.

I get out finally and Mom meets me halfway back to the car. I stand, cradling her head in my left arm, my palm cupping her head, which is protected by her raincoat cap. I feel bigger than she is.

I continue alone toward the gravesites. Miya, Grandpa, Debbie. Huddled beneath my umbrella. I just want to dive in and pull her out. Completely unrealistic thought.

And again I'm thinking of everything else I need to do just as I was at her burial. Want to run away. Even if it's just to a bathroom.

I was not only writing for myself by May, but was also fully engaged in the Holocaust Survivor Project. The project sprung from our family's need to belong and connect with others that understood our pain. Hundreds of elderly Detroit-area Jews had guarded their stories, their past with shameful guilt, not wanting to burden others with their pain, as well as protecting themselves from reliving their Hell over and over again. Concentration camps, death marches, starvation, hiding, physical abuse, and rape, their lives ripped from them in an instant.

It was a project we could create as a family, together, utilizing everyone's individual strengths. Mom as photographer, I as interviewer and writer, Kacee as Mom's assistant during the portraits, and Emma as the business mastermind. We did not want each survivor's story to die with him or her in old age. We wanted their voices and faces to always be remembered. And in turn raise money through the sale of the published coffee table book to provide for those less fortunate survivors who did not "make it" in America.

It was a little known fact that many Holocaust survivors in the Detroit-area were poverty-stricken. They had been overlooked and disenfranchised. Providing financial aid to them was not only necessary, it was dutiful. The Jewish community had always been known to embrace their own. Jews, for whatever reason, instinctively have always felt obligated to care for one another.

I was a survivor. Or, at least I was trying to survive. Hadn't really mastered how to do that just quite yet, but I was getting there. What I had realized during my journey was that we're all survivors. Some of failure, some of heartbreak, some of the death of a loved one. What experience was the most difficult to survive? How could you put a value to such a thing? Who's to say I was hurting 100 times more than someone else? Shouldn't we always embrace each tragedy—small or great—with as much compassion as the next?

Journal Entry, May 13, 2008:

After the cemetery, Emma, Kacee, Mom and I met at Panera to organize for the project...Emma has completely organized the logistical aspects of the whole thing, spreadsheets upon spreadsheets, detailing costs, numbers, goals and how every element will be affected by different changes in any of the sales/finances of the project. Kacee now wants to do some of the interviewing. She has to assert her value, in my opinion, and doesn't like it that I'd be showcased so dominantly in the hard copy publication. I wasn't going to put up a fight. If she wants to, go ahead. I'm both excited and nervous to do the interviews and write. Will I write good pieces? What sort of voice/style do I use?

Emma, Kacee and I are now taking different photo shoots—the numbers weighed more heavily on how many I'm signed up for.

In the beginning I met with the survivors about once a week in the afternoon, sitting at their kitchen tables or on the sofa in their living rooms. Offering me freshly baked cookies and juice. Opening up their home and soul for a complete stranger. With my voice recorder running and sheets of paper with my leading questions printed, I allowed them to open up, welcomed their horrific tales of watching their mother and youngest sister being led to the gas chamber, or the infamous Dr. Death raping them, or being forced to carry orphaned babies down two flights of stairs and hold each in his arms as a commander shot each in the head.

At times I had to pinch myself as a reminder that this was real. That, just like my writing, their tales were not fiction. That those identification tattoos were not drawn up, but instead etched into their forearms, a branding of their "worthlessness and inhumanity."

Their stories saddened me, but I felt grateful that we were creating an opportunity to honor their beauty and individuality by making their written stories speak to what made their experience unique and by making their portraits showcase their character.

In theory, Kacee and Emma were supposed to take on a number of the interviews and write those articles, but that was far from what happened. In fact, after one or two interviews each, both of them refused to write anything and engage in the project any longer. All responsibility was thrown into my lap. This made me feel bitter and resentful. I did the work though because the project itself was vital. Plus, I was the writer; I had an obligation, which everyone assumed was his or her job to remind me.

I did it at times, clenching my teeth, because by doing it, I was succumbing to the shame I felt, as if I was 12 years old, of not doing what Mom and my sisters wanted of me. Part of me wished I had it in me to drop the ball, like Emma and Kacee had, and be unruly.

The "family-ness" of the project disbanded.

Chapter Eighteen

Journal Entry, June 5, 2008: "To Matthew"

Do you wake up every morning and wish you could turn and kiss her? Do you miss receiving all her calls? All her gourmet meals? All her letters and long-winded emails? Her 50-activity day plans?

Because even if you don't, I do. And there's nothing I can do to replace that joy. That joy you stole from her and from me.

I want to hate you so much. I want to stand in front of you and scream and punch. But only if it would bring her back. And I know it won't. Even though I convince myself otherwise. Just as she wrote, I take a breath and hold it. Hope the pain will stop. But it won't. I exhale and realize it's just one more breath I experience without her.

And I hope and pray and plead for her to come to me, to show herself. But she never does. I believe she really is sitting next to me, or hugging me, or wiping the tears dripping from my cheeks. But is she really? Or is that just my mind cashing in on all that spiritual hoo-ha?

When will this pain go away? How could I ever really accept her decision?

That's something I have never really thought about until now. Her decision. It was her decision. Impulsive? Or, planned out?

Because Matthew stopped speaking to Steve, one of his business partners and best friends, in February, Miya's things (originally stored in Steve's garage) had been relocated to a storage unit a few blocks away. At first Matthew wanted to inconvenience us by refusing to give us her things. Yet, by May, he considered paying the monthly fee at the local storage unit too costly and more of an inconvenience for him. The five of us flew out for three days to pack it up and ship it out.

On one hand, the trip to Gunni was enjoyable, a chance to get away from home. On the other, it was miserable because not only were we sifting through Miya's things, but fighting with Emma and Kacee seemed to be at an all-time high.

Journal Entry, May 20, 2008:

Today is Tuesday, our second day in Gunni. Yesterday's main event was the storage unit. The attorney Dad's been coordinating with here got the code to the padlock. The facility was right down the street from the airport, close to Matthew's condo. I sat in the backseat of the minivan, door wide open, watching. Boxes stacked high, wooden, aged furniture cocked this way and that way. The old bed frame from Mom and Dad's room in the cottage, a funky, exhausted chest, a book case, 2 bikes (her racing one and her townie get-up), other sporting goods, lamps, vases, CDs, TONS of yoga mats, picture frames, art pieces, and boxes + boxes of clothes.

> *Dad stands to the side of the unit, crying, face covered, shielding his body from, in essence, Miya. Kac, Emma and Mom slowly and gently maneuver up and over each area of stuff, brushing their hands over some of the golden Miya possessions. I remain collapsed in the car's back seat. The sun is beaming—about 75 degrees. But the unit is shaded, chilly.*

> *I was ready, just as Kacee was, for Miya to pop out from behind the old bed frame or the five-high stacked boxes or the old bookcase. "Ta-da!" she'd sing, flailing her arms in the air, a delicious smile on her face. "Did you miss me?...You missed me?...Yes, you missed me!" she'd exclaim, thrilled that we really did miss her. I was certain this was all part of her ploy. But I kept waiting, and waiting. Not moving from my seat in the minivan. Waiting. Come on, Miya. Shouldn't you be making your grand entrance...now! No. I was forced instead to get up and pick up the pieces with the others.*

We loaded four of the clothing boxes into the minivan to sift through them in the hotel room, away from the dust of the storage unit. Dad thought we were going to be allowed to take Miya's car, load it up, drive it back to Detroit, sell it and then put the money into Miya's estate to pay off the funeral and any other debt, which Matthew was refusing to pay. That, of course, wasn't going to happen because Matthew still wanted control over something. It would have actually helped him since he kept crying bankruptcy (as though as owner of the Gunnison Directory he didn't make one of the highest incomes in Gunni).

Personally, I was against Dad's plan, since I didn't want to help Matthew out in that way. He had made it so difficult to get her things and tie up all the loose ends. I figured why should we help pay off his debt? He wanted to be in charge and have control over when we could get her things. Now he should take on the financial burden.

Journal Entry, May 20, 2008:

> *While we hiked the trails above Western's campus, the city and Miya's house, Mom said to me today, "We could have done all of this six months ago if only Matt would have allowed us to pack up her things and have possiesion of everything Miya. We could have spared so much time, money and tears."*

> *And she's absolutely right. We wouldn't have had to waste trips to Gunni to get the dogs, her things, etc. But what I did realize once Mom said that was that if it hadn't played out as it has, we would never had returned. We would have always held a huge grudge against Gunni; the city/community*

would have never embraced us as they have and seen Matthew's true colors. After Matthew wouldn't let us see the dogs, have her things, or talk w/ us, Gunnison realized there was much more to Miya's death than a "sick" Bipolar woman falling off her rocker.

At the storage unit, I hopped onto Miya's townie bike—wide handle bars, kick back stopping style, wide seat. Filled the tires with air and began strolling the city, the sun beating down on me, smiling and singing to myself. Can't wait to have this shipped back home, so I can ride into Birmingham or the WB or Sylvan and write all day—do my Baltimore thing.

Twenty minutes later, the five of us convened in Mom and Dad's hotel room.

Journal Entry, May 20, 2008:

The hotel room floor was covered w/ Miya's clothes—as though Miya herself had unpacked and a tornado had blown through. Every two minutes, it seemed, one of us would declare, "That's mine! Miya, you took this 3 years ago!" as though she was sitting in the room with us. Which I know she was—just not in the physical sense.

The best was Kacee saying, "Ah, we fought over these shorts for years. I'd steal them, then she would, then I would steal them back. And what's funny is that they're actually Mom's!"

Dad didn't stay in the room—not just because he wasn't interest in claiming one of Miya's standard, run-down Old Navy V-neck sweatshirts or khaki skirts since fitting into a size small or 4 would never happen for him— but because he didn't want to look at it. Didn't need to be outfitted in Miya, didn't need her to physically engulf his body with her smell and touch if she wasn't physically here. So he left.

I somewhat enjoyed it—shopping in Miya's Closet. Which seemed more like a Salvation Army rack. A lot of it shit, worn out, plain ugly clothes with the rare, occasional spectacular find. And it's those "spectacular finds" that make the search worth it! Miya had the worst taste. What she thought looked good—random khaki jackets and skirts, random tanks—was what I liked in 8th grade. I loved how Miya used to compliment me with, "Why do you have such cute clothes? Dress me!"

At one point Emma had asked, "Has anyone else noticed that every thing is inside out...like she's tried it all on?"

Mom and I laughed in response, "Yeah, that's cause she did!" When Miya would get dressed, she'd try on each and every piece of clothing she had. One shirt, then the next, then a skirt, then some pants, then those pants in a different color, then back to the skirt, then back to the original shirt.

I was never convinced that the dryer ate my missing sock, or my favorite shirt, or my favorite spandex, or my favorite swimsuit top, or my favorite rain jacket. It was never the dryer; it was always Miya. Whenever she would ask my advice on what to wear, her 15 potential outfits were sprawled across the floor.Odds were that some piece of every one of those 15 outfits were either mine, Emma's, Kacee's, Mom's or one of our friend's.

"Miya, that's mine! I lost that two years ago!"

"Oh, I thought that was mine!"

"No!"

"Oh, well I thought you left it for me."

"No!"

"Oh, I thought it was Mom's."

"No!"

"Well, can I wear it tonight?"

I'd try my best to stand my ground, but her unrelenting pleas and pouts were somehow successful. She always got me. Mom used to call her "F. Lee Miya," because she could convince anyone of anything.

In the hotel room, Emma continued, "I don't know if we should organize it by shirt, skirt, pants, tank top...or by ugly, uglier, ugliest!"

Journal Entry May 20, 2008:

The 4 of us looked through her things, organizing it into piles—the repossessions, pieces for the blankets Linda's going to quilt out of the clothing pieces that are so Miya—Yoga Room T-shirts, bike racing jerseys, her beach-style shawl that I love. I completely disagree with putting the shawl into a quilt. I want to be able to wear it. It was the piece of clothing (in addition to Miya's gray Lullelemon hat) that I begged Ashley to grab when she packed a suitcase on Nov. 16. That Mom, Kacee + Emma want it in just frustrates me because I feel when I want something it's overlooked, put down, considered an issue and selfish…which is only that way b/c I want it.

Kacee kept harping on the "rules" we're making about Miya's things…so things don't get lost or worn out. The "rules" are directed toward me, since when I want something it's "Sabrina's being possessive." But when she or anyone else wants it to be a certain way, it's all fine and dandy.

I left at about 2 p.m., biked close to the hotel to the baseball fields and laid out—sure Miya was yelling at me to throw on clothes. No one was around in the middle of nowhere—pretty much nude—needed my sun therapy. Then went back to nap in Mom's hotel bed—she soon joined me—so nice!

Nice to see Ashley. I know how lonely she must be. It was like Miya was the glue of their whole social group—she was the peacemaker, did therapy between them all—did intervention often—the social coordinator. When she died, it was like there was no foundation left. As Emma said, "Can't build a house without a foundation. It's like you take one brick out and the house all crumbles."

Without Miya there was no group. Everyone dispersed—went into their own shells. I feel lonely for Ashley. Found out also from her that Brad's dating some girl from Denver pretty seriously. Must be the reason he's not returning my calls/email. Maybe it is how he's dealing with this all or maybe it's what Emma thinks—talking with me is awkward for him, or even a bit off-limits, since he is dating someone. Maybe he realizes I don't want to see him to rekindle some old fling, or maybe he doesn't. I just want to see him to make sure he's doing ok. To talk about Miya—to laugh about her.

After dinner I grabbed the bike back at the hotel and met Mom at City Market to buy Tupperware packing cases for the clothes for shipping. Then I biked back to the hotel, a full moon blessing the sky, being choosy about which star was allowed to shine. I picked out My Radiant Miya. The brightest, highest one.

I was ready to get back home to see Koh and to sort through the trip emotionally, as well as my written notes. As I pieced all of it together, I found myself huddled over my computer, writing and editing alongside Koh. Reliving every memory sparked even greater emotion.

Journal Entry, June 4, 2008:

What happened from the time I hung up the phone at 4 p.m. to the time Matthew found her dead? I just want to know. I just want him to tell me, "I was torturing the dogs and it drove Miya over the edge. Because she finally realized how horrible I was. I told her I didn't care if she killed herself. I told her I didn't love her, never did, that my love was never unconditional." I just want him to tell me those things.

I'm so sad for her. I feel her pain. Heart-wrenching pain in the middle of my chest, nestled beneath my ribs, tucked away into the black hole, gets deeper and deeper. Sad for how much she suffered with this sadness. But also sad for myself. Because I see that I often feel the same. And I don't want that sadness to ever drive me to do what Miya did. And I also don't want my sadness to make Mom/Dad worry/sad as they were/did for Miya. And mostly don't want Miya to be watching me and having to watch me suffer. Because I know that seeing that and not being around to heal me would also break her heart.

Chapter Nineteen

By June, I needed to experience the drop, the fall, the plunge downward. Toward something, knowing that the fall would eventually end, but that I had no idea how it would turn out. A jump, a leap, a tumble even.

Sammi's request at 6 p.m. on a Saturday seemed crazy. The sort of crazy I was craving. I needed it, needed to do something that would test myself and prove that I was in control of my life. By 10 p.m., I called Sammi to confirm for the next day.

Skydiving, the ultimate risk.

I knew Mom and Dad would be angered, so when they called on Sunday to check in and see what I was up to, I simply answered, "I'm just hanging out with Sammi. Got to go! Talk later." Leaving out details was key to saving them the headache.

Journal Entry, June 25, 2008:

Dad was enraged. "I have enough fucking heartbreak in my life! You have to go jump out of a fucking airplane?!" I had popped the DVD into my Mac on the kitchen island, as he headed out to dinner.

"Dad, this is what I did today," I invited. Explosion upon seeing me, geared up for my preliminary interview prior to the jump. "At least I waited to tell you after the fact," I said, justifying it. As he slammed the back door shut, I yelled, "Well, I'm alive, aren't I?!"

I completely understand Dad's reaction. It would enrage me to know another of my daughters could possibly die, skydiving of all things. Yet, I don't want to feel stifled by the guilt Dad instills in me if I do something of which he disapproves. Because I am living. Yes, part of me died when Miya died, but a bigger portion became enlivened, awakened. By the fear of not living w/ the goal of happiness. Of not overcoming any issue I have or allowing another to make me question my joy or need to survive any longer. I want to be fuller for me + Miya.

Journal Entry, Later That Day:

Anger. Toward Miya. For deciding to do this. For forcing me to move home, for making me feel like I've been pushed up against a wall, trapped—by Emma and Kacee mostly. Emma's criticisms for what I say, do, and wear will not let up. And Kacee's judgmental stares will not either.

I was angry!

"Finally," Burch told me today during our one-on-one session.

Angry about Lauren leaving the country for one and a half months in May and not telling me, not being there for me the past 8 months when I should have seen her at least once a week since she came home <u>every</u> weekend *from Ann Arbor. Angry Mom told her when she drove past a few nights ago, "You know Sabrina. She won't hold a grudge."*

No!!! I DON'T WANT TO FORGIVE and FORGIVE and FORGIVE!!! I can't keep absorbing all the hurt caused by my inconsistent friends and my sisters' criticisms. Sadly, as I mentioned to Burch, I will for some reason probably end up forgiving her. It enrages me that everyone feels justified to tell me what is and is not appropriate. I want so badly to be able to address these issues at family therapy—but I don't think I could emotionally keep it together. Would sit, choked up, crying instead, and once Emma and Kac would begin arguing, I'd become a snail and hide in my shell.

Skydiving didn't do the trick, so I sought an escape elsewhere in July, visiting Hopkins friends who had moved to New York after graduation.

I was homesick for Baltimore and the freedom and ease I felt while living on my own. As July hit, I couldn't take living in Detroit anymore, and since most of my friends were no longer in Baltimore, I headed to the big city.

Most people would never guess I'd be a city girl. "You? You like New York?" they would ask in shock. Yes, yes I do!

Journal Entry, June 25, 2008:

3 p.m. today decided to hop on a 7:30 p.m. flight to New York. I wanted so badly to escape somewhere with Koh—but I honestly needed the city, my friends, utter lack of responsibility. Getting away for 5 days for the second time in almost 8 months since Nov. 14 is not too much to ask, considering how difficult it is for me to be home.

I'm going directly to Benny's place in midtown and then either meeting up w/ Jeff + his soccer buddies or Figi boys on the west side. So, great to be so spontaneous.

As I told Burch, I almost want it to be read as a statement by the family. I think Mom realizes how painful it is for me at times, how lonely, how much E/K attack me. When she answers the phone or welcomes me home, there is a softness to her voice, a sensitivity.

Excited to be out w/ friends, walk Manhattan ALL day tomorrow, feel sexy and just have fun!

A night out with the Hopkins boys was all about enjoying life. No bullshit, no drama, all fun (especially since Chrissy, acollege soccer teammate and favorite playmate, would often come into the city those nights just to see me). Eight-hundred dollar tabs at the bar, shot after shot, beer after beer. While I instigated every dance montage, every other minute the boys offered a sip of this, a shot of that, but they knew my deal. I was the 100% sober one (unless, of course, they could coax me into taking a swig of their beer to prove I still didn't enjoy the taste), who seemed to outsiders to be the most intoxicated, because I'd be dancing off the walls. Such nights out were taken to the max, mostly because all of them were incredibly miserable at work. They needed to release their unhappiness in some way and somewhere.

Their investment bankingjobswere the equivalent, as one of their colleagues described, as "being a Brazilian waxer for a 300-pound, hairy chick 24 hours a day, 7 days a week. You don't want to accept the job but you do with a smile because the pay's superb, and therefore you simply drink nights away to forget."

In addition to the Hopkins party crowd, Jeffrey and Ben were also on my to-do list. Having played soccer in Israel with Jeffrey during the 17th Maccabiah games in 2004, we bonded. We continued our friendship in the proceeding years, randomly running into each other on the beaches in Barcelona and meeting up in Thailand. After Miya died, Jeff was very much present, checking in on me, especially supportive of my writing. He was the sort of guy you knew would make it huge. Innovative, charismatic, handsome, a guy's guy with a feminine, confident touch. The guy you call to pitch a business idea in order to get an even stronger one.

Journal Entry, June 27, 2008:

Lunch w/ Jeffrey. Discussion about what my writing is doing for me. Got into how my work connects with huge global issues and how anyone deals with heartache/destruction.

Now watching video on TED about prioritizing global issues. How you <u>never</u> really understand "it" until you've lived it. Like what's it like to not <u>really</u> have clean water. I can see young boys pushing bicycles down the street on their daily 10-mile trek w/ water jugs attached. See it in process and how such an issue affects their life, but do I even <u>really</u> understand it, driving past in my SUV, driven by our Rwanda tourist guide? No. Because I didn't wake up to my screaming 2 yr. old sister, starving and having no water to brush my teeth, wash my body, drink… I wouldn't until I've lived it. Until I've sweated and exerted myself while pushing that bike alongside my older brother, barefoot, sun blazing, or possibly in the midst of a tropical storm. Just like I couldn't until I've lived through my very own sister's suicide. Not just read about it, heard about it via CNN, or witnessed my closest friend deal with it.

You don't know until you've lived it.

Ben was also a friend from Hopkins. Having graduated early like I did, he moved to the city in January 2008, selling his soul to Goldman Sachs. He loved the drive of the market, the structure, or rather insanity, of his work schedule. I couldn't think of anyone better suited for such a job.

We have always acted (and probably will forever) like husband and wife, actually calling each other Hubby and Wifey, arguing most of the time over who's right and who's wrong. Arguments aside, I knew Ben like no one knew Ben. There was no front; he would strip himself down in front of me, allowing himself to be completely vulnerable and open. And I liked to think that was because he knew I would always be there for him unconditionally. Drugs and alcohol never were the glue for our friendship to thrive; our friendship was grounded much deeper than that superficiality.

Not only had Ben driven me to the airport on the morning of November 15 and was the one who opened up and read the 3 a.m. email from Mom as he booked my airfare, but I routinely stayed at his apartment whenever in New York. The trip in June was no different.

On June 30, my last day in the city, I spent the entire day journaling in his apartment. Emotionally stirred from the phone conversation I had with Mom the previous night, I wrote entry after entry almost every hour of that day.

Journal Entry, June 30, 2008:

I feel like I'm back in bed w/ Emma + Kacee playing our game of Clue as we were in November. Mom's newest theory on the actual events of November 14…Mom thinks that Matthew + Miya had a fight. She told him she was going to kill herself, he either watched her or went upstairs, let her do it. Then ran outside screaming for help. It's just like that Desperate Housewives' episode of the woman staging her suicide (hanging herself), timed perfectly for her husband to come in and save her.

Hollywood's not reality though. Miya didn't realize there wasn't any "lights, camera, action" in her plot. Her "savior" and the "hero" instead let it happen.

It's never going to end—the speculation, the need to know exactly what went on between them. Is that the key I must attain to let go? The truth? Mom had prefaced the conversation with some news story on a honeymoon couple. While scuba diving together at some tropical getaway, the husband drowned his wife. There was no direct proof. And it took some time for it all to unfurl. But when it cracked, it all made sense. Based on circumstantial evidence. They pressed charges on him.

Circumstantial evidence: how the husband acted, what he said, and what he didn't. Just like Matthew…Mom reminded me that the only 2 times Matthew has spoken to us was in the police station—(which was only "Yes, I'd like her to be buried next to Grandpa Billy," without even looking at us)—and then in Gunni in May when Mom + Dad tracked him down on his bike w/ his attorney present whom we were meeting ourselves in an hour anyway. Mom asked him, "You going to be there, Matthew?" and he replied, "I wasn't planning on it."

That's it. 2 conversations. How can his actions not inspire skepticism?

Journal Entry, June 30, 2008, 10a.m.:

Did he walk upstairs and leave her? Did he? You asshole!!! How could you? I write these questions over and over and over and over. ANSWER ME ALREADY!!!! Just like your mom yelled at me in the police station, "She was your wife!" Exactly! I wouldn't even have it in me now to do that to you if you were in Miya's position. I'd have enough decency to talk you out of it, or at least cut you down.

Journal Entry, June 30, 2008, 11a.m.:

I never would be writing about all of this if Miya had not died. I wouldn't be sitting in Ben's chair, scribbling feverishly as thoughts race, emotions fluctuate, eyes tear up and then dry up. Wouldn't need to escape to New York like I needed to—I'd be living the life in South America.

Journal Entry, June 30, 2008, 1 p.m.:

Sitting in Ben's apartment, journaling and playing through my iTunes. Dave Matthews "Pay For What You Get." Hmmm…really? What am I paying for by Miya dying?

The only thing wrong I can remember ever doing is snagging a handful of grapes for a snack as I grocery shop, or walking out of a market in the middle of nowhere Washington state when I was 13 on a Wilderness Ventures trip, walking out absentmindedly w/ a Dove candy bar in hand…But that can't really be counted as wrong b/c once I noticed I was still holding it, I got scared + snuck back into the store to properly purchase it.

Pay for what you get? It has no monetary value. So is it in pain? What am I paying for? What are any of us paying for?

Journal Entry, June 30, 2008, 2 p.m.:

I don't want to feel this pain. Deep in my chest, causing me to hunch over whenever I stop a moment and take it all in. When I realize this is my truth. I'm not writing fiction. This is Miya, this is me. This is why I think I was so eager to jump into something with Carter. Who'd want to feel this pain willingly? So much easier to find distractions.

Why couldn't I stop liking this kid? 1 month, 2, 3 after it ended? Only thing which makes sense is that I couldn't lose something so abruptly again and be okay w/ it. I lost Miya in a split second. Everyone else has to "stick" more.

Of course, as though I didn't have enough shit to deal with, somehow, I was back on Carter in July, feeling just as heartbroken. I would replay those moments kissing him when my entire being would melt. I lost track of how many nights I laid in bed certain it was his footsteps walking down the hallway toward my bedroom at the Big House. I just craved his company in my bed. I couldn't let it go.

Returning from New York, I found myself with Heidi and Lauren at a July 4th party with him and his friends. Having to watch Carter skinny-dip and then make out with some random girl in front of me was too much.

Journal Entry, July 6, 2008:

Do you ever just feel lonely? Even when from an outsider's perspective your life may seem perfect? As though everything isn't just because there is that one piece missing? The piece which you're certain would solve and fix all your shit. All your insecurities and anything that takes up and wastes your time when instead of just living and enjoying yourself you get caught up, dealing with that loneliness and filling that void by whatever means you have taught yourself over the past 22 years? Whatever's so ingrained in your subconscious thought and activity pattern.

Is it wrong to think/desire that one person in whom you could absorb yourself and with whom you could share yourself could be that missing piece? Is that just putting a Band-Aid over the wound? Is that what Miya did when she so desperately and entirely fell in love with another? Was she just temporarily dealing with her issues? Is that why she hasn't answered my prayers to her to "find me someone" with whom I can fall in love? Because she doesn't want me to live how she lived...never actually facing and overcoming her issues before she gave herself to another?

Because isn't it true that in order to completely give yourself and all your beauty to another, don't you have to unconditionally love and know yourself? What if that takes an entire lifetime?

I watch and hear person after person "in love," in a relationship... "This is my girl/boyfriend." How is that possible? Is everybody just settling? Or are they actually finding someone who really gets them? Am I just utterly unlucky and always screwed? How is it possible that I can never find anybody I'm interested in?

And, when and if I do, that one person doesn't want me and doesn't want a girlfriend. Which inevitably proves to be a falsehood, because the next thing I find out is that in fact he is dating someone a week later. It's just ME he doesn't want. And then I fall into an even greater trap of questioning myself and pleading to know: What's so wrong with me? Why not me? Why does this happen to me over and over with men?

Questions that are very destructive to anyone's well being, because it allows that person to devalue him or herself. And, as I already said, in order to love, you must unconditionally love yourself. Something which isn't accomplished if you are asking those questions of doubt.

Chapter Twenty

For months after Miya's death our family dynamic was rocky, very rocky. Emma was living in Royal Oak at her boyfriend's, Kacee was at the Kids' House with Henley and Billy, and I was still in the Big House. Sometimes we'd go weeks without seeing each other. We would speak at sessions with Burch about doing more as a family, but it never came to fruition. I would be coaching or busy interviewing a survivor for the Holocaust Project. Kacee might have been busy with a client or might have just had a bad day. Dad would be 20 minutes late. And Mom would have a photoshoot, which wouldn't end until 8:30 p.m. Emma was left angry and frustrated, trying to schedule something. But times together were almost avoided like the plague.

If Kacee or I were having a bad day or even week, Emma just didn't seem to understand. She seemed to be dealing with too much anger herself. Mom and Kacee were not getting along, Emma and I were not getting along, Kacee and I were not getting along, Dad and Kacee were not getting along, Mom and I were not getting along. There always seemed to be some conflict or ill feelings.

But all the rockiness was necessary for our own discovery and healing, as each of us tried to find our voices in a place where we never imagined moving back. Trying to latch onto our adult lives, personalities and ways of being, despite our parents trying to package us up in our youthful ways—since that would have been the easiest means to have us exist—to help them cope. They wanted us to be what they were most accustomed to and comfortable with.

My writing was as emotionallyinspired as it ever had been. There were times when I could separate and unbiasedly recreate relationship dynamics, but even when doing that, I still was capturing how real life was playing out—emotions involved. Where I was at that time or that moment was honored. Struggles with Kacee and Emma were not fabricated, but real; heartbreaking realizations were stumbled upon.

It was all about boundaries—emotional boundaries. Understanding how all five of us operated without any, and how that had affected the vitality of many of our relationships. Therapy as a family and individually began to untangle those poorly woven threads and give us the tools we all needed so desperately to relearn to form healthier boundaries for healthier communication. One therapist wasn't enough. Two, three, four was much more effective.

What I found through my writing, the day-to-day at home, and many, many therapy sessions with Burch was that Miya's death merely exposed everything, leaving me raw and unprotected. I craved support from my family. Yet such support was limited because of two main issues: the Kids' House and my writing.

Both issues, however, were just distractions. It could've been anything. We just needed something on which to take out our pain and rage. And who better than the ones you love the most and you know will never go away?

When we purchased the Kids' House in February 2008, Mom, Kacee and Emma decided I would not live there. Partially because Miya's dogs would murder Koh, but also because Kacee and I were "at each other's throats," as Mom always said. Kacee claimed the Kids' House as her own space.

Journal Entry, July 8, 2008:

> *She would claim I had invaded "her space." "Her" house. "Her" life. I can't believe I am being made to feel as though I don't belong in my own house. That "my space" should only be the upstairs of the Big House—as I deal with Mom reminding me what I should be cleaning up and when/how to feed Koh and clean up after him, while having to walk past Miya's bedroom everyday, with Koh typically sleeping on her bed, and still feel uncomfortable being in/around Emma's room.*
>
> *Why does Kacee hate me so much? Is she just taking all her anger and insecurities out on me? Is it as everyone tells me: "She knows she gets to you and you're her sister, so she knows even if she's this mean, you'll always be around"? Probably. But, it sure as hell makes me feel like shit. And, I notice myself the past couple days falling into bad habits of not taking proper care of myself and feeling anxious—mostly feeling as though I need to prove something to her.*

By the summer, I was no longer obsessively writing at cafes, but instead escaping into Sylvan. Either I'd lie out on the Friedman's dock or spend time at the Kids' House. If Kacee was not home, I'd tan and write on the patio, which was ideal for sunbathing nude, hidden by the wooden paneling around the deck from our oh-so-close next-door neighbors. If she was home, I'd retreat to the basement.

Originally, Emma and Kacee were each assigned one of the two bedrooms on the main floor. In the basement, Emma also had a reading room while Kacee had an office. There wasn't a square foot of that house that was mine. Pathetically, it took about two months until my family realized, "Well, maybe Sabrina could use the closet under the stairwell for a writing space." My room was the previous owner's storage room. I was the modern, American-Jewish version of Harry Potter. The only difference was that I didn't seem to have any magical powers…even though my name was

Sabrina.

Journal Entry, July 9, 2008:

I feel like I'm 15 again. Sitting at the Kids' House in my writing room in my big armchair. It feels like spending nights in the library in Dad's armchair at the Big House. Listening to Kacee and her girlfriends get ready to go out and then watching them proceed downstairs, past me, saying goodbye and leaving for the night. Then, the house would fall silent.

Now, Kacee's friends won't even come downstairs to say hi. It's as if they give me the time of day, Kacee will disown them. Kacee won't let me in. Anything I do she finds fault with and defines as an invasion of her space. As she said to me Wednesday, I'm "intrusive!" When I asked her: "Why do you hate me so much?" she bitterly, yet confidently replied, "It's not hate; you may perceive it that way, but it's not. You're just intrusive."

How can Kacee really believe that bringing Koh into the Kids' House in the basement, door closed to the laundry room and her work room where the dogs aren't even allowed to step foot in, is a big deal? It is shocking. Seriously, can she REALLY think it is a big deal? When I did walk upstairs to say hi to Becca and Katie, I said: "Hi, Kac," when she walked into the dining room. No response to that, only "Do not bring Koh over here." Threatened calling Dad, so I simply said: "Well, I just spoke with him and he says it's fine."

By July, I needed another escape from the emotional heaviness on the home front. Spending a week coaching up at Sauk Valley gave me such an escape. Pre-season training was held at Sauk Valley for the girls teams of the Force, a premier soccer club I was helping coach in Bloomfield Hills. Each day at camp consisted of three training sessions, complemented by meals, rest period, swimming hour, and evening activities (such as volleyball or the talent show). Before this week, I had only met the U-17 girls at tryouts a month prior and held agility training sessions a week beforehand. It was safe to say I knew none of them, could not remember any of their names, could not recognize any of their faces. A fresh slate from which to work. Within a day or two, I was to them what I was to my Cranbrook hockey and Marian soccer girls. I fell in love with them quite quickly.

But the fresh air, dense forest and bug-infested, 30-year-old exhausted carpet and bed cots did not cause amnesia. Things were still erupting back home. Only a phone call away during family therapy that week I was just as affected, as I would have been if I was within eyesight. The physical distance helped me voice my truth more than usual, but the criticisms from Emma and Kacee got to me just the same.

Journal Entry, July 10, 2008:

*Participating in our family therapy session last night was much easier
than usual because I was on conference call. The emotional intensity of being in
a room with Emma and Kacee, dealing w/ family issues, was lessened to such
a degree that I finally had a voice, felt confident enough to initiate conversation
and articulate my feelings surrounding my writing (and Emma and Kacee's
bitterness toward publication) and Kacee's abhorrence about me moving into the
Kids' House.*

*I've heard it before from Emma and Kacee. "Sabrina, this is not
about you or your fault, but…" and then they outline every incident where
Mom or Dad favored me. And how those situations only act as a disservice to
me, making me the "loser," [as Emma put it]. I completely respect and hear
their frustration that they consider Mom and Dad to favor me. That when
Emma or Kacee attack me with criticism Mom and Dad do come to my
aid/defense. I do think some of it comes w/ being the youngest, some of it is
due to my personality and what I need, and some of it is because of how Emma
and Kacee are and therefore anyone in my position would need their parents to
back them…Especially when Miya is no longer here to cushion the effects of
their judgments and remind me how wonderful/beautiful I am, like she always
did.*

I was the first to admit I was obsessed with writing. If I was not
physically writing or typing, I was brainstorming ways to connect one
anecdote to another, or analyzing the newest twist and turn in the "story."
Was my obsession healthy? Probably not. Would I eventually get to a point
where there was nothing else to write about related to the book, and would
have to ask myself, *What next?*

I had used this project as my main distraction and coping tool, a
way to have purpose and direction while living in Detroit. It served this
purpose all winter, spring and summer, but in eight months, or five years,
or even fifteen years, would it turn against me? If it was published, I
assumed everything I wrote thereafter would be compared to it. Everything
I ever did or said would be takenin the context of "the girl whose sister
hung herself." It would all be documented. In print for the world to read.
And my wound would be forever open in another way. Exposed to
whomever wanted to examine it, touch it, or even try to heal it. Would it be
worth it?

Journal Entry, July 11, 2008:

*I don't feel that just b/c Emma and Kacee feel it's inappropriate to
share with the public it's not necessary. So, now I'm extremely torn. Will
Emma and Kacee come around and respect what I am doing? And see it as
something I'm doing for us as a family? Or will they really always hate the*

thought of me writing a book? Is it worth losing my 2 living sisters just to honor my 1 dead sister? What would Miya want me to do?

Also, it's 7/11. I thought today is supposed to be a lucky day. Not when everything falls apart at the seams and forces me to question everything.

Linda was one of *those* people whom I hoped to touch. She was, in a sense, part of our family, her daughter being Miya's first childhood friend, and in recent years Mom's portrait assistant. She was, despite being in her sixties, also one of my girlfriends. Someone that cherished me for being me and reminded me to stay true to myself—despite other peoples' putdowns.

She joined me one of many nights at the Bean and Leaf in Royal Oak in February. Stress was stamped all over her. She smacked the newspaper on the table. A Detroit newscaster had hung herself. One more blow to women everywhere.

I sat there, saddened, thinking about that newscaster, wondering, *How could someone actually do that to him or herself?* And then I remembered. I knew first hand. Could I have forgotten Miya so quickly? Was her truth so fleeting? Was I repressing reality so much?

Months later, after I returned from Sauk Valley, Linda also joined me at the Big House. It was Miya's eight-month death anniversary. The sadness of that time-marker only the start of my shitty day.

I didn't leave the house all day on the 14. Hadn't even woken up until 1 p.m. Eating and lounging, lost in my own thoughts and insecurities surrounding Emma and Kacee...torn.

Having called Linda, she was out her door a minute later and collapsed onto the couch next to me in the library 15 minutes later. She knew most of the drama, but I filled in more specifics. She was disgusted. "Why wouldn't they want you to write this?" her disgusted look accentuated by her even more pissed off tone. "You're stifling your feelings about this, and they're basically saying, 'Shame on Miya.' That's what they're saying."

And she was right. All Miya ever felt was shameful for being "sick" and being too "inappropriate." My own sisters were making me feel the same way, as though I should be ashamed of my past, my story, Miya's story, our story.

I told Linda also about the last night at Sauk Valley, sitting up at 1 a.m. with my three women coach roommates. They begged me to read something I had written, which I willingly did, and which in turn gave them the green light to open up as well. As I finished sharing the section about seeing Miya on the coroner's table and answering their inquiries about Matthew and who he was, the floodgates opened and I sat quietly. Stories of their abusive relationships, drug addicted ex-boyfriends of four years who made each of them feel like nothing. One admitted, "I was tolerating everything about this guy that I hated...Huhhhh!" she sighed. Women...like Miya, like Linda, like me.

It could be anyone though I realized, since even men could feel this way and question themselves.

Linda continued to preach to me about not stifling my feelings, because, as she said, "I've spent my whole life doing what other people wanted. Doing what was acceptable." Linda knew firsthand the importance of writing such a book. Of giving people the okay to open up, express their emotions, share their failures and learn from them. Not stuff the skeleton in the closet. She asserted, "This is about how you perceive the interactions of your family. Aren't we all losing touch about what this book is about? It's about feelings. Haven't we all lost someone?"

She was right. As she put it, "It's about sharing. These women probably all hide it. Why do we do that?"

I decided at that moment that I would not be stifled.

Chapter Twenty-one

Journal Entry, July 26, 2008:

     Rebecca had told us that the first person Miya saw when she died and crossed over was Grandpa Billy. That he was waiting for her. And then Debbie was there. And also Great Aunt Sally, who also committed suicide.

     I knew Grandpa would have been there to comfort her and show her "the way." But that doesn't justify it for me. Doesn't stop me from being completely angry with him.

     Why didn't he warn us? Why didn't he stop her?

     I don't care if it came down to Miya's decision, Miya's time to go; he should have used all his energy, even if merely impossible, to cut her down himself and intervene with free will. Shot some magical lightning bolt powered by love and force her back toward earth.

     Didn't he realize how much pain his inactivity has and would cause?

     During our memorial service trip to Gunnison, while at the police station reading through her journals, Emma, Kacee and I mentioned to Thompson what Rebecca told us.

     Thompson said, "Well, that's interesting, because in her office downstairs, next to her suicide note and the computer screen with the last email communication between Miya and Matthew, there was a photo of her and your grandpa. Face down. Lying on the carpet."

     Did Miya know he would be waiting for her? Was turning the photo of the two of them facing the carpet her declaration of "Here I come" and then she hung herself?

     Or, had she been sitting there crying, shaking, asking for Grandpa's help and love to comfort her and make a better decision, praying to him?

     And, when he didn't answer, did she turn the photo over so she didn't have to face him? Felt too guilty about what she was thinking of doing and what she ended up doing?

     I have asked Grandpa over and over, how could you let this happen? You were supposed to be our protector. Which causes me to even feel guilty too because I know in my heart that he is just as pained knowing that he was unable to save yet another of his little girls.

The only loose ends I liked to keep were with boys. I was content with not spoiling my friendship with a past romantic fling in case that ever became something more in the future. I kept my options open. Plus, I usually wanted to stay friendly because I genuinely liked who those boys were as people.

     Loose ends surrounding my sister's death? Not so much. Knowing exactly what, when, and how something happened in such a situation seemed compulsory, which probably was why I was obsessed with piecing together the 14th over and over again.

By the eight-month anniversary, the case still remained open. Thompson didn't want to shut any doors or windows. He knew what Matthew was all about. He had experienced his temper first-hand a few days after Miya's death, saw his rage, similar to the outburst the night before the memorial service in front of their friends. As the dust began to settle a week or two afterward, Thompson became one of our biggest Gunnison allies. I most appreciated how open and respectful he was with us regarding specifics and uncertainties surrounding her death. He listened to our "hoo-ha" concerning Rebecca's reading and considered any and every theory we postulated over the months. He also recognized the importance of protecting Miya's journals—which he promised to hold as evidence for the entire ten years if needed so Matthew could never touch and destroy them.

I had investigated all family, Miya, and relationship histories, as well as the process of coping and post November 14 details. I was ready for the next step. I called Thompson one lazy Monday afternoon at the Kids' House to request copies of Miya's journals, which he had promised he would copy and send during our last visit to Gunni. We ended up speaking mostly about Mom's new "theory."

This was what Thompson had to say about it:

"*Because of the way your sister passed away—the clenching, the bracing for it, the way she had herself positioned—her muscles were tight, and that enhanced the rate of stiffening. So rigor mortis probably set in rather quickly. That was consistent with what the people that were there said. They were telling us how stiff she was. And that, according to the pathologist, is very typical of somebody who hung herself. Because of that we said: Okay, she had been deceased for a significant amount of time because the body had stiffened up. If it would've been within minutes, her whole body would have flattened out on the floor, other than maybe her clenched hands. But because it had been some time, an hour or so, they had walked in when her body was inflexible.*

By the time we actually started taking pictures and doing stuff with her, we were getting close to midnight. She had been there quite a while by that point in time. But she had been moved by the people that had tried to save her within a couple of hours of her passing away. And when I say a couple, that isn't a scientific fact, it's just an estimate. It could be an hour, it could be a half hour. There isn't an exact science for placing that time back. I really hope I didn't mislead you in this way before. An hour or two in a death investigation is extremely fresh because you're not really getting the next stages of death when your life is over. Your body starts to decompose…and so that's why I say fresh. Five hours would be fresh.

I didn't want to tell your mom she's absolutely wrong, because she was saying things that could be possible. But what I explained to her was that the physical evidence we found was absolutely consistent with your sister taking her own life. And there was absolutely no evidence of the contrary. She thought maybe he would've known your sister was doing this. I'm sure she shared all of this with you.

What she proposed to me was maybe he actually looked down there and he watched her die instead of trying to save her. I can't rule that out, because that would be an act of doing nothing and that wouldn't leave behind any type of evidence. That's a definite possibility. But everything else that surrounded your sister, (and I talked in length with the pathologist about this,) if something had happened to your sister and she was put in that position unwillingly, she would have fought. And there was absolutely nothing to indicate those acts.

Actually the positioning of the ligature and everything else was 100% consistent with her doing it to herself. And her fists being clenched was an indicator that she was conscious during the time this took place. There was no question about the method of her death. And I guess there were some thoughts on the suicide note. I don't disagree with your mom, but I guess it was her handwriting and her thoughts at that time. It wasn't written by him, and she wasn't forced to sit down and write it."

I explained to Thompson what confused us was the brevity of the note and the fact that Miya did not mention her sisters. It seemed very un-Miya, but I did admit to Thompson that I realized when a person was in that state of mind he or she was obviously not being very rational. Thompson continued:

"Everybody would agree she was very emotional at the time. And she was acting on, an irrational mind. But anything's possible. I'm still looking and making sure things do make sense. Nor am I trying to close something just because of appearances. What I shared with your mom is that there was no rush to finish this up. We wanted to be complete and we wanted to have all that information and didn't want to discount anything your mom was saying.

But there are facts. Those aren't up for interpretation. That's the way it was. The physiological things that had happened to your sister, there was no confusion. He said, No, this was a conscious act and definitely the only injury and the only cause of death.

If Matthew knew she was going to do it, because she said it, and he allowed it to happen, then we can look into that. Time would be our friend. Maybe he ends up talking with somebody and shares that detail with somebody. Maybe he ends up having a moment of weakness, and it leaks out to me.

There was nothing about his demeanor or actions he took that night that was suspicious. How Matthew acted honestly wouldn't be the way I would have, but I'm not going to put my thoughts into something. He did what he did for whatever reason. I never got the impression he was real strong of character. So it wasn't surprising at all that he came across something like that, and it scared him to death, and he ran out of the house like a scared child, screaming and crying for help. That didn't surprise me at all, especially once I got to know him.

That's not especially what we hope that a grown man would do at that point in time. But that's why some people are firefighters and some people sell phone books."

Next, I contacted the Gunnison coroner, Frank Vader, for his report. Two weeks later, I received a copy. It was everything I already knew, but with a much more unaffected, scientific tone and approach.

CORONER'S REPORT
GUNNISON COUNTY, COLORADO

Frank Vader
Gunnison Country Coroner
118 N. Wisconsin
Gunnison, Colorado 81230
NAME: Miya J. Fotel
DATE OF DEATH: November 14, 2007
PLACE OF DEATH: 314 S. 11th Street
DATE OF CALL: November 14, 2007 **TIME:** 9:20 PM
DATE ARRIVED AT SCENE: November 14, 2007
TIME: 9:38 PM
DATE OF DEATH: November 14, 2007
TIME: unknown PM
DATE PRONOUNCED: November 14, 2007
TIME: 9:44 PM
To wit:

I was called by dispatch about 9:20 P.M. on Wednesday, the 14th of November 2007 and was told that at 314 S. 11th Street law enforcement was going on scene to investigate a hanging.

I arrived in town some twenty minutes later and went to the location. Several members of the Gunnison Police Force, including Investigator Dan Thompson, met me. Connie Smith, the local Victim's Advocate who was just leaving, also met me. She stated that they were taking the husband of the lady that was hanging in the house to the police station, and that she was going there to be with him. She told me that it was a very traumatic incident and there were a lot of friends of this couple in the area. The traffic was such that the police had to get into their traffic control mode to some degree to keep everybody out. That was the reason that they took the deceased's husband, whose name is Matthew Fotel, away from the scene. He was not necessarily a suspect in this death, but to just get him out of the crowd.

I went in and talked briefly with Dan Thompson, who told me that he himself had just arrived. He asked me not to touch anything as he was still in his very preliminary stages of looking around and photographing. I agreed that was fine, as I too needed to take photographs myself.

We proceeded to do so. We walked throughout the house taking pictures, and eventually I got downstairs. This was a three level townhouse. We walked in on the middle level, there is a master bedroom and bathroom in the upstairs level, and then downstairs there are a couple more bedrooms and another bathroom.

When I went downstairs, the deceased was lying on the floor in a supine position with a short chuck of roughly three eighths diameter nylon rope that appeared to be either around her neck or entangled in her hair. I looked up on the railing of the stairs and saw the other part of the rope, which had a knot tied around a spindle of the staircase.

I was informed at that time that when Matthew, the husband, arrived home around 8:30 P.M., he found her in a hanging position, and he freaked out. He ran next door for help. The next-door-neighbor happened to be a Deputy Marshal from the Mt. Crested Butte Police Department, and this is where he lives. He was an off duty cop who ran with Matthew back over to the house. Not realizing she was long gone, he cut her down.

Closer inspection of the body revealed that lividity was consistent with the supine position, not the hanging position. She was in a narrow hallway, which was not very well lit, so we had to bring in a flashlight to get a closer inspection of the body. I noticed that the lividity was set and non-blanchable, which means she has been in this lying down position long enough for the lividity to set. This caused some concern to me, because I knew that at this point in time it had only been about two and a half hours since she had been cut down. My feeling was that this was not enough time for the livor mortis to set in this particular position. The body was very rigid, which could be a little more consistent, because at this point I did not know how long she might have been hanging. With the flashlight, I checked the whites of her eyes for petechial hemorrhaging, and in the dim light I was not able to determine much of that, which caused me further dismay. I expressed my concerns to Dan Thompson, and we photographed as best we could in that light.

After another look through the house, I went ahead and bagged the body and loaded the body in the van.

As soon as I could get to a phone, I notified John Baier with the D.A.'s Office of this death.

The following morning I took the body to Montrose for autopsy. Dr. Canfield was in the process of performing an autopsy on a previous case of mine. I watched that for awhile, all the time talking about this case of Miya, and my concerns about the livor mortis being set in the supine position, not the vertical position that she had apparently been in due to hanging.

Once we got Miya laid out on the table and upon closer inspection with much better light, we were able to see petchial hemorrhage in the eyes. In the lower portion of the legs, we did see extensive petechial hemorrhaging, which is consistent with asphyxia deaths in a vertical position.

Dr. Canfield explained to me that more than likely, Miya was very worked up physically, as well as emotionally when she hung herself. People who are worked up physically, for example, joggers who are out jogging and die of sudden cardiac arrest or something, it is known and well documented that they enter into rigor mortis state very quickly. All the natural post mortem processes do occur very rapidly in someone who has been under a lot of physical exercise you might say.

Miya Tofel was very slim, obviously in very good physical condition. She was a yoga instructor, I think also a climber, a runner, everything, so he said, obviously, being that worked up physically and emotionally at the time of death would explain the rapid onset of both rigor and livor mortis.

I felt much more comfortable after his explanation of the likely occurrences. Also, by this point in time, I had learned much more about what was going on with this young couple preceding this death. Apparently, Matthew had informed his wife the previous day that he wanted a divorce. We have come up with some e-mail messages back and forth from their computer at home which substantiate an ongoing dialogue between the two of them, most of which occurred on the morning of the death, explaining extreme hurt feelings on both sides. On his part he explained a need to live apart for a while or to live apart starting very soon.

Also, we did find a note that appeared to be a suicide note that I did not photocopy. I rewrote in my own handwriting, because Detective Thompson did not want me to touch the note. He was even afraid to photocopy the note at that point in time. I felt it pertinent to bring this note or at least the message of this note to autopsy, as well as the rope ligature that she had around her neck. The note is included in my file.

Upon arriving back in Gunnison that evening I met with the parents of the deceased. The dad's name is Joel Must who is Jewish. I do not have her mother's name. He explained to me that she had been a troubled daughter. At the age of 14, she had overdosed herself on Tylenol. However, afterwards she did come to their bedroom and woke them up. She told them what she did, and they sought help. They were able to save her. Another time at the age of 19, she had overdosed on illegal drugs and was found in a comatose state by a friend who sought help for her. However, this was felt at the time, to be an accidental overdose. She was a very emotional person and had a very troubled childhood and adolescences.

She had also told Matthew that upon him telling her that he wanted a divorce, "She wanted him to fell the pain that I am feeling." We feel that this is in some part retribution to Matthew for his notice of divorce intent, as well as the note states 'tired of the pain" and "I can't go through another two years." She said that she had been in this position before, and it is becoming much harder. "I am in too much pain."

Due to the Jewish beliefs and the wishes of the family pertinent to those beliefs no autopsy was requested. Dr. Canfield and I agreed to do a very minor procedure, which involved a collection of both blood and urine for toxicology testing. An incision below the neckline was also made to where Dr. Canfield could get up to the ligature mark on the neck to examine that to make sure that it appeared on the inside as it did on the outside, and to make sure that everything in that area was consistent with ligature compression of the neck. It was, and that is the extent of the autopsy that we did.

I am still calling this an autopsy because the definition of autopsy is to see for ones self. This was not a full-blown autopsy to any degree. Furthermore, pertinent to the Jewish beliefs and the wishes of the family, the body was not embalmed. The body was packed in a special airtight container and shipped back to the east coast for burial.

174

The more we got into the investigation, we felt the time of death probably turned out to be later than earlier. According to Matthew, he came home around 5 P.M. and did not see his wife, but he did notice both her engagement ring and her wedding band on the bathroom sink. After this unfolded, she was wearing her engagement ring, so we know she died after 5 o'clock, and we feel that it was probably closer to 8 o'clock than 5. However, for death certificate purposes, I have gone with "Unknown time of death" on November 14.

I do have photographs. I will have a toxicology report. Cause of death is hanging and manner is suicide.

Chapter Twenty-two

I thought I had learned what it meant to really grieve.

Losing Grandpa Billy and Papa Mike, my mom's best friend, Cindy, to cancer, two of my high school hockey coaches (both in their 30's), two dogs (Sadie and Tessa), Great Uncle George, Great Aunt Ruth, Great Aunt Millie, Cousin Essie, Bobby (Kacee's best friend from high school, who drowned), Vince (a friend from Cranbrook, hit by a drunk driver walking across the street). And, Miya, of course. Those were the big ones, with countless others in between.

It almost seemed illogical. So many deaths…especially in an 11-year span.

In a weird way, I was thankful for all my misfortunes. If I hadn't been used to funerals and loss, saying goodbye and the lack thereof, dealing with Miya would've been impossible.

Some were sudden, others expected. Some I had prepared myself for for years, waiting for them to finally cross over and not be in pain any longer. Some I would never be able to explain and grapple with. Maybe that was the biggest difference. Maybe learning to cope with the sudden ones never got easier, only harder depending on who they were to you. Maybe if they did get "easier", you were no longer as alive and connected as you should have been. Maybe the expected ones only taught you what it was like to lose someone, not how to actually deal with it because was there really a "right" way to grieve?

Had I really learned how to properly grieve though? Was I shocked, then sad, then angry, and finally had I accepted Miya was no longer alive? I think I fell short. I didn't think I could ever let myself accept Miya was not alive any longer.

Journal Entry, August 1, 2008:

I called Miya this morning. On my drive out to the lake to swim with Mom before heading to the last day of the Marian soccer camp. Called just to see her name on my phone screen: "Miya Must."

Knew she wouldn't pick up. Expected to see "Calling…" on the screen as it searched + searched for something to connect to on the other end. Expected to hear the phone company voice recording: "Sorry. The phone number you have dialed is no longer in service. Please check the number and try again." Expected it because it's what I have had to listen to every time I've called the past 8 ½ months. But it was different this time.

It rang. Ring, ring, ring, ring, voicemail recording. "You reached ----. Leave a message and I'll call you back."

"----" Was it Louis or Lans?...I don't know. The guy's name was muffled. Was I wishfully hoping Miya would pick up on the other end right when I heard an actual ring. So, all my prayers asking for it all to be a dream/nightmare would be answered? Has it been that long? Has enough time passed that her number could be recycled? Reincarnated in a way? Does that guy know that he may get calls asking for Miya?

I just wanted to hear her: "Hi, Boopers!" amidst screams for "Henley James, come here!" and "Billy, go get the stick!"

I'm not ready for her to be "over"—not ready for the phone company to decide that it's time. Not ready for xxx-xxx-xxxx to be someone else's. Not ready for the rest of the world to move on when I haven't.

With Mom, it was like we were constantly playing a game of "Catch Monni." She would move from one activity to the next—from swimming to walking the dogs to yoga to lunch on the go or with girlfriends to a photo shoot to returning 50 missed voice messages from only one hour away from her phone to walking the dogs again to dinner to going over her day's photos on the computer. She was potentially the busiest person I knew. Her days were as jam-packed as could be—wonder from where I got it!

If I could ever convince Mom to come up and put me to sleep, or sit on the couch with me and just chat, she couldn't simply sit and just be. No, she had to also be scooping up Koh's litter box, while wiping off counter tops, while checking her emails on my laptop, while discussing our exercise plan for the morning. I was forced to fight for alone time with her anal tendencies. Definitely a game of "Catch Monni."

When she got an idea in her head—like buying the Kids' House in February—she would bulldoze her way through until she accomplished what she set out to do. If she needed to check her emails, nothing else could be done beforehand. If she needed to eat, she had to do it right then. Same was true for Miya's memory book. We either offered to help, or she would have done it alone.

Journal Entry, August 3, 2008:

Memory book making/organizing in Dad's office at the Big House. Mom, Kacee, Katie and I are sitting, cross-legged on the floor, all the letters/cards/newspaper clippings unfolded and scattered all around us.

Mom giggles in between tearful sniffs.

"Here, Bein," Kacee says, handing me a baby pink envelope. Miya's handwriting crowded the entire envelope. A line circling our home address. With mini-messages all around. "Kisses and Hugs from your big Sister Miya," "I Miss you!" "Say Happy," "Have fun at Camp!"

Then the letter on baby boy blue paper.

Miya's Letter, 1993:

> *Dear Bupers,*
>
> *I miss my littlest sister so much! Did you get any homeruns at the games that I missed? Hope your having fun in basketball. I heard you were better than all the boys. I'm never going to forget you and maybe might be coming home at the end of August. Keep on reading and so one day you wouldn't be needing any help reading the letters I send you at all. At the next visiting day I want you to come up and visit me. Tell Logan and Lizzie I say hi! Give Sadie a hug for me. Have fun at camp when your sad and homesick just think of me and be happy. I know your going to make so many new friends. Don't let Jonne and Jenny get to you. If you have a problem go to Emma, Kacee, Lizzie, or Logan. I know you feel comfortable with all four of them. Go to the Bulk food store and get me hard candy like: chocolate mint, coffee, lime, lemon, grape, apple jolly ranchers, and send it. Sharon will keep it for me! I love you + miss you!*
>
> *Love, Miya Jo.*

After I finished reading Miya's letter to me, Mom found and unfolded a huge banner style letter Miya also had made me on 2x4 foot white paper.

Miya's Letter:

> *Beiners,*
> *How is my littlest Sister?*
> *I miss you so much.*
> *I'm doing really good.*
> *I can't wait to see you.*
> *You light up my life. I'll always*
> *Be here for you. I <3 U.*
> *We'll be sisters forever.*
> *Monkey.*
> *Somewhere over the rainbow and into my heart, you will always be.*
> *[Each line written in a different color of the rainbow.]*

Journal Entry, August 3, 2008:

> *Dad walks in from his bike ride, sweating, lifts his yellow faded T-shirt over his head, bearing all. His stomach hanging over his shorts. "She was hell on wheels at that age," he jokes, as he listens to Mom read a report card from Temple Beth Ami Sunday School. Grade E.*
>
> *Dad jumps on the computer, his way of being part of the scene, yet distracting himself enough, sort of like deflecting any question or criticism. Finally, stumbling out of the room crying, as Mom reads memories Miya wrote*

down in a notebook from childhood, like Mom rolling up a toilet roll with a present in the center for her.

Then I was handed yet another letter from Miya while she was at Mt. Bachelor, colored markers decorating this envelope, addressed to "Sabrina Beiners Must" with "You are my sunshine my only sunshine, you make me happy when skys are gray, you'll never know Beiners how much I love you, I will never let them take you away" written in blue pen on the back.

Miya's Letter:
Dear Beiners,

Hi cutey! I miss you so much. Last night we watched this movie and this little boy named Sullivan reminded me of you and your soft heart, so I cryed for you. I can't wait to give you a hug. I hope you survive it.

As I wrote Emma + Kacee, I threw up on Friday night [because of the flu], and today is Sunday the 14ᵗʰ of November and I feel a lot better. Toworrow is Emma's big day and the next is Adie's. Yesterday was Amerisan's Bat Mitzvah, too bad I wouldn't be there. It snowed yesterday but today the sun is melting it. I can't wait to skiing but it will be different w/o you there needing my help. God I love you beiners. Is the hockey season going good for you, how about indoor soccer. Your probably the best on both teams, but that doesn't surprise me at all. I can't wait to see you were going to have so much fun at Marco, but this time no fighting. So, well about me my second life steps "The Bridge" is coming up so soon. I can write me friends. I can't wait. Are you making a lot of friends in school? Any girls your friends with or are you still my little tomboy sister who is friends with all the boys? How are reading? I'm sure you and your brain are the lead reads of the class. In that part of school you definitely don't take after me! Well my little sister I have to go write dad. I miss you!

Write back soon!

Love you so much, Miya Jo

XXXOOXXOOOXX

In Dad's office there was also a huge bin of photographs of Miya and Ben on the floor, photo after photo of the two of them, as well as their engagement announcement in *The Jewish News* from September 13, 2002.

Marriage Engagement Announcement:
Monni and Joel Must of Bloomfield Hills and Lisa and Jim Klein of Boston, Mass., are proud to announce the engagement of their children Miya Jo Must and Benjamin James Klein.

Miya and Ben met at Western State College of Colorado where they are both graduates. Ben graduated with a degree in economics and is in pilot school. Miya graduated with a degree in clinical psychology.

The couple is planning to be married in June of 2003.

Chapter Twenty-three

Living somewhere in which I never wanted to start my life made me feel antsy about when and how I could get out. I had made jetting off to a new, exotic destination a habit whenever boredom or anything uncomfortable set in, especially while traveling by myself throughout Europe and Southeast Asia in 2006. In essence, I was running from myself.

From September to December 2006, I had lived in a house in Bangkok with 25 other kids. I loved being a *farang*, a foreigner. Loved I was usually the only white girl for miles (especially with sun-kissed blonde hair). Loved that I was able to schedule classes *only* on Tuesdays and Thursdays, leaving me with four-day weekends, more conducive for getaways to Laos, or Vietnam, or Cambodia, or Myanmar, or the south or north of Thailand. Loved I was able to get past feeling overwhelmed by the smog and craziness of Bangkok and really appreciate the beauty of the city.

Every second was an adventure. I could go from sleeping on a cot, engulfed within a mosquito net on the wooden floor of a bungalow in Siem Reap, Cambodia for $1 a night to storming into the most exclusive, model-saturated clubs, such as Bed Supperclub in Bangkok, alongside my Austrian roommates, partying all night with the flawless Brazilian male models.

I knew I would always be an explorer, loving to hop on a bike and toot around, checking out unknown streets. But as freeing as exploring could be, I would sometimes explore out of my overwhelming push to move, to go, and to be as efficient and productive as I could be. I would change what I was doing in fear that there was something better or greater waiting for me. I found that I rushed through life from one activity, one thought, one emotion to the next.

Being home, where doing those activities or having those thoughts and emotions were intensified, made it even more difficult to just sit and be with what was. Especially since there was nowhere to escape.I reached a point in July when I could not function any longer living at the Big House. Living there had turned from comfort into destruction. I had no space. Nothing I could claim as mine, and to go home to at night and have the silence I desperately needed. Mom was still ignoring my pleas not to come into my bedroom at 7 a.m., cleaning out Koh's litter box, or walking into the library and before she could sit down and talk to me automatically picking up any cup or bowl on the side table, whether I was done with it or not, and taking it directly into the kitchen. I was a 22-year-old living at my parents as if I were a 13-year-old.

"What's so difficult about living at your parent's house? When I was your age, I didn't have any other choice," Dad would interrogate. What my parents could not understand was that I just needed my own space. I had tried so hard for nine months to deal with all my issues while living at the house, and the pain and hurt and loss surrounding Miya's decision. These were issues that had been brewing since I was a child and they began to finally surface and ferment. They tasted bitter and overwhelming. At first I figured, if I could deal with everything living where those issues were most poignant—my parents' house—I would overcome and fix all my demons for good. But what I realized was that I couldn't break free and fully surrender myself if I was living where most of those issues were fostered.

Journal Entry, August 10, 2008:

What is best for me? All I want is to escape, runaway. Just drive. Anywhere, everywhere other than here. I'm starving for inspiration. An adventure to inspire me to embrace life again. Mom and I got in an argument this morning—"Don't blame me and Dad for your unhappiness living here," she scolded.

What she has been unable to recognize is that I'm not blaming them. I do own my issues. Know that no matter where I am those issues will follow. However, why being/living at home is so difficult for me is because it adds a great weight to my already tipped scale. And trying to deal/surrender to what I feel overpowered by is made 100x more difficult simply b/c I also have to deal with issues surrounding home. I can't isolate myself and sit with uncomfortable emotions and thoughts and urges when I routinely relinquish myself to those destructive habits of lounging around in a confused/lost state.

Why am I living here? Is it to be home for our family? And, if so, how far/long will I willingly allow myself to struggle to satisfy others' needs?

Or, is it to stay put until I'm finished writing? And, if so, what if that doesn't unfurl? What then?

I was set on South America for years. Since the moment I moved home in December 2007, I'd say, "Well, I might only be here a month or two months." Which by the end of winter turned into, "I'll be gone after my girls' soccer season." Which by the end of spring turned into, "I'll be gone by October when my freshmen soccer boys' season is complete." I couldn't put my life on hold any longer. Miya wouldn't want that. And I was falling apart emotionally. I'd go weeks without working out, just eating pizza and sleeping all day, not writing. Doing everything that did not work for me. I was certain it was my way of rebelling. Doing everything that Mom had never done...and what Dad had.

I had always done the right thing. Always brought home those gold-starred papers, always followed through on my word. I was sick of it though. Through therapy, I realized that my anxiety to rush and rush and feel like I never was in the right place, doing the right thing, needing to chase something I could not define, was very much rooted in the way I was brought up. Learned to go, go, go from Mom, years and years of scheduled workout mornings and errands and running from one activity to the next.

I never wanted to change Mom. I loved her just as she was—can't-sit-still Monni. And same went for Dad. He would always be content coming home from the office, sitting in his chair in the library, eating dinner in front of the television, hollering, "Come here, Beiners! You gotta see this!" enthralled by some random Discovery Channel special, as he also coaxed me into massaging his calloused feet and hands, and his thick, tight shoulders.

Still, I became bitter that I couldn't quiet myself. I could consciously tell myself: *This is the way it is. And there is nowhere you have to be, just enjoy being.* I was bitter toward Miya for putting me in this predicament. Feeling guilty to not be living the way that Mom or Dad expected of me. To not have a place in a home I partially owned. To not have developed the relationship that I had wanted so badly from Emma and Kacee. In part due to their criticisms, but also because of my fear and inability to function as an adult and break away from that middle school conception of myself while in Detroit.

Journal Entry, August 13, 2008:

> *I'm so angry at Miya. Disappointed in a way. Bitter that she's not here to fix this for me. One bender seeping straight into the next, only giving myself just enough time to pop my head above the surface, gulp up a breath of the crispest air, feeling SO great, and then being dunked right back under, as though someone, possibly my mind, my unconscious, is saying: "Too bad! Can't have it!"*
>
> *I wanted so badly to call Miya for her help yesterday. Needed her to hear me out. Listen to how shameful I feel about letting myself go and falling into such a depressive state. About dealing with her absence, struggles of living in Detroit, about family situations (which, luckily, have been much better since our last family meeting Mom facilitated in the Kids' House two weekends ago), and my own means of drowning myself in my own emotions through food. Like I need to punish myself. Think that I won't fall victim to what I always do. But that trigger gets pulled every time and I'm sent straight into a downward spiral, uncontrollably. Hating it and myself, yet at the same time there is a sense of utter freedom. Like, finally I can just let go.*
>
> *I mostly loathe these benders because I feel like I just wasted wonderful opportunities to do so many other great things. Like I'm purposefully limiting myself.*

I had close-to-no support system. Miya was dead. Emma and Kacee were obviously not an option. I was trying to hide from my parents. I had randomly hung out with Lauren maybe only five or six times in the past nine months. Sara was in Virginia. Sammi was dealing with her own shit. Ben was in New York. And I wasn't completely open with Heidi, Jordan or many of my college friends, like my freshman year roommate Shanna. The people who knew me best and fully were unavailable.

Email to Lauren, August 15, 2008:

I have had three of the most consistently shitty weeks I've gone through in a while. I felt so stuck. Was about to book a next day one way flight to Costa Rica and start traveling. Needed to escape, runaway. And it hit me that the two people I would really take advice from on these types of things would be you and Miya. I knew that both of you would give me the truest, most Sabrina minded opinion because you both think very similarly to the way that I do. And I couldn't call you.

I've been going to so much therapy over the past 7 or 8 months. Connecting all the dots. And I couldn't share it at all with you. I want someone to explain to me how you cope with losing your closest sister and best friend all at the same time. I want to meet with you and go for a walk and have you explain to me why you did this to me. What did I ever do to you to deserve you not being around to help me grieve?

I stood in the kitchen late one night with Dad and he affirmed, "You can't just run from your issues. They go wherever you go." And he was right. But sometimes when you hit your limit, change for a bit would help clean out the guck, so when you did try again, it would be a bit less mucky. At what point should a person separate what's good for the family and what's good for herself?

I moved into Linda's on a Wednesday afternoon. She had somehow successfully guilt-tripped me into not booking a flight to Costa Rica, reminding me that I had obligations with coaching and the Holocaust Project, with which I must follow through.

A bag of clothes, some toiletries, Koh's liter box and toys, and the little man himself.

The address: 10777. Luck number triple-7. The happy, yellow two-story house with wooden floors, cute white drapes, bedspreads, and decorative photos covering every inch.

I would sit in the extra bedroom upstairs, my room, fan buzzing, writing all afternoon and evening after a morning Holocaust interview (which I had now increased to four or five per week), leaving for only two hours to run practice for the freshmen boys—no distractions. Only Koh occasionally smacking my dangling foot with his paw out from under the bed.

Journal Entry, August 16, 2008:

I biked up and down Woodward from Linda's house during the Woodward Dream Cruise today. Thousands of car-fanatics decking out their old-time rides for their annual glorious meander down the most famous road in Michigan. The hub of car making (which really is no longer since the industry has plummeted in recent years due to the piss-poor economy) still boasts a great line up of muscle cars, street rods, custom, collector and special interest vehicles—everything from souped-up Corvettes to old school ambulances and fire trucks.

I met Kacee earlier at 7:15 a.m. yoga for Debbie's class. Debbie is soft, elegantly verbose, and has an amazing touch. She commented that the Dream Cruise is just like yoga in that it is an event which people with like-minded interests come together and share their joy for that thing or activity. And she was right. The 20 or so students in the studio were there together, joined as a community to embrace everyone's energy, breath and heat.

Debbie's words stuck with me. When thinking about my desire to run. To be by myself.

To pull an "Into the Wild." Sort of like I've done in the past when traveling. But this time I'd have no time frame. No reference point. The world would be mine.

Yet, would I be missing what is most important? Sharing my experience with a friend? I remember many moments while traveling by myself two years ago where I was extremely, extremely lonely. I accepted it, felt it, because I considered such loneliness part of my journey of self-discovery. Of learning how to just be by yourself. But there were many moments I knew certain experiences or places would have been more fun if I had someone else with whom I could share it. Sort of like the boy's realization at the end of "Into the Wild."

Chapter Twenty-four

I remembered a conversation I had with Sherri, one of our best family friends, who lived two doors down from the Lake House, late that spring. She told me about how she and her sister Cindy didn't speak from the time they were 12 to 18 years old. Eventually though, they became best friends. Sherri told me, "Just give it time."

She was right—in time, everything started to heal itself.By August, Kacee and I hit common ground and became each other's grounding force.

Journal Entry, August 22, 2008:

I sat in the Kids' House yesterday on the sunroom couch in my towel after swimming. Kacee leaning up against the kitchen doorpost. First time I can remember really talking for the past 7 or so months. Spoke about fears and issues and how you must completely bury yourself in those feelings and insecurities, allow them to take control, in order to understand them and take control of yourself eventually. To give up resistance finally. To stop limiting and just let go.

I didn't want to stop talking. She cut our conversation short because she was meeting Mom at the water to swim the dogs. She told me: "Just write it all down," assuming I just needed to get it all out. Which I did. I needed to be heard, understood. But not just by means of my writing, like I usually do. I needed HER to hear me. Needed her to know that I heard her. That so many things that both of us struggle with are the same. That there is a common background and train of thought behind our thought patterns, beliefs, emotions. That, yes, you can speak about the process of overcoming your issues with friends. But family is indispensable.

h   The most influential thing we did to mend our wounds was going to a couple's therapy session with Kacee's therapist, Danyelle (whose work was alternative—a bit off-the-beaten-path).

Journal Entry, August 23, 2008:

Kacee and I saw Danyelle today for the first time together. She positioned us in comfortable bar stool style chairs, facing each other with two feet apart. Then with paper and pen in hand, each of us separately and quietly wrote down situations/events/words that have or had caused pain, hurt, anger and sadness in the past. Of course, being a writer, I wrote and wrote—for about 10 or 15 minutes. Then I was asked to go first and read one of mine. I choose the time a month and a half ago when Kacee screamed, "This is my fucking space!" in reference to my desire and need to be allowed to spend time at the Kid's House. I jotted down on the paper that her words made me feel hurt because I felt like no one heard/realized how badly I needed an escape, too. That it was hurtful especially since the house was supposed to be for the sisters, something to share.

Danyelle had me state the example and how it made me feel. I was crying and it was difficult to continuously look into Kacee's eyes. I hold my breath when I cry or am upset. Which limits the pain I can and allow myself to feel. Danyelle kept directing me to breathe from my lower belly. She noted that my belly is filled with unsettled emotion. I know that—it's where I hold all my fears and insecurities. And why when I do binge or eat something that isn't "good" for me, my digestive tract shuts down out of shame and as a means to punish myself.

When I was done expressing which emotions were brought up surrounding the situation with Kacee, she then asked Kacee to relate what she heard. Then she asked Kacee to say which emotions she felt while I was speaking. I looked right into her eyes. She felt sadness and anger. Sadness that she made me feel that way and anger with herself for being "bad", as she was taught or made to think she was as a child. I had to answer what I heard Kacee had just said to me. And then Kacee had to own her words.

In between, Danyelle also made note of what was Fact versus Judgment surrounding the Kid's House and how the decision was made concerning who would live there. Essentially, acknowledging that it was Mom, Kacee and Emma deciding that I would not live there does not work. Instead, it should have been the 3 people who own the house, not leaving until a decision was agreed upon fully by every person. Then we hugged.

I felt joy. I was happy Kacee felt open enough to share her insecurities, especially since it was confusing to me why I always feel like I am being judged by her. We heard each other. She saw my sadness. I understood her anger and fear. My assumption that I was to blame anytime we didn't get along was wrong. It was her struggling with her own stuff and vice versa.

Mom's birthday was a few days later on August 26. A year before was the last time the six of us were all together. That night at dinner was an emotionally taxing event for Miya and me personally—Miya neck deep in Matthew issues and the family criticizing me about the usual shit. (The hardest part for me was that Miya was a main contributor to those criticisms, instead of defending me.) History seemed to repeat itself this year unfortunately.

Journal Entry, August 29, 2008:

I was busy all day with a Holocaust interview, writing the article, and then my boys' team soccer game. I didn't spend any time with Mom during the day. Which I felt guilty about, yet relieved that I conveniently had an excuse because of work…In reality, I had been on a 3-day binging bender which ended Monday, so I didn't have the strength.

I did make it to the salon in Birmingham after the game for a massage while Emma, Kac and Mom also got pampered. The massage was exactly what I needed. To cleanse my body and push the bad energy from my muscles, skin and internal systems. Feeling content, not rushed, my mind quiet for the first time after those 3 days. I joined them at Cameron's Steakhouse…I just needed to sit. Didn't want to eat. Wanted to observe, which I knew comes from a bit of bitterness. I didn't want to eat just because I was supposed to. I wanted to start fresh and clean tomorrow.

Kacee finally announced, "This is bothering me, and I just want to put it out there. I'm upset that you're not eating, Sabrina, at Mom's birthday dinner. Is there a reason?" I quickly told her I have been binging for the past 3 days and finally feel quieted, relaxed. I could see she understood right away.

While conversation switched focus, Emma piped in, whispering to me, "What exactly is a binge, Beins?" My eyes began watering, focused my attention into space to the right of the table and when the kettle burst, snatched my keys and phone and walked out. I felt bad, horrible actually, because I was ruining Mom's day. Mad at myself too though because I was having flashbacks to a year before as the family attacked me about how unhealthy I am. How I sat mute at dinner in Ferndale, too.

Dad followed me out, yelling my name as I crossed the street. Worry quivering between each forced breath. I drove off. Straight to Linda's into bed with Koh. Music playing downstairs, lights off. My phone buzzing and buzzing—Dad, then Kacee, then Emma, Emma again, then Mom, then Linda and a text. Ignoring all of it, phone on silent.

Dark, dark thoughts. Thinking about Miya's method.

Terrified by my own thoughts. How much easier to just end the pain.Everything feeling so hopeless. Nothing's getting fixed. Still binging all the time. Still wallowing in my own pain and confusion.

Twenty minutes later, Mom and Kacee came over and crawled into bed with me. Kacee stroking my arm, Mom cradling/spooning me, brushing my hair with her fingertips.

Journal Entry, August 29, 2008:

Kacee spoke mostly. About understanding how I am feeling, asking what they can do to help. "Support?" she assumed. I nodded my head.

"How dark are your thoughts? On a scale from 1 to 10, 1 being the lightest, 10 being the darkest." Tears streamed down and I shut my eyes harder. Kacee understood. Shame. Because if I did, I'd be doing just what Miya did. And as difficult as it has been for our family to survive, would they really be able to survive if I was to do something, too?

There was a bond formed that night at Linda's. A deeper understanding than ever before between me and Kacee. I had never made any suicidal thoughts known before. Now mine were out in the open, as were Kacee's.

Journal Entry, September 1, 2008:

> Kacee and I are getting along so well [which makes me feel calm and understood]. Talking about anything and everything, learning how to be supportive, non-judgmental, respect each other's boundaries. I feel like Emma is still a bit removed from the family right now, but I'm giving that time, too.
>
> I feel as the seasons change now—summer to fall—we are, too. The air a bit crisper, less muggy. To break free finally. A time to slow down and prepare for the winter. A time, in a sense, of letting go, as the leaves transform, allowing their built up energy to seep through, to undress, and become less inhibited.

My Cousin Marla's wedding celebration in downtown Detroit was a momentous event. Emma, Kacee and I were left to entertain ourselves since Mom and Dad had to leave directly after the ceremony for another wedding.

Journal Entry, September 1, 2008:

> At one point, we went into the photo booth—snapping those old-school photo slides with four shots running down the bookmark-shaped page. Making funny faces, kissing each other's cheeks, legs and arms in the air, laughing. Like we were kids.
>
> Finally as Emma, Kac and I were getting ready to leave, "My Girl" came on. We jumped up and hustled to the dance floor in unison. Holding hands, encircled, singing along, smiling exuberantly. When Uncle Alan cut in as a fourth, it hit me. Like he filled that void. Something snapped in me and I began crying. 4 just made such better sense. Kacee and Emma embraced me, continuing to dance and giggle. Miya would've loved seeing us dancing as a unit.
>
> Maybe Kacee is right. Maybe change is approaching. Maybe after all these months and months of struggle, we'll each be more enlightened and let go of a lot of stuff that is limiting our happiness. And maybe letting Miya go is part of that transition.

I moved out of Linda's into the Kids' House in mid-September. Kacee and the dogs upstairs; Koh and I downstairs. I had a halfway door at the top of the staircase put in as an extra security cushion from the cat-killing beasts, Henley and Billy.

I finally was able to create the silence and serenity I needed.

Journal Entry, September 20, 2008:

Moving into the Kids' House has been far beyond wonderful. We are creating a life together, just like Miya would have wanted. Emma is definitely still separate from us, which saddens me. But I know that too with time will work itself out.

We are creating a space that is safe, warm, unconditional...attempting to fill that void of Miya with each other. We have built another version of the Gunni Cabin

I knew there was a reason I had to stick it out in July and August when I wanted to run away. I needed to create this with Kacee. She is so wise and open and true.

I was working with the freshman soccer team at Brother Rice, the all boys' Catholic high school adjacent to Marian's campus, during the Fall which helped me get through those months. "You're coaching freshmen boys?" people would exclaim upon hearing the news between whoops of laughter. "Can't wait to see how that turns out! Those boys are all going to fall in love with you, Sabrina. They definitely won't be thinking about soccer!"

Due to the Catholic Church sex scandals, Rice faculty, administration and parents were extra paranoid about maintaining appropriate relations with the boys, void of any sort of emotional or physical abuse. To the extent I had to watch videos about their reform program. My motto for the season was: "You're in my bubble!" as I scanned my arms in a circular motion around my body, creating a visual warning for my boys if any one was too close and therefore would cause me to be under even greater scrutiny by their parents.

"Sabrina, you can't wear that. Sabrina, you can't say that." Constant rules and regulations.

Despite all the cautions, I bonded with those kids. Just as my girls' teams did, the boys mocked me in every way they could: my height, my size, my fashion sense, my appetite. It seemed only my foot skills were left untouched. The boys would pout if I jumped in on the scrimmage. "This is so unfair! Stop scoring!" they'd lament. I couldn't though, since it was the only way I could keep tabs on them. I kept my credibility as a coach by consistently reminding them I could school any day of the week.

I also took the boys to Raina's yoga class halfway through the season, which was just as fulfilling as it had been with the girls. (I had however miscalculated the amount of chatter, groans and farting.) We won only three games the entire season, yet I considered it a great success.

I wanted more than to just distract myself though. I wanted to connect with my body, heart and soul, too. I wanted to live from my Higher

Self, not my Ego, which had developed over the past 22 years from each and every interaction, particularly among my parents and sisters. I wanted to learn how to better react to anything or anyone that triggered my childhood wounds. I wanted to deal with all these demons, as I started to do with Burch, now...not spend another 30 years in therapy, talking about the issues. I wanted to learn how to surrender, free myself, and let go of everything that did not serve my greatest good.

Journal Entry, September 22, 2008:

It's about owning your own issues. Any words or reactions or judgments you may have with or about someone else is only your own stuff.

Relearning how to share feelings. How to breathe from our stomachs and not suffocate those deep emotions—to welcome and embrace all the joy, love, excitement, as well as the fear, anger and even shame.

Danyelle knew how to coach me through this.

Journal Entry, September 24, 2008:

I want to individually work with Danyelle to seek out better coping tools so as not to act on these emotions and thoughts whenever I feel the need to lose control or prove something to myself or other people. Feel like Burch is great to talk it out and help have these breakthroughs, but doesn't help me learn those tools. I'm desperate.

Chapter Twenty-five

It was my ignorance to think that I could schedule an appointment with Danyelle, be told what to do, how to do it, and have it magically fix me. It would be as if I, as a medical student, assumed I could read textbooks and observe my professors in surgery and become the best version of the doctor I aspired to be. In hindsight, months deep into working with Danyelle and her transformational tools, such an expectation was unrealistic and a bit humorous.

I was also wrong to assume that Danyelle would coach me how not to allow certain behaviors to manifest. Instead, she was trying to inspire me to embrace every part of myself, not repress any urge. As she explained countless times, if the urge was there, it was there for a reason, so I needed to explore it and surrender to it. Being open to face and heal such wounds of shame, sadness and fear was just the start. Actually allowing myself to completely welcome in every emotion was what was most draining. Nothing was "right" or "wrong", just truth. I needed to let go of my need to rush, as well as eat and exercise a certain way.

I needed to love myself even when I was not acting "perfectly."

I wanted to specifically fix my binging behavior because I was so sick of it ruling my life. I wanted to continue to beat it down. I wanted to shame it and shame it and shame it as bad, bad, bad. Such belief systems were even more detrimental, though, because, as was the case with anything, the more I shamed it, the more I would do it. Danyelle's transformational therapy work taught me to recognize that if someone triggered me, he or she triggered me for a very specific reason, which would have been connected to a childhood wound. As Danyelle would say, "Bring it back to you." She wanted me to be triggered, so that I could examine the effect it had on me, and then be able to identify the wound and validate my pain.

Her work was like peeling an onion. As I peeled one layer and then the next and then the next, life got stickier and more invasive. As I released my own poignant smell, which was in a sense my own wounds, I'd tear up and recoil.

When I would have an urge to binge, Danyelle would say, "So then binge! Enjoy it! Don't shame it! Sit with how your body feels and what emotions eating all that food brings up."

I hated her when she would say this; I actually wanted to punch her in the face. I couldn't understand how I was supposed to not hate overeating.

But it was so important for me to do so because the act of binging meant so much more than just the food. Just like any other bad habit, it was trying to fulfill some emotional need. What void was I trying to fill? From what emotions was I trying to hide? I didn't have all those answers just yet.

It took a while to get to this point:*So I ate all this crap. Okay, no big deal. Sit in your body. Why did you do that?* I didn't want to eat out of fear, fear of becoming Dad, as well as the fear of not satisfying Mom. I needed to determine what worked best for me, something which no one other than myself could decide. I didn't want to continue to associate fear and anger with certain foods. I didn't want to limit myself. *So what if I wanted this chocolate bar, maybe even three of them, or an entire loaf of bread, or this pint of ice cream, or this entire pizza despite being allergic to milk, or whatever else it was.* I knew I could balance it out later or tomorrow with healthier choices.

But I kept doing it and doing it and doing it. The cycle seemed never-ending. As much as I tried to convince myself it was no big deal, I still hated doing it—snacking and eating all evening, well into the night, throwing off my energy level.

I wanted to fix and rid of it…yet, at the same time, as much as I wanted to deny it, part of me was really not completely ready to not do it. Binging was in a sense freeing and uncontrolled, doing what I wanted. If I didn't have this need to be uncontrolled, I wouldn't have the need to behave in this way. That was why the episodes no longer lasted just an evening or two days, but four or five or six days.

I had tried to use my head to rationalize, justify, and explain my behaviors. My technique, according to Danyelle, wouldn't work. I needed to observe without judgment. Because if I judged myself, my body would recoil, yet want to do it even more. Just if you tell a child not to touch the stove, the child will do so, secretly, because he or she needed to test it out for him or herself. *You said, No. Well, why is that?* Maybe it was to feel the pain and then become vulnerable in another way.

Just as I had many nights, I stayed up late one evening (after eating all day), writing, having tapped into a memory I had yet to revisit from childhood. I finally connected how I was with food now and how I was with food as a child, and why binging and sitting and eating by myself was such a comfort, holding onto the habit subconsciously.

I began revisiting those lonely weekend nights during elementary school, middle school and high school when I'd hang out at the house. My sisters were busy socializing and partying with their best girlfriends and on occasion my parents would leave me to catch a movie or have dinner with friends. Mom and Dad would invite me to tag along, but it got to a point where I felt even more pathetic being out with my parents than home alone. Sports had always occupied most of my time, but I also yearned to be socially "normal" and hang out with girlfriends. Repeatedly over the years, I heard, "Sabrina's only friends with the boys. Sabrina doesn't get along with girls." Those statements made me truly believe not only was I not a good friend, but that girls didn't want to be my friend.

I knew that was not true; I was friendly with everyone at school. There were few, if any, girls with whom I did not get along. Developing those friendships outside of school was difficult for some reason though. "What're you doing tonight, Beiners?" Dad would routinely ask. "It's Friday night, shouldn't you be going out with friends?" That was when I realized: *I'm supposed to be going out, so because I'm not, I'm a loser.*

When I wasn't busy with a sports obligation, I would stand in the kitchen at the Big House, mentally scrolling through my list of "calling friends", hoping at least one could hang. I didn't want to spend yet another night alone…or, better yet, have to see Mom and Dad's disappointed, saddened faces when they realized I had no plans.

I used to have these lists in my mind, depending on with whom I was closest at school at that moment. One month it would be: Sheila, Kathleen, Jordan, Joan, Sarah. Another month it would be: Steffi, Chelsea, Margaret, Hillary. I'd dial and dial one after the other, dreading answering Dad's "What are you doing tonight?" with "Nothing."

If my parents went out, they'd hand me $20, and I'd call Dominos to place my usual order: two medium pizzas, one plain cheese, the other extra, extra mushrooms, and breadsticks. Thirty minutes later, I'd set myself up in Dad's recliner in the library, channel surfing between Lifetime, HBO, Fox Family, TBS and TNT movies, chowing down on my dinner.

It hurt. I believed I was a loser. I had never healed that loneliness from years before, so now I was trying to process, validate and heal it all.

I finally got why this need was so deep.

I really was mirroring Dad. I had used my weekend pizza eating ritual as my social outlet, my comfort for years, which during sophomore year of high school became an ice cream ritual. But then I began hearing that "five pound" warning. So I became even more conflicted, as I mentioned before. Months after Miya's death I still didn't know for certain if this was really the reason for all my binging hang ups, but it was part of it.

No wonder why it had hurt so much through the years to constantly pick up from Emma her judgment that she thought I was a loser. When that need to feel wanted and accepted as a child and adolescent was most crucial, I had felt neglected.

Two months into moving into the Kids' House, Becca, one of Kacee's best girlfriends and a sister-like figure to me, also moved in, taking over the second bedroom upstairs. The three of us were all doing Danyelle's work at that point, Becca actually in my weekend workshop group. It was like a commune. Each trying our best to trigger, support and focus one another on living from our Higher Self.

What I realized, with Kacee and Becca's help, was that when I spoke the words out loud, "I struggle with binging," they became less scary, less shameful, and more human. I did so with the intention of releasing my fears, embracing them, and then letting them go. I was also working with Danyelle to program these thoughts: *I am being seen and have nothing to hide. I have the courage to show this part of myself.* It was intense work.

Kacee especially was a huge support for me…and I for her. She would remind me, "What would you ever had to write about if you didn't have any struggles? You grew up, went to college, had kids…great. Surface level, surface level. It's not until you really look at yourself that you're like, *Fuck, it's not really fine.*" She made me feel sane and beautiful even when I felt as ugly as could be.

Yet, as much as she made me feel okay about doing whatever I was doing, she also didn't want me to feel that my creativity was reliant upon experiencing that darkness. "Writers find that creativity in darkness. But you don't have to be creative in the dark." I appreciated her support. Still, as much as I would try not to fall victim to a binge when I would write on the topic, I would almost every time.

Burch had opened up Pandora's Box for me; Danyelle was teaching me how to play that music shamelessly and not try to tightly seal it again.

Not only was I dealing with insecurities about food, but I was questioning everything else: *Why did Carter not want to date me? Why did this happen to me again and again with men? Why did I feel shame if someone said or did this or that? Why did I feel sadness in this or that situation?*

As I continued working with Danyelle, I realized I should have outwardly thanked Carter for breaking my heart. It exposed me to every emotion I could have possibly felt and every wound I have that could be triggered: not feeling good enough, my overwhelming sadness, my desire to fill that void by whatever means possible.

I remembered Carter himself once even jokingly claim, "Sabrina, you're like a child." I didn't respond other than with a slight giggle; instead, I internally pined over his words.

He was right. I was like a child. I couldn't get enough of his affection and attention. If he held me in bed, even if every inch of his body was touching me, it wasn't enough. I literally wished he could have swallowed me whole. It seemed I was starving for love, which didn't logically make sense because I was never abused as a child but instead adored by my parents.

Carter helped me to understand why I desired a man in my life so badly. I wanted someone to distract me from that sadness.

Journal Entry, October 4, 2008:

It's illogical. I miss her so much. Crying fits that overcome me and wipe me out. Feel her sadness then. Feel anger, but more a disappointment in her for leaving me. Then part of me really has faith she'll miraculously appear. As though if I allow myself to express all my sadness and force her to watch it and sense it, she'll swoop down and come back to life. She was only temporarily gone, I tell myself. A sick, practical joke.

It wasn't until October 11, 2008, Miya's 29th birthday, that I had these realizations. I had not fallen for Carter just because it was he. Yes, he was fun and handsome and affectionate, but he really could've been any guy. I just needed someone last winter, someone to soak up my pain. Make me forget how badly I was suffering, how very sad I was. The touch of a man had always lifted that deep, inherent sadness from me. For a moment, for a week, for three weeks. Whatever it was, it allowed me to breathe easier, not feel as rushed, and feel a bit calmer in my mind.

Journal Entry, October 5, 2008:

Came to Port City Java to meet Dad...With my legs draped over his thighs, massaging his coarse hands, I shared with Dad why it's been so hard without Miya. How I believe sadly if I cry enough she'll come back. How when I'm sad, it's been hard not to have her to call. How I replay that last conversation with her over and over. "I know, I love you, too, Miy." How could I not have seen it coming?
I made Dad cry.

After escaping our family day on Miya's birthdayto visit Carter, (even though I told everyone differently,) I was in essence escaping that pain. I needed to feel loved, validated, worthy of happiness. The kid couldn't give me what I needed though, what I wanted. And, as Schuette, one of my best friends from Cranbrook, told me on the phone while driving that evening, "You're the strongest person I know, Sabrina. You deserve someone that will do anything to be with you." And he was right. I had lost sight of my truth, chasing after this kid, just because I did not want to lose something I was not ready to let go of.

Journal Entry, October 6, 2008:

I'm trying to let her go. Trying so hard. Allowing myself to exist in these dark places right now, sadness so overwhelming, which transforms into anger as I get frustrated that it won't go away. I need her here. What a stupid decision, Miy.

Part of Danyelle's work involved the letting go process. During my first workshop weekend, Miya actually came through during my regression.

Journal Entry, October 7, 2008:

*Standing across from her, looking into each other's eyes. I feel
sadness, anger she is no longer here. Then shame because I am angry she left
me. Danyelle directs me to tell her, "It was your decision to leave me." Telling
Miya that makes me sadder.*

*At the end of it I must tell her, "I am letting you go, and no longer
need you for comfort." I did it, but still holding on some because so much of me
doesn't want to lose that connection with her.*

*Then I had to tell her how much I love her, "I love you. Thank you
for understanding. I love you, love you, love you." Really felt her presence; could
see her being.*

It was difficult for Mom and Dad to see me in this space, so sad, so
dark during those months. It had always been, just as it was for them when
I was a sophomore in high school and at times during college, depressed
and confused.

When I was 15 years, Dad would crawl into bed with me at night
while I cried. He once told me about how throughout his twenties he was
deeply depressed—years of therapy, work, and sleeping all weekend. A haze
of sadness and unhappiness. He needed me to know he understood. He
needed me to know that he was worried, but would be there, unlike his
parents, who were quite absent during his childhood. There was a bond
formed those nights with Dad in bed, something I may never have even
fully expressed and told him for which I was thankful.

My parents saw in us what they feared so deeply in themselves. Not
only did Grandma Maggie abuse Mom emotionally, causing her to seek
refuge in California when she was 17, living on her aunt's farm before
studying photography in Santa Barbara, but Dad was abused in a way, too. I
was triggering their self-doubt more than ever.

They were trying to fix me, wanting me to consider going to an
actual MD and taking medication. Dad would call and check on me, leaving
me voice messages, many just to try to humor me, such as: "Beiners, this is
your father. Call me back…This message has been approved by Joel Must."
A sly wink off the recent election campaign.

I didn't blame them. It wasn't a joking matter anymore. Miya's
decision had taken that sadness that seemed to thrive within us to another
level. Suicide was now part of my vocabulary. Losing another child would
completely destroy my family.

Chapter Twenty-six

By November 2008, I was involved with a new boy, Chris. As embarrassing as it was to admit, I met Chris my first night as the only shot girl at Stan's Sports Bar. Thursday nights were college karaoke nights, as well as Chris-nights. He and his high school buddies were weekly karaoke customers. Chris was shameless. He'd stand, belching out song versions of the *Rolling Stones* or *The Band* in his Pendleton button-down shirts.

I was intrigued right away because when he spoke to me or I spoke to him, he would really look at me, right in my eyes, genuinely interested. He was engaged by whatever I did or whatever I said. Plus, he allowed me to be in whatever space I needed to be in. If I was down, that was okay. If I wanted to go for a run at 6 a.m. before subbing, he'd be racing me down the icy, slick December streets. It was so easy and organic with him.

By interacting with and trusting Chris, I got to know myself even deeper. I realized how my food issues did limit so many aspects of my life at times: socially, romantically, and physically. If I binged, I would not go out and see friends. If I binged, I would limit how much physical exercise I could do. If I binged, romantically, I didn't want someone touching me and loving me when I was not loving myself. I didn't want them to feel my bloated, curvier mid-section as a result of the day's cake, pizza, and candy eating extravaganza.

On the flip side, when I felt balanced and confident in my body, I wanted my boyfriend, at this point Chris, to touch and love me completely. Touch, in a sense, became my reward for not having given in to those destructive binging habits. But if I didn't feel perfect, I would punish myself further by not letting anyone touch, see, or really even socialize with me, Chris included. I had learned to hate my body if it wasn't balanced.

Journal Entry, November 12, 2008:

I didn't feel completely disgusting in my body…but more anger toward myself for letting myself go today and yesterday and the day before that. And that affected my relationship with Chris and not wanting to see him/hook up with him tonight. I told him on the phone earlier, "I don't want you to really touch me tonight. I feel gross."

He definitely doesn't completely understand why. How do I explain to someone when I almost can't admit it to myself that I binged and therefore have outrageous shame for how I'm not properly caring for myself?

Why do I let food dictate my life? Shame on me! I want to scream that.

But then I feel shameful for thinking that because again I have allowed the food and my emotions surrounding eating to be more powerful than my own higher self.

That was why I loved Koh so endearingly—because he loved me without any judgment. I never felt like I had to be or look any specific way. He looked at me like a child, unconditionally and intriguingly. It was just like Miya used to look at me, or at least when she was in a good space and not projecting her own struggles onto me.

But Chris was that way as well. He wanted to be around me even when I was in that space, (even if he didn't completely know why). So I worked rigorously to re-teach myself that such behavior was not so shameful, and that shutting people out would only add fuel to the fire. When I was more carefree with what and when I wanted to eat, I realized my body did not shut down as intensely. That realization was freeing.

After Miya's death, Dad was gaining more and more weight and Mom seemed to be shrinking. (This was not because she wasn't eating, but because she never sat still. Plus, she had a very high metabolism so her over-activity and high stress level was causing her to literally shrink.) Dad was using food and Mom was using movement to escape the pain and deny the grieving process. It seemed they were just as far from letting go of Miya a year later as they were the day they found out about her suicide.

I felt angry about this. But it wasn't just about their health; it was also about how present they were. Or how not present. I was no longer just grieving Miya, but grieving the loss of my parents, Mom specifically. Danyelle repeatedly referenced an Oprah episode she once saw when two mothers were interviewed, both of whom had lost their son in a homicide over ten years before. While one had let go and continued living, the other mother looked disheveled, revengefully fighting to bring her son's killer to justice.

I feared this would become Mom. That ten years from now she would still be fighting to know the truth of the 14th. I, too, wanted to know that, but I wanted my mom back more. I wanted her to be what she was before Miya died. I knew as an adult I needed to detach and not rely on Mom, or Dad for the matter. I needed to learn to clean my wounds myself. Cutting that emotional umbilical cord seemed impossible though.

By the fall, I barely spent time with Mom. I'd get a "How are you feeling this morning?" as she rushed out of the locker room at the Sports Club, while I sauntered in. Or get a phone call to give me the most up-to-date interview list for the Holocaust survivors.

Soon, she purchased a Blackberry. I was convinced this was the death of her. It allowed her to be even more distant, using text messaging as a means of preferred communication.

She was completely engrossed in her photography; she seemed to give more compassion and attention toward her clients. Same was true toward her girlfriends.

I wasn't stupid. I was aware dealing with people other than your own children after a life-altering loss was easier. I had hoped Mom was stronger than that. She didn't seem to be.

Our family had fallen apart.

Journal Entry, November 13, 2008:

I'm sitting by the pool. The mother criticizes her younger daughter, 14 years old she told me, as the girl goes to eat her Powerbar. This daughter is plump, awkwardly shaped. "That's for after your workout, after you do laps. Put that away!" The mother next turned to her 18-year-old daughter who is still doing her laps and is not as physically out of shape as the 14-year-old. "How many laps did she do?"

The mother dressed in workout gear is physically strong and muscular. Obsessive. How can she expect her daughters to aim for such perfection and obsessiveness? She is instilling eating disorders and skewed self-images into her teenage daughters' minds. The mother's own insecurity was never healed, and now she is manifesting it in her own children. That is so unfair.

The mother starts arguing with the younger daughter thirty minutes later about something (probably about her weight); the daughter fights back: "I started eating my vegetables every single day, Mom!" I continue watching the girl examine herself, then examine her sculpted mom and then her older sister. Such insecurity.

An hour later the mother has the girls pose for a photo in their bathing suits by the pool. An innocent, loving request, but after you've berated your daughters, how could she expect the girls to feel comfortable taking a photo in the most revealing clothes possible?

I watch the older daughter stand somewhat confidently, as the younger daughter hunches, her hands twitching awkwardly and insecurely at her side in semi-clenched fists.

Then I observe the mother sitting a few minutes later at her lounge chair, reviewing the photo. I could imagine her zooming in and out, examining each of her daughters' imperfections. Such motherly love! I want to shout and scream, but mostly cry. My sadness and fear and shame are so triggered.

I want to go talk to the daughter, hug her, tell her she's beautiful and it's not her fault if she feels ugly and unwanted and not good enough. But I don't. I don't want her to feel even more shame and as though she deserves to be pitied.

It was a sick cycle. I would observe one generation struggle in a certain way, and because they never rigorously worked to heal those insecurities, they would pass it down to their children. It couldn't be helped unless that generation worked rigorously to become more conscious and aware with how they truly operate and interact. These 30, 40, 50-something mothers and fathers were so insecure themselves and never appeared to be healed, all they knew was how to pass their insecurities onto their children. When did we begin to promote judgment and self-hatred as opposed to unconditional love?

I never would have connected all of these things unless Miya died. I never would have forced myself to sit and be with my emotions—my fears and anger and shame. I would have continued repressing it and repressing it in the controlled manner I was taught. I had tried for months through my writing and journaling to understand Miya's decision. What I didn't acknowledge and comprehend until over a year after her death was that her decision was one so inherently made. She didn't value herself enough because she believed she was sick, ugly and unwanted. She didn't value herself enough in her marriage to say, "Goodbye, Matthew. I am through. I will never let someone treat me so badly. I am worth so much more!"

Endorsing her desire to stay and work it out with Matthew was done out of love. I didn't know any better. I had no real experience in relationships. So, in a way, I was angry with Matthew because deep down I was angry with myself and also felt shame for being angry with Miya.

It was her choice.

Her choice.

Her choice.

To stay, and also to kill herself. Yes, Matthew was abusive, but she needed to have empowered herself. She needed to have healed herself.

I could not have saved my sister.

I knew firsthand how hard that journey could be. A journey which was not only difficult necessarily for an emotionally abused wife, but for any person wanting to free him or herself from anything which didn't serve his or her greatest good, whether it was drinking, smoking, drugs, overeating, under-eating, self-mutilation, or self-doubt.

The two extremes—Mom versus Dad—were in constant battle with each other. I was working therefore to create my own tapes, my own balance, my own truth. I was on a journey of my own. There were definitely times during the year I thought about cashing in, because it was excruciatingly painful to sit and be in those emotions and memories, working to heal those wounds and restructure my life. I needed to learn from Miya's mistakes and break this familial cycle of not valuing myself enough to do what would be best for me.

Miya's story was universal. Different numbers, but all part of the same equation. I couldn't speak on behalf of Mom, Dad and Emma since I did not know the extent of the work they were doing to heal themselves (which I assumed was minimal), except for Kacee. She and I were working intensively to create a new pattern, one from which we hoped our future children and families would benefit by not being affected as we were by this vicious cycle of self-destructive behaviors and thoughts. As Kacee put it, "This work is difficult. If it wasn't, every single person would be doing Danyelle's work. We are changing this pattern, a pattern which took decades to create. Now, in a year or two, we are destroying it and building a new. How beautiful is that?"

My writing no longer could simply just be about love and loss, but also about acceptance and healing. I needed others to be empathetic toward me, and then in turn be accepting toward themselves. I wanted to inspire change on a greater scale than just my microcosm of a world.

If only one person read what I wrote and it spoke to them and made them feel sane and human, not de-humanized by the power of the mind's destructive thoughts, I would have considered my writing to be a success.

Chapter Twenty-seven

Journal Entry, November 14, 2008:

Never-ending sadness. Painful jabs at my chest. Fists clenched. Tears endless. One year. One year. Wish I could rewind and just start all over again. Fly down there, stop her.

I had assumed my life would return to normal after the one-year anniversary. I imagined November 14, 2008 as a finish line, crowds of people in the stands, cheering, holding up congratulatory signs. "You're almost there! One more step, another, another. Yay! You made it." Ripping the tape, arms jetting toward the sky in celebratory relief, collapsing to the ground due to exhaustion yet also elation. *Now, I can let go,* I would tell myself since I finished the race.

But whether it was today, tomorrow or 15 years after the one-year, this reality would still be mine. Just as one of the Holocaust survivors told me, "Anniversary here, anniversary there, it hurts forever."

Leading up to the one-year, I wanted to fix everything that was wrong in my life…quickly, as fast as possible. Attending a Vipassana mediation retreat in Illinois, held at the end of October 2008, was my desperate attempt to do such a thing. Ten days of noble silence, meditating for a total of 11 hours each day. No talking, no interacting, no eye or physical contact. Complete self-observation. I figured if I forced myself to be and sit, I could just fix it all.

A day and a half into the retreat I realized I didn't need the schedule and serenity of the rural location to rediscover my already tapped resource. Instead I needed to work on how to live with myself and all my baggage and grief…in the real world.

Journal Entry, October 23, 2008:

I did not need to come to Vipassana to explore and get in touch with the depths of my mind. That's where I live everyday, curled up next to my computer or journal. If someone had not done all the work I have on myself, thanks in most part to my writing, I can see how ten days in noble silence meditating would be beneficial. But for me it simply is a space where I can rest. Not have all my triggers going off at home w/ family…

I don't feel like I'm running away as I did in Thailand at Udi's Vipassana retreat—because there I was uncomfortable sitting with all my thoughts and my anxiety and "rush." Here in Illinois, however, I am aware and conscious to what and how I struggle. Where I am on my path is not to determine my issues and navigate my mind. It is instead to learn better coping methods and how to deal with all my triggers and childhood wounds.

I left by morning of the second day. I didn't feel shameful for not finishing the retreat "successfully"; I actually felt joyful, because I finally was clear about what my next step had to be to heal and self-discover.

As time passed, anniversaries came and went, and we hoped more and more information from that ambiguous night would surface. The one-year anniversary proved this to be true.

If we had heard these things a year before, closer to Miya's death, we would not have been able to rationally digest it. Emotions would have contaminated our minds, impeding us from operating in a strategic, calm manner.

We just simply wanted to know the truth. We needed to know. What exactly happened the night of the 14th? Minute to minute, thought to thought, emotion to emotion, word to word, action to action. It was all speculation, what was and was not said and done. All the evidence was consistent with Miya taking her own life. But we couldn't continue to disregard our inclinations as well as what Rebecca Rosen and the Gunnison dog whisperer said and believed. That Matthew played a bigger hand in her death than he admitted.

Mom, Kacee and I flew back to Gunnison on Sunday, November 16, 2008. We were more than eager to visit Caren, Little Kari, Ashley and of course Thompson, as well as just feel the freshness of the sunny-skied air.

At dinner that Sunday night, Little Kari revealed what Matthew had actually said the night before the memorial service, when he had exploded in front of family and friends. We had always assumed Matthew's piercing words a year before were directed toward Ashley; we were wrong. Ashley never wanted to share it with us. *What good would telling the Musts do?* she figured. In truth, what wouldn't it have done? It was proof there was more to the night of the 14th than a mentally ill woman committing suicide.

"She fucking deserved what she got! Fuck her, fuck her!" Matthew had shouted vehemently. "Nobody's worried about me! This service should be about me, not her! Fuck Miya!"

My mouth fell agape, my body froze…wow. Why hadn't anyone told us this a year before? Had any of Miya's friends at the house that night realized what such biting words really meant?

She fucking deserved what she got!…? What Matthew gave to her? By means of kicking the chair or leaving her hanging? By egging her on and then leaving her alone downstairs? By dying and disappearing from his life permanently?

Ashley told Kari the next day what he had said, commenting, "I didn't really believe he was that type of person until that came out of his mouth last night." And truthfully most people didn't and probably never will.

At dinner, we further discussed how Matthew presented himself as this cool and collected, handsome, laid back sort of guy. Nothing ever seemed to be a big deal. People wanted to be around him because they wanted to understand how he could go through life so carefree. Or so they thought. When something set off his rage, though, he would disassociate from that part of himself and morph into the abusive Matthew.

The next day we met Caren for lunch and she explained, "He has the ability to compartmentalize this rage to such an extent that what happened to Miya was just one part of what was happening. And the most important part was not what was happening to Miya, but what was happening to him."

This is just how Matthew reacted to Miya's eating disorder. He hated it and believed she was weak if she binged and purged. He probably would have reacted in a similar way if Miya had threatened or staged her suicide. (Her note seemed to be more a scare tactic than anything. *Matthew's going to find me, realize what he's losing, and want to save me.* I assumed if she had been really serious about committing suicide, the note wouldn't have seemed to be an afterthought.)

Her eating disorder was a way to self-destruct, just like suicide (or at least in the physical sense, since suicide may ultimately be a way to free oneself). Matthew most likely would have considered any such threat an act done against him. "God, fucking damn it! Why are you doing this to me? You're weak!" he probably would have shouted.

He had a pattern of exposing himself to women who would willingly take the abuse. He thrived on the control he had over their emotions and neediness; therefore, when he lost control of the person who struggled the most—Miya—he might have gone berserk.

I imagined when he realized what he had done (whether it was kick the chair from under her, stand back and watch her die, or walk upstairs after they fought, knowing what she was about to do), he paced back and forth in the basement while she was hanging dead, thinking, "Oh my God! What did I do? My life is ruined!" And then, in an effort to save himself, he went screaming for help. Not to save Miya, his wife, but himself. "Somebody save me!"

He had played with our family's emotions since the beginning—by showing up with an attorney, by keeping us out of the condo, and by keeping the dogs from us, knowing that would have been the last thing Miya would have wanted. He wasn't just abusive toward Miya; he was abusive toward our entire family.

If Kari's confession wasn't enough, the second blow was finding out about Carla. This girl was a friend of Miya. In February, 2008, when

Kacee and Emma were in Gunnison to pick up the dogs, Carla had joined my sisters on a hike and confessed how she even witnessed how abusive Matthew was. How she herself had been in abusive relationships before and saw all the telltale signs whenever around Matthew and Miya. Somehow from February to April she forgot; she began dating Matthew and moved into the condo soon after. Only five months after Miya died. A grieving husband? Sure wasn't acting like it.

Kari rhetorically asked, "How could he start a life there with someone else?" In the condo where his wife committed suicide?

But that was the idea. *I'm going to start my life and forget everything and not have anyone get in the way of what I want.* Miya's time was up and Matthew wanted her done and over as quickly as possible. Having his mother pack up her things 24 hours after her death wasn't enough; he also had to paint all the walls and pollute the condo with the paints' pungent smell...in an attempt to rid of Miya's toxic energy and make room for his new life and girlfriend.

We next met with Thompson at the police station on Monday afternoon—Mom, Kacee, Kari and I. Kari came to testify and recount the events from a year ago.She explained to Thompson, "Not once did he express sorrow, not once did he express pain for her. Not once. At first I thought it was the situation of finding someone like that and how horrific it would be. But the next day, I never once heard him express pain for her being gone. It was always about him. I was there when he had to call Monni. He didn't want to have to do that; he simply asked, 'Have you heard? Did someone call you? Miya hung herself.' I have never been in contact with another human being that didn't have the capacity to feel, to not feel pain, to just not feel. He just doesn't give off any sort of inclination that he is capable of those things."

Again, time had to be our best friend. As much as we didn't want anything to happen to Carla, we were hoping her relationship would untangle to be just as abusive as Matthew and Miya's. And just as abusive as Matthew and Paige's. Maybe he'd slip up and admit to Carla what really happened between him and Miya. Or maybe if we ever ran into him we could provoke his rage and he'd stumble, admitting the truth.

After our meeting, Thompson led me separately into one of the interrogation rooms. He had not yet copied Miya's four remaining journals which he had promised to do when he sent me the first batch in September, 2008. The journals were still being held as evidence; so even though I could not physically remove them from the police station, Thompson allowed me to spend as much time reading them as I wished...especially since the station was open 24 hours a day. After a few hours on Monday afternoon, I returned on Tuesday from 3 p.m. until midnight. I sat in that 3x4 interrogation room feeling paranoid because of the one-way mirror. Crying, shaking, frustrated. Like I always was when reading her thoughts because it reminded me of how wonderful, brilliant and true my sister was, as well as being reminded of how similar she and I were.

Miya's Journal, May 10, 1999:

Sabrina and I are so, so close b/c we are so much alike, so I helped her at a younger age so she grew up that way and her friends learned.

Sabrina's Journal Entry, November 18, 2008:

At the police station with my laptop, transcribing her journal entries. Any entry that relates to her deep sadness, childhood pain, abusive relationship with Matthew, her own self-destruction.

I'm realizing how similar we are. I mentioned it before in my writing, realized it months and months ago. But really, it's like I use her exact language to describe my sadness and hurt at times.

And I feel her pain concerning relations with Kacee and Emma because I was there.

It's like there was this untouched bond between us since I was born. And that could never be touched. And I miss her more than ever, because her words are just so damn wise and truthful. And I fucking hate Matthew for doing this to her and taking her from me.

Whenever I occasionally popped my head into Thompson's office if I needed help deciphering Miya's horrendous handwriting, (which, I hated to admit, was quite similar to mine), the two of us would walk through the details of the 14th again. We considered all the new evidence surrounding Kari's testimony. We also seriously considered the possibility that Miya had the intention to stage her suicide to elicit a response but Matthew kicked the chair.

As midnight rolled around and after two trips to the vending machine for dinner, I cleaned up my work area and stumbled back to the hotel, exhausted. I slept until 11 a.m. and headed back over to the police station at 12:30 p.m. with a box of Firebrand cookies and muffins as a thank you to the officers, especially Thompson, for being so accommodating and welcoming. Once again, Thompson and I reconvened in his office. He walked through all the evidence for the hundredth time so I could obsess about even more and clear up any last uncertainty.

He wanted me to understand even if Matthew had stood there and watched, doing absolutely nothing other than screaming in a rage, he could not be criminally held accountable. Matthew probably falsely assumed if someone found out she had threatened suicide and he took no action to stop it, he would be charged. This was potentially why he sought legal protection before facing Mom, Dad and me at the station.

As much as I wanted to believe that it was all staged, I knew I needed to be as objective as possible. If it was a stage, there wasn't a pair of scissors or a knife to cut her down. Also, for the first time, Thompson disclosed more specifics to me about the state of Miya's body. He explained not only were her arms bent, but her legs were also, as though she had lifted them up. These two specifics helped to demonstrate her intention. Thompson was now also investigating the condition and nature of the rope: its length and positioning around her neck. Depending on the rope's elasticity (which very well might have been quite elastic considering the rope was used for yoga), Thompson suspected Miya might have positioned herself with her tippy toes grazing the carpet. Once on the chair, she would have gradually stepped down to stand on her tippy toes and then lift her feet. That descent would have eliminated the jerk of the fall and lessened the violent, sudden nature of the act.

Maybe her hands were clenched as if she was on a rollercoaster. She was thinking of going on the ride, but when she heard the cart creak against the tracks, she might have decided she didn't want to go on any longer, yet realized it was too late, so she was clenched out of fear and pain. Or maybe she really was determined from the start to carry it out and was lifting her legs and clenching her fists to make sure she was successful.

What did all this continued speculation do for me though? Matthew was still Matthew; Miya was dead.

Epilogue

Some of the hardest moments for me were sitting alone with Mom in her office downstairs, looking at her day's photo shoot material, photo after photo, sifting out the best ones. Beautiful, precious kids. Kids who remind me of what we never got a chance to experience with Miya.

I assumed within a year of getting married Miya would've been in full-bloom, belly popping out. I was waiting for that morning I'd wake up, Miya snuggling next to me, excitedly whispering, "Auntie Beiners! I'm pregnant. I'm pregnant!" But come on, that will never happen.

Journal Entry, August 29, 2008:

How do you grieve? Is it a process done alone? Or with your family and loved ones? Is there a set time frame or is it person-specific? Is Danyelle right that our family has not properly grieved? Have we not allowed ourselves to be really sad, then angry, and finally let go? I feel like I deal with my emotions constantly, and in a sense, drown myself in my own misery, thinking and thinking, writing and writing about Miya.

Maybe we haven't had a chance.

Every couple of weeks and sometimes every week there seems to be something. First the funeral, then shiva, then the memorial, then my birthday, then December 14, then New Year's Eve (Miya's engagement anniversary), then January 14, then Kacee's birthday, then February 14, then March 14, then the Kadima luncheon, then March 31 (the wedding anniversary), then Dad's Annual Food Show, then April 14 (the 6-month anniversary), then Mother's Day, then May 14, then Gunnison again for Miya's belongings, then June 14 and Father's Day, then July 14 (8 months), then Heather's wedding ceremony, then August 14, then Mom's 54th birthday (a year ago, being the last time the 6 of us were together).

No break. No room to breathe or "forget" about what anniversary or event is lurching around the corner.

Not only did I revisit journal entries from the days and months after Miya died, but also from long before. Anything I found related to Miya, visiting Miya, or previously thinking about death was intriguing to me. My biggest fear growing up had always been losing Mom or Dad. I wouldn't know how to survive without them. No matter if I was living in Prague or hiking the Grand Teton or studying in Baltimore, home had always been defined by where they were. And, so, for some strange reason, even before November 14, I had often concocted scenarios in my mind, made-up stories about losing one of them and sometimes even one of my sisters or best friends. It was a weird way I experienced how I might react if one was to ever die. I thought about death, and even thought about how other people would react if I was to ever die prematurely.

While I was in Laos in September 2006 for a long weekend, I read Alice Sebold's *Lovely Bones*. I jotted down two quotes in my journal, questions that the narrator had and questions that strongly resonated in me then—and even more so now. They were:

1. *When was it all right to let go not only of the dead but of the living—to learn to accept?*
2. *Ruth, who wanted everyone to believe what she knew: that the dead truly talk to us, that in the air between the living, spirits bob and weave and laugh with us. They are the oxygen we breathe.*

Journal Entry, September 30, 2006:

 I cried last night while lounging in bed finishing Alice Sebold's book. I imagined receiving a call back in Bangkok that Mom had died. I reacted in hysteria. It's a mystery why I constantly create scenarios like these—wondering how I would react if this was indeed true. Reading this book about death reminds me of Grandpa. I sat reading in bed earlier today and found myself talking to Grandpa and asking him to show himself. I feel like quote #2 is so right on.

When was enough really enough? When did we have to stop crying? When were we supposed to move on and live our lives? Did we have to forget our pain? And, was it healthy to live with the belief that the spirit world was actually "living" among us and never fully "let them go"? Rebecca's reading seemed to prove that such a spiritual existence was present. Therefore, if I didn't believe and didn't joyously "breathe" in Miya and Grandpa and everyone else, was I doing them an injustice? Would I regret being ignorant once I died and realized what was really the truth?

Then, while living and interning in New York City in the summer 2007, I read JoanDidion's *The Year of Magical Thinking*. Her autobiography was about how she dealt with mourning the deaths of her husband and daughter in the same year.

Journal Entry, August 8, 2007:

 I continued to read Didion on the Great Lawn. I love her voice. Quick, confident about her thoughts, truthful about her emotions, uncertainties, mistakes, memories. She recounts the events of her husband's sudden death, followed by the death of her daughter (sick from the flu, turned into pneumonia then falling into a coma). She recounts her actions/thoughts step by step through each incident.

 I like how she breaks traditional literary technique and tucks in—somewhat in anatomical form—bits of poetry/letters. She speaks of grief, about what it means, how it's manifested, how it's caused, how it's denied (unsuccessfully).

I've thought about Mom and Dad, and Kacee and Miya and Emma dying, and most of all Lauren. How'd I deal with it? I couldn't. It makes me cry and recoil just from the thought of it.

I was able to sort of find an escape in her words, enjoyed the sun, but still felt overpowered by time and the "need" to do something—why couldn't I just be content with doing what I was?

Now I wondered, had I done the same? Did I create a book that would speak to its audience in the same way that Sebold and Didion did for me?

Just as Caren told me in May, 2008, "It's ongoing. The struggle to come to grips with her death, understand it, accept her decision…The most difficult is figuring out where to end, because it's ongoing. So I guess I'll just end it here."

Journal Entry, September 13, 2008:

If Miya hadn't died, I wouldn't have moved home. If Miya hadn't died, we wouldn't have purchased the Kids' House in Sylvan. If Miya hadn't died, I would never have had to live in such a close proximity to Emma and Kacee again and really learn how to be sisters and try to be the "best sisters" as Miya claimed the 4 of us are. (Must • Girls • Love, right?) If Miya hadn't died, I would never have connected all the dots concerning ways and issues I have with how Mom and Dad are and how they taught us to be (consciously and unconsciously), which also affected ways and issues Emma and Kacee and Miya also have. If Miya hadn't died, I wouldn't have had that groundbreaking insight, which I believe will with time, great effort, and continued therapy, allow me to surrender, as Kacee says, to whatever does not serve my greatest good. If Miya hadn't died, would I have ever been tested to such a great extent and known of what our family and I are capable? If Miya hadn't died, would I have ever really known what it means to fall straight to hell and what it takes to pick myself up, climb out of that darkness and find light in life again?